Bridge to
IELTS

Pre-intermediate–Intermediate Band 3.5 to 4.5

Teacher's Book

Roger Scott and Kate Fuscoe
with Vickie Pastellas
and Sophie Walker

NATIONAL GEOGRAPHIC LEARNING | **CENGAGE Learning**

Australia • Brazil • Japan • Korea • Mexico • Singapore • Spain • United Kingdom • United States

Bridge to IELTS Teacher's Book

Roger Scott and Kate Fuscoe with
Vickie Pastellas and Sophie Walker

Publisher: Jason Mann

Senior Commissioning Editor: John Waterman

Editorial Project Manager: Karen White

Development Editor: Heidi North-Bailey

Head of Marketing and Communications:
  Michelle Cresswell

Project Editor: Tom Relf

Production Controller: Elaine Willis

Art Director: Natasa Arsenidou

Cover design: Vasiliki Christoforidou

Text design: Maria Papageorgiou

Compositor: Maria Papageorgiou

Audio: Soundhouse Studios, London

ISBN: 978-1-133-31749-4

National Geographic Learning
Cheriton House, North Way, Andover, Hampshire, SP10 5BE
United Kingdom

Cengage Learning is a leading provider of customised learning solutions with office locations around the globe, including Singapore, the United Kingdom, Australia, Mexico, Brazil and Japan. Locate our local office at **international.cengage.com/region**

Cengage Learning products are represented in Canada by Nelson Education Ltd.

Visit National Geographic Learning online at **ngl.cengage.com**
Visit our corporate website at **www.cengage.com**

CREDITS
Although every effort has been made to contact copyright holders before publication, this has not always been possible. If contacted, the publisher will undertake to rectify any errors or omissions at the earliest opportunity.

Cover: Shutterstock (leungchopan)

Illustrations
The publisher would like to thank the following sources for permission to reproduce their copyright material:
p.110: The Franklin Institute for the illustration diagram 'The Kodak Brownie' www.fi.edu, copyright © 2012, The Franklin Institute, All Rights Reserved.

Printed in China by RR Donnelley
1 2 3 4 5 6 7 8 9 10 – 16 15 14 13 12

Bridge to IELTS Contents

Introduction to *Bridge to IELTS* Teacher's Book

WHAT IS IELTS?

IELTS (The International English Language Testing System) is a globally recognised exam. It tests the language ability of candidates who need to work or study in an English-speaking country. The test is skills-based and has four parts: Listening, Reading, Writing and Speaking.

IELTS is accepted by more than 7 000 institutions in over 135 countries. These include universities and colleges, immigration departments and government agencies, as well as multinational companies and professional bodies. The test is jointly owned by the British Council, IDP: IELTS Australia and the University of Cambridge ESOL Examinations (Cambridge ESOL).

The test is available in two formats: the General Training and Academic module. The General Training module is for candidates who want to migrate to an English-speaking country, and for those who want to undertake non-academic training or study at below degree level. The Academic module is suitable for those who want to enter an undergraduate or postgraduate study programme in an English-speaking country. The Listening and Speaking tests are the same in both modules, but differ in the Reading and Writing.

For more information on the exam, go to the IELTS website *www.ielts.org*.

WHO IS *BRIDGE TO IELTS* STUDENT'S BOOK FOR?

Bridge to IELTS is specially designed to help lower-level students who plan to embark on an IELTS preparatory course in the future. It is aimed at Students who are pre-Intermediate/band 3.5 level. The course focuses on both the General Training and Academic modules and bridges the gap between general English and the IELTS test.

In order to achieve a higher score in the IELTS test, students at this level need to build their language base as well as develop their reading, writing, speaking and listening skills. *Bridge to IELTS* works systematically on these four elements as well as building key study skills, such as learning outside of the classroom, thinking about study habits and using reference material.

In addition to the above, students also need to understand and deal with an IELTS course in terms of topics, texts and task types, and exam strategies. The Student's Book slowly introduces students to all of these areas so that by the end of the course successful students will be able to move confidently on to an IELTS preparation course such as *Achieve IELTS* or *IELTS Express*.

WHAT IS IN THE STUDENT'S BOOK?

12 IELTS-orientated, topic-based units
The units cover topics such as **Education**, **Urban sports** and **Conservation**. Each eight-page unit develops students' grammar, vocabulary and pronunciation as well as integrating and building their reading, writing, speaking and listening skills. The last page of the unit focuses on students' writing skills from sentence through to short text level. Answer keys and audioscripts are embedded in the Teacher's Book to ensure the teacher has them when needed.

Grammar
Over 25 key areas of grammar are covered. They are all drawn from reading or listening texts and the grammar focus is on meaning, use and form. A range of activities get students working with the grammar. If students need further clarification and/or practice, they can refer to the **Grammar reference** at the back of the book.

Vocabulary
Vocabulary areas such as **Meeting people**, **Academic subjects and higher education**, and **Adjective and noun collocations** provide students with the type of language they will need for the IELTS test and for life in an English-speaking country. Tasks usually move from meaning to contextualised usage followed by personalised practice.

Regular reviews
Each two-page section begins with a review of grammar and vocabulary. This is followed by the *Bridge to IELTS* feature which teaches students how to recognise and then perform an IELTS task type, such as labelling or guided summary completion. The Review ends with a focus on an area of **Study skills** to help students learn more effectively.

The Writing bank
In addition to the 12 writing lessons in the main units, there are 12 writing lessons at the back of the book. These lessons relate to the contents of each unit and build students' writing from word, sentence and paragraph level, to short texts. They can be used in class or given to students to work on outside of lessons.

The Communication activity bank
There are regular pairwork activities in the Student's Book units. The Assignments section of the book houses the Student 'A' and Student 'B' communication activities.

Audioscripts
All of the audioscripts, apart from the IELTS Practice Test, are at the back of the Student's Book and provides a valuable resource for students who want to review the content of the listenings in class or at home.

Grammar reference
The reference section at the very end of the book gives clear summaries of all the grammar points as well as additional practice activities.

How does the Student's Book prepare students to embark on an IELTS preparation course?

Although IELTS is a skills-based test it is crucial for students to have a language base that will support them when working through the four tests. The Student's Book presents and activates grammar, vocabulary and pronunciation. The IELTS exam tests students' language skills, so it is also very important to provide students with exposure to the range of texts and task types that they will meet in the actual exam. For example, as IELTS is internationally focused, students will have to listen to accents from around the world. *Bridge to IELTS* takes account of this by exposing students to a range of accents in the listening passages.

It is also vital that students understand how each of the four tests work, how long they last, how they are scored and what they have to do in each test. For example, in the Listening test students need to know they will only hear each recording once. In the Reading test they must write their answers in pencil and in the Writing test they will lose marks if they write less than is required by the word count. To further help students prepare there are three key features:

- The *Living IELTS* feature teaches key functional language related to the Speaking test.
- *Discussion* develops the student's ability to deal with different parts of the Speaking test.
- The *Bridge to IELTS* element teaches students how to recognise and then perform IELTS task types such as the guided summary completion.

What's in *Bridge to IELTS* Teacher's Book?

The Teacher's Book is divided into three sections: the Teacher's notes, the IELTS practice test and the Communication activities bank.

The Teacher's notes
The notes provide teachers with clear and comprehensive guidance on how to use the 12 units. Each unit opens with a **Unit overview** which allows teachers to understand the main elements of the lesson very quickly. The units contain background information on the IELTS tests for teachers as well as tips on how to work with IELTS-orientated materials. The Teacher's notes also cover the five **Reviews** and the 12 **Writing lessons**. In addition, the book provides the answers to all the exercises in the **Grammar reference** section.

The IELTS practice test
The 20-page, photocopiable Practice Test should be taken at the end of the course. This provides an opportunity for students to put everything they have learnt about the IELTS test into practice. An introduction to the test provides information on the format of the test and how to administer and mark it. Answer keys, including model writing answers, and the audioscripts are provided as well.

The Communication activity bank
The bank provides 24 information-gap style activities, two per unit. These activities either revise and practice key areas of language or provide speaking practise to build students' ability to deal with different parts of the Speaking test in the exam.

What other components does *Bridge to IELTS* have?

The *Bridge to IELTS* Class audio CDs
The two audio CDs have all the unit listenings as well as the listenings for the IELTS practice Listening Test.

The *Bridge to IELTS* Workbook + audio CD
The Workbook provides systematic revision and recycling of all the language work and topics in the Student's Book. In addition, students are given further reading, listening and writing skills development work. Each eight-page unit has six pages of language and skills work, a **Study skills** page and an **Exam study** page. The **Study skill** pages encourage students to become more efficient at studying by working on topics such as **Time management**, **Checking your work** and **Using a dictionary**. The **Exam skills** pages help students to prepare for exams by examining the strategies they will need for each of the four tests. The Workbook also contains all the audioscripts from the listenings as well as a full answer key, including model texts for the Writing activities.

The *Bridge to IELTS* ExamView
This easy-to-use software allows teachers to print out ready-formatted tests for every unit or to create their own tests from the bank of test items. The material tests grammar and vocabulary, reading, listening and writing.

Home

UNIT OVERVIEW

This unit looks at the topics of **homes** and **making friends**. The main **grammar** focus is on the present tense of **to be** and **there is/are**. The **vocabulary** focus is on the **home** and **socialising**. The **speaking** aims are to be able to **greet** and **introduce** people in a casual social context, say **where you come from** and ask **where someone is from**. Students also learn how to **describe a room** and **give a talk** on where they like to study. The main **writing** focus is on writing a **description of the town** where you live.

WARM UP

Ask students to look at the picture at the top of the page and discuss these questions: *What do you think the photo shows? What does the word 'home' mean to you? Where is 'home' for you?*

READING

1 Tell students they're going to complete a conversation between Ana, Sergei and Eva. Ask them to individually write the correct word in each gap in the dialogue. Ask students to check their answers in pairs but don't conduct feedback as they will listen and check.

ALTERNATIVELY

With a stronger group, ask them to cover the wordlist and complete the dialogue.

1 Hello	**2** How	**3** Fine	**4** well	**5** this	**6** Nice
7 meet	**8** from	**9** new	**10** student		

2 **1.1** Tell students they are now going to hear the conversation and they should listen and check their answers. Check the answers as a class. Then put students into groups of three to practise the conversation.

ALTERNATIVELY

If the class do not know each other, you could ask them to make the sentences true for them and hold the conversation in groups of three.

 1.1

A = Ana, S = Sergei, E = Eva

A: Hello, Sergei!
S: Hi, Ana! How are you?
A: I'm fine, thanks. And you?
S: I'm very well, thanks.
A: Sergei, this is Eva. She's from Argentina.
E: Hello, Sergei. Nice to meet you.
S: Nice to meet you too! I'm from Russia.
E: Are you a new student?
S: Yes, I am.
E: I'm a new student too!

3 Ask students to read the text quickly. This is skim reading, so tell them to look for the answers to the questions only. (*How many universities are there in Australia?* and *Who is O-week for?*) Check their answers as a class.

1 41
2 O-week is for new students.

4 Tell students they will now read the text again more carefully. Read through the four questions. Then ask them to read the text and choose *Yes* or *No*. Ask them to underline any problem words as they read. Put them in pairs to compare their ideas. Check the answers as a class and go through any problem words.

1 yes   **2** no (it's the first)   **3** yes
4 no (they know the university well)

LISTENING

1 **1.2** Tell students they are going to hear a conversation between Fouad, Agnes and Yibo at the O-week meeting. Point out the list of subjects A–E and tell students to listen and tick the things they hear talked about. Play the recording.

B (food) and **D** (family)

2 **1.2** Tell students they are going to listen again for more detailed understanding. Ask them to read the questions and then listen and choose the correct answers. Ask students to check answers in pairs before checking as a class.

1 a	2 a	3 a	4 b

 1.2

F = Fouad, A = Agnes, Y = Yibo

F: Hello. I'm a new student. I'm here for the new students meeting.

A: Hi! Welcome to O-Week! What's your subject?

F: Chemistry. I'm in the science department.

A: You're the first student to arrive at the meeting! I'm your student host. My name's Agnes. What's your name?

F: Fouad. I'm from Saudi Arabia. I'm Saudi. Nice to meet you, Agnes!

A: Nice to meet you too, Fouad!

F: Are you from Australia?

A: No, I'm not. I'm a student here in Melbourne, but I'm from Germany – I'm German.

F: Oh. Where are you from in Germany?

A: Berlin.

F: Berlin? Is Berlin the capital of Germany?

A: Yes, it is. Oh, excuse me. Here's another new student. Fouad, this is Yibo. Yibo, this is Fouad. Yibo's a science student too.

F: Hi, Yibo. Nice to meet you.

Y: Hello, Fouad. Nice to meet you too.

F: Where are you from, Yibo?

Y: I'm from China. I'm from Beijing.

F: Really? My brother is a student in Beijing. He thinks Chinese food is very good!

Y: Yes, it is. It's very nice.

A: Australian food is very good too. There's a free barbie at the student union carnival on Friday.

F/Y: 'Barbie'?

A: Oh! I'm sorry! 'Barbie' is an informal word for 'barbeque' in Australia. We cook meat, or fish, or vegetables outside over a fire.

F: I'd like to go. What about you, Yibo?

Y: Yes, please!

A: OK, that's great. Now, let's just wait for a few more students to arrive and then we can start our tour of the campus!

Living IELTS

INTRODUCING PEOPLE

Emphasise that this section is very important for the spoken component of IELTS. Here students will practise the basic functions of meeting and greeting.

 1.3 Ask students to listen and put the sentences in the right order. Play the recording and check the answers as a class.

Now put students into groups of three to practise introducing each other.

ALTERNATIVELY

Use the recording to practise the dialogue in chorus line by line. Draw attention to intonation, rhythm and word stress.

1.3 and answers

A: Fouad, this is Yibo. Yibo, this is Fouad. Yibo's a science student too.

F: Hi, Yibo. Nice to meet you.

Y: Hello, Fouad. Nice to meet you, too.

GRAMMAR
PRESENT SIMPLE OF *TO BE*

Introduce the grammar by writing these example sentences on the board:
The students in the class are from all over the world.
I'm tired.
Australia is a really big island and it's really hot.
They aren't from Sydney.
Are they from Germany?
Yes, they are.

Ask students to underline *to be.* Ask 'What is the verb doing in the sentences?' and elicit or explain that you use the verb *to be* to give/ask for information about yourself, things and places, etc.

Point out the pronunciation features of your last three sentences: *aren't* is a single syllable /ɑːnt/; *are* is /ə/ in a sentence but /ɑː/at the end of a sentence.

Ask students to read through the grammar box and check their ideas.

Note: If any student's language does not have the verb *to be,* explain that in English it must be used and cannot be left out.

> If students need more help, refer them to the Grammar reference on page 138.

Note: There are no answers to the Grammar reference in the Student's Book, so be sure to go over the answers at some point if you have asked students to do the exercises.

1 Ask students to complete the sentences individually with the correct form of the verb. Check answers in pairs, then as a class.

1 is	2 are	3 aren't
4 'm/am not	5 isn't/is not	6 is

2 Put students in pairs to order the words to make questions. Conduct brief feedback. Ask students to read the questions out to you.

Answers (to activity 2 and 3)

1 Is he German? (d) *No, he isn't …*
2 Are you a new student? (a) *Yes, I am …*
3 Is she from China? (b) *Yes, she is …*
4 Are they on the tour? (e) *Yes, they are …*
5 Is your name Yibo? (c) *No, it isn't …*

3 Ask students to complete the answers using the words in the box. Then ask them to match them to the questions in activity 2. Check their answers (above). Then ask them to practise the conversation in pairs.

Communication activities

1A *see Teacher's notes page 128.*

PRONUNCIATION
VOWEL SOUNDS – /ɒ/ /eɪ/ /aɪ/

1   1.4 Introduce each sound. Play the recording and ask students to match the words to each sound. Drill chorally and individually.

1.4 and answers

1 b /ɒ/ what
2 c /eɪ/ name
3 a /aɪ/ I

2 1.5 Tell students to complete the table as they hear each word. Play the recording, pausing after each word to give enough time to write the answer. Write the table on the board as you check the answers.

/ɒ/	/eɪ/	/aɪ/
from	make	nice
on	day	my
not	they	fine

1.5

from	nice	make	day	on
my	not	they	fine	

3 Practise as a class. Drill the words as a whole class, using the table on the board to help.

VOCABULARY
MAKING FRIENDS

1 Ask students to match the words to make phrases in pairs. Point out that the first one has been done for them. Check answers in pairs, then as a class.

1 e	2 d	3 b	4 c	5 f	6 a

2 Ask students to complete the sentences on their own and then briefly check in pairs. Feedback by asking students to read out the sentences to you.

1 introduce yourself to someone
2 say hello
3 start a conversation
4 go out with friends
5 chat to someone
6 meet people

READING

1 Ask students to match the words with the pictures on their own. (This provides a vocabulary check by asking students to provide the titles to each of the pictures.) Pick up on any significant pronunciation problems. (*Choir* /kwaɪə/ might be a problem.)

1 Internet	2 sports club	3 band	4 choir

2 Ask students to briefly read the passage and number the pictures in the order they are mentioned. As this is a skim reading activity, you might like to set a short time limit for the reading.

1 Internet	2 sports club	3 band	4 choir

3 Ask students to read though the list of questions. Then ask them to read the text again, this time for detail, and decide if the questions are true or false. Tell them to underline the text that helped them find their answers. Ask students to compare answers in pairs before checking with the class. Ask for the reasons for their answers.

1 F (there are many different ways)
2 F (it's a good idea to keep the conversation light)
3 T
4 F (some good friends are different)
5 T
6 T

4 Emphasise that **two** of the choices in each question are right. Ask students to read the text again, and then work in pairs to complete the activity.

1 a, c	**2** b, c	**3** a, b

5 Ask students to work on their own to find the words in the text and choose the correct meaning. Point out the line references which are there to help them. Conduct feedback as a class.

1 a	**2** a	**3** a	**4** b

Discussion

This activity gives students practice in using the vocabulary. It also helps prepare them for PART 4 of IELTS: the Speaking test. Put students in pairs to ask and answer the questions. Bring to an end by asking a couple of groups if they agree with each other.

VOCABULARY

ADJECTIVES TO DESCRIBE ROOMS

1 Check students understand: *student hall* and *bedsit*. Point out that 'flat' and 'bedsit' are British English. American English uses *apartment* and *studio*. Then match the pictures to the words as a class.

1 house	**2** bedsit	**3** flat	**4** student hall

2 It is important for each student to have a correct version of the table in activity 2. Therefore, ask students to complete this on their own and make sure they write down their answers. Circulate and monitor. Check answers in pairs, then as a class.

chair	big uncomfortable comfortable small
room	big bright cold uncomfortable comfortable noisy small tidy warm quiet dark
bed	big cold uncomfortable comfortable small warm
house or flat	big bright cold uncomfortable comfortable noisy small tidy warm quiet dark

3 Do this activity as a class by asking selected students to volunteer the opposite of a word you choose. Ask which word has no opposite in the list. Tell them to find the opposite in their dictionaries.

ALTERNATIVELY

Set as a contest, with the first student to finish reading out the answers to the class. Students complete as they hear the answers.

big/small	comfortable/uncomfortable
bright/dark	cold/warm quiet/noisy

No opposite given: tidy/(untidy)

4 Ask students to complete the sentences with the correct answers in pairs. Conduct brief feedback.

1 comfortable	**2** bright	**3** noisy
4 small	**5** tidy	**6** warm

Discussion

Put students in pairs to decide which place in the photos they would most like to live in. Why? Feedback by selecting individuals to say what they prefer and why.

LISTENING

1 🔘 1.6 Tell the class they're going to hear a conversation between two new students, Hassan and Etsuko, talking about where they live.

Ask students to read the questions, then listen and choose the correct answers. Play the recording, repeating if necessary.

1 b	**2** a	**3** c	**4** a

2 🔘 1.6 Tell students they are going to listen again and tick the items they hear mentioned. Tell them to read through the wordlist before they start. Play the recording straight through, repeating if necessary.

desk	table	laptop	sofa	bookshelves	window

🔘 1.6

E = Etsuko, **H** = Hussan

H: Excuse me, are you Etsuko?
E: Yes, I am.
H: Remember me? At the tour of the university – on Wednesday?
E: Oh yes! Of course! You're Ahmed!
H: No, I'm not. My name's Hassan.   ➥

E: I'm sorry, Hassan. I remember now. You're from Turkey.

H: No, I'm not. I'm from Iran. And you're from Japan!

E: That's right! You've got a good memory, Hassan! How are you?

H: Fine, thanks. And you?

E: I'm OK too. There's a lot to do – O-Week is such a busy time!

H: Yes, it is and I'm looking for a place to live too!

E: Oh really? Where are you at the moment?

H: I'm in a room in a shared flat. It's right in the city centre and I can walk to the university in ten minutes. There are three of us in the flat.

E: How many rooms are there?

H: Three.

E: Is your room big?

H: No, it isn't. It's very small. But the other students are very friendly so I can practise my English! But it's very noisy. There isn't a quiet place for me to study.

E: Is there a desk?

H: No, there isn't but there's a small table for my laptop. I go to the university library when I want to study. And there aren't any bookshelves so all my books are under the sofa. It's not ideal! What about you, Estuko? Where are you?

E: I'm in a room in a student hall. It's a single room. It's a bit small but there's everything I need. There's a big desk for my laptop, there's a lamp and there are bookshelves, so there's lots of space for all my books. I love reading! There's a small sofa too – it's very comfortable! The best thing is that it's very quiet – and I can see the park from my window!

H: I want to find a room like yours!

GRAMMAR
THERE IS / THERE ARE

Introduce the grammar. Write these examples on the board:
There is a sofa.
There are three people.
Underline *is* and *are*.

Ask 'What is the rule?' (you use *is* with singular nouns and *are* with plural nouns). Elicit how you form the negative *There isn't a sofa. / There aren't three people.* Elicit the question forms and answers.
Is there a sofa? Yes there is. / No there isn't.
Are there three people? Yes there are. / No there aren't.

Ask for more examples, using items in the classroom as prompts. Then ask students to read the grammar box and check their ideas. If you like, play Etsuko's final description of her room again to highlight *there is/are* in action. 🔘1.6

> 📖 *If students need more help, refer them to the Grammar reference on page 138.*

1 Ask students to look at sentences 1–4 and decide if *there is* or *there are* is correct. Go through the first one as a class. Students compare answers in pairs, then check as a class.

1 There is	**2** There is	**3** There is	**4** There are

2 Ask students to complete the questions, then compare answers in pairs. Check answers with the class.

1 Are there	**2** Is there	**3** Is there	**4** Are there

3 Ask students to put the sentences in the correct order in pairs. Point out that 3 and 4 do not test *there is/ are*. They are in preparation for activity 4. Circulate and monitor.

1 Is there a window in your room? (c) *Yes it is. There's a lovely …*
2 Are there shops near your home? (a) *Yes there are. There's a big …*
3 Is your home very quiet? (d) *No it isn't. It's very noisy.*
4 Is it a good place to live? (b) *Yes it is. It's right …*

4 This activity complements activity 3. Ask students to work individually to complete the answers with the words in the box. Check answers in pairs, then as a class (answers above).

5 Ask students to work in pairs to ask and answer the questions in activity 3. Move around and monitor. Pay particular attention to question intonation, rhythm and stress.

SPEAKING
DESCRIBING A ROOM

1 Model the conversation by asking three different students one of the questions, working through the points mentioned. Then put students in pairs to practise each conversation. Ask them to reverse roles when they've finished. Move around and monitor, paying attention to students' intonation and stress. To finish, ask them to feedback anything interesting they learnt about their partner to the class.

2 🔘1.7 Tell students they are going to hear Marisa talking about where she likes to study. Tell them to decide as they listen which of the two pictures is of Marisa's room. Allow students time to look at the two photos and note the differences. Play the recording. Ask the whole class for the answer. Play the recording again if necessary.

The first photo is of Marisa's room.

My ideal room to study in? It's my bedroom at home. It's a big room and it's blue. Blue is a very calm colour. There's a big window, so it's very bright. There are three bookshelves, there's a large desk for my laptop and there's a red sofa. It's a good room to study in because it's very quiet and it's very tidy!

3 1.7 2 Tell students to listen again and choose the correct answers. Ask them to read the questions before they start. Play the recording. Check answers in pairs, then as a class.

1 b   2 a   3 a   4 b

4 Ask students to work individually and make some notes on their ideal room to study in. They will need these notes later in the lesson.

Bridge to IELTS

STARTING YOUR TALK

The talk is an important component of the IELTS Speaking test. Ask the class to read the box. Ask *What is a good way to start your talk?* (Repeat the words on the card – emphasise 'slowly and clearly'). *Why?* (It gives you time to think about what you can say next).

5 Ask students to read the topic card. Tell them it is like one in the IELTS exam. As a class, rehearse the opening in chorus. Practise the language for the talk as a class. Invite volunteers to answer the questions: where the room is, what colour the room is, what there is in the room and why it is a good place to study in.

Then put students in pairs to take turns giving the talk. Remind them to use their notes. Move around the class and monitor.

WRITING
A PERSONAL DESCRIPTION

1 Tell the class they are going to write about themselves. Ask students to study the photo and to guess which sentence might describe the city. Briefly check their ideas.

2 Then ask students to read the text to check their answers. Conduct feedback as a class.

True of Novgorod: 2, 4
True of Natalia's flat: 5, 6

WORD ORDER

3 Do the first one as a class, then ask students to work on their own to complete the activity. Check answers in pairs, then as a class.

1 What's your name?
2 Where are you from?
3 Where is your city?
4 Where is your home?
5 What is near your home?
6 What is your home like?

4 Ask students to imagine they are Natalia and write down her answers to the questions. Ask them to compare answers in pairs before checking as a class.

1 My name's Natalia.
2 I'm from Norgorod.
3 It's a small city in the west of Russia.
4 My home is in the centre of the city.
5 There are lots of shops, restaurants and cinema's near it.
6 My home is very comfortable, warm and bright.

6 Now ask students to complete the text using their own ideas. When students have finished ask them to read or show their paragraph to their partner. Conduct brief feedback.

 Communication activities
1B *see Teacher's notes page 128.*

Writing Skills

Festivals

UNIT OVERVIEW

This unit looks at the topic of **festivals**. The main **speaking** aims are to talk about important festivals. The main **grammar** focuses are **the form and use of the present simple tense**. The **vocabulary** focus is on **adjectives to describe festivals and the feelings associated with them**. **Writing** covers some aspects of **the use of capital letters and full stops**.

WARM UP

Get students to look at the photo at the top of the page. Ask them to discuss these questions:

1 *Where do you think this festival is?*
2 *What do you think you can do there?*
3 *Would you like to go to it? If 'yes', why? If 'no', why not?*
4 *Do you have a favourite festival in your country? What is it called? When does it happen? What can you do there?*

READING

1 Ask students to read the words in the box and check they understand them. Ask them to work in pairs and to use the words to talk about the pictures. Conduct quick feedback.

ALTERNATIVELY

If you think students need more help, hold a general class discussion about the pictures before they start.

2 Ask students to read the questions and then read the webpage text quickly. This is scan reading, so tell them to look only for the answers to the questions. Check the answers in pairs, then as a class.

1	January or February	2	two weeks
3	ice	4	Bonhomme

3 Tell students to work alone to choose the correct meaning of the words in the text. Ask them to compare answers in pairs. Drill the words as you feedback and check the vocabulary. For example, ask them to show you the picture of the mascot.

1 a	2 b	3 b	4 a	5 a

GRAMMAR

PRESENT SIMPLE

Tell students they are going to look at some grammar. Write the two examples on the board:
It's one of the largest festivals in the world.
Every year she goes to the Quebec Winter Carnival.

Ask them what the verb is in the first example and underline *it*. Then ask them about the second sentence and underline *goes*. Ask them if they know the name of this tense and write 'Present simple' on the board above the examples. Tell them that a tense can mean different things.

Give them time to look at the grammar box and the two meanings of the present tense here. Ask students to give you more examples of these two different uses. If their examples are correct, write them on the board under the examples from the Student's Book. If they are wrong, ask them questions to guide them to the right answer. For example:

Student:	*I work in a bank.*
You:	*Ok, is that always or generally true, or is that a habit or a regular activity?*
Student:	*It is always true?*
You:	*'Always true?' In 5 years, 10 years, 20 years … always true?*
Student:	*No.*
You:	*Correct. But is your job in the bank a regular habit? Something you do now?*
Student:	*Yes. So it is the second example, right?*

Now focus on the form of the third person singular. Point out the form of *I/You/We/They live in Quebec* and *He/she/it lives in Quebec*. Elicit or tell students that with the present simple we usually add -*s* to the third person.

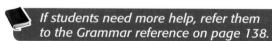 *If students need more help, refer them to the Grammar reference on page 138.*

1 Do the first example in activity 1 together. Then put students in pairs to complete the other examples. When you check the answers, point out that some verbs don't follow the same rules, for example *goes*.

comes	enjoys	goes	likes	lives
says	speaks	visits	wants	

2 Ask students to read the sentences and choose the correct answers. Check answers in pairs, then conduct feedback by asking individuals to read out each sentence.

3 Ask students to work alone to complete the text with the correct words from the box. Check in pairs, then as a class.

1 come	**2** takes place	**3** lasts	**4** want
5 enjoy	**6** look	**7** watch	

Discussion

This feature of the Student's Book gives students practice in using the grammar. As such, it is an accuracy and fluency-based activity. It also helps prepare them for PART 4 of IELTS: the Speaking test. Model first. Tell students to talk for as long as possible. Put them in pairs and move around as they talk, noting down examples of correct and incorrect English for a brief feedback session at the end.

LISTENING

1 🔘 1.8 Tell students they are going to hear two students, Etsuko and Ahmed, talking about the winter carnival in Quebec. Ask them to read through the statements and then choose the correct answers as they listen. Answer any questions before playing the recording. Check answers as a class.

1 a	**2** b	**3** c	**4** a

2 🔘 1.8 Tell students they are going to listen again and decide whether the questions are true or false. Play the recording. They may need to listen more than once. Check answers in pairs, then as a class.

1 F (he really doesn't like winter)
2 F (he loves the weather in Canada)
3 T
4 T
5 F (he feels cold just thinking about it)

 1.8

A = Ahmed, **E** = Etsuko

E: Hi Ahmed! How are you?
A: I'm OK, but I'm freezing. It's minus 10 degrees today!
E: Yes, I know it's very cold, Ahmed. But, it IS January and Canada is the coldest country in the world!
A: I really don't like winter. It's awful.
E: No, it isn't! It's fantastic! I love it. The winter carnival starts this weekend – on Saturday! Do you want to come with me? ➥

A: I'm not sure. What happens at the carnival?
E: Well, there are amazing snow sculptures all over the city and there is even an ice palace! It's very beautiful – especially at night when the lights shine through the walls of ice. I really want to see it!
A: Well I don't! What's interesting about an ice palace? It's boring.
E: OK, but you like sport – there's a canoe race across the St Lawrence River. It's one of the main attractions – it's very exciting!
A: I like playing sport – I don't like watching it. And I hate watching sport in the cold!
E: So you don't want to see the snow bathers then ...
A: Snow bathers? Do you mean people actually have a bath in the snow!
E: Yes, can you imagine? Isn't that awful?
A: I feel freezing cold just thinking about it.
E: OK, Ahmed, do you want to come to the winter carnival or not? All you need are warm clothes!
A: I've got a coat and a scarf but I don't have a hat ...
E: I've got a red one you can have. Come on, Ahmed! I really want you to meet Bonhomme!
A: Who's he?
E: He's a snowman! And he wears a bright red hat too!

Living IELTS

TALKING ABOUT LIKES AND DISLIKES

This feature of the Student's Book focuses on functional language which will be of use to students in PART 4 of IELTS: the Speaking test.

Talking about likes and dislikes is something we do all the time, so it is important to learn how to do this properly. Explain that word stress is very important in English. It carries a lot of meaning.

🔘 1.9 Tell students they are going to listen and underline the stressed words. Put the first sentence on the board. Show students how they can mark the stressed words in the sentence by underlining them. Ask them to listen and mark the stress. Then listen and drill the sentences.

🔘 **1.9 and answers**

I <u>really</u> don't like winter.
I <u>love</u> it.
I <u>like</u> playing sport.
I <u>hate</u> watching sport in the cold!

VOCABULARY
POSITIVE AND NEGATIVE ADJECTIVES

1 Put students in pairs and ask them to decide which adjectives are positive and which are negative. Drill as you check the answers.

> **Positive:** interesting, exciting, beautiful, colourful, fantastic, amazing, delicious
> **Negative:** awful, boring, freezing

2 Put students in pairs to answer the questions. Check their answers as a class.

1	delicious	**2**	fantastic, amazing
3	awful	**4**	freezing

3 In the same pairs, ask them to choose the correct adjective to complete the sentences. Check their answers as a class.

1	delicious	**2**	beautiful	**3**	freezing
4	exciting	**5**	fantastic	**6**	amazing

4 Ask students to circle the odd one out, then compare answers in pairs. As feedback, ask them to explain why each word is the odd one out.

1	awful (negative)	**2**	interesting (positive)
3	freezing (negative)	**4**	awful (negative)

5 Ask students to work individually to complete the sentence. Ask them to read their sentences to each other in pairs, before conducting whole class feedback.

PRONUNCIATION
SYLLABLE STRESS

1 Say or tap out on your table the three stress patterns (Oo, Ooo, oOo). Ask students to match the words with the stress patterns, and then check their answers and drill.

1 c	2 a	3 c

2 📀 1.10 Tell students they are going to listen and put the words in the correct place in the table. Play the recording, pausing after each word. Then play the recording again without stopping. Get partners to compare their tables. Check answers as a class by making a table on the board.

Oo	Ooo	oOo
awful	interesting	fantastic
boring	beautiful	exciting
freezing	colourful	amazing
		delicious

3 📀 1.10 Play the recording again and ask students to repeat. Drill chorally and individually. Insist on *interesting* as three syllables, not four.

📀 *1.10*

awful	interesting	fantastic	exciting
beautiful	boring	amazing	colourful
freezing	delicious		

💬 **Communication activities**
   2A see *Teacher's notes page 128.*

READING

1 Ask students to read the phrases, look at the four photos A–D and tick what they can see. Ask them to match each photo with each phrase. Check answers as a class.

A	picnic in the park
B	barbeque on the beach
C	masquerade party
D	fireworks display

2 Tell students they are going to read a text about New Year's Eve in Australia. This is skim reading so ask them to read the passage quickly, and put the pictures in the same order as the text. Stop them after three minutes. Ask them to compare answers in pairs before conducting class feedback.

1	picnic in the park
2	barbeque on the beach
3	masquerade party
4	fireworks display

3 Ask students to read the passage again and answer the questions. Elicit the answers individually. The exact form of words is not important, just the ideas.

1 **1** 1 January
2 special events (parades, music, entertainment), barbecues, parties, picnics, firework displays
3 Sydney and Melbourne
4 over 1.5 million
5 They mark the end of the old year and the beginning of the new.

4 Tell students to work alone to find words from the text that match the meaning in each sentence. Check answers in pairs, then as a class.

1 celebrate   **2** exciting   **3** massive   **4** impressive

Discussion

Explain that the ability to discuss is highly important for the spoken component of IELTS and socialising in an English-speaking environment.

Read through the questions and put students in pairs to hold the discussion. As the first question is a closed yes/no question, you can add to the interest by asking the class to discuss how the celebrations are the same or different. Encourage them to expand on the reasons for their answers to question 2.

LISTENING

1 Put students in pairs. Ask them to label the pictures with words from the box and then group the words as 'people' or 'things'.

people: 1 clown, 6 musician, 2 dancer, 7 acrobat
things: 5 float, 3 stall, 8 kite, 4 puppet

2 Ask students to read the poster and work on their own to answer the questions. Check that *most* is understood. Check answers in pairs, then as a class.

1 Festival of the Winds   **2** 9ᵗʰ September
3 Bondi Beach   **4** 11 am
5 (it's) free

3 🔘1.11 Tell students they are going to listen to two friends, Jing and Fouad, talking about the Festival of the Winds. Ask them to listen carefully and tick the questions in activity 2 that they hear answered. Play the recording. They may need to listen more than once. Ask students to compare their answers in pairs before checking as a class.

All questions answered.

4 🔘1.11 Tell students they are going to listen again and choose two answers. Play the recording. If necessary, pause when the answer to a question is reached and ask for the two answers. For question 1, you may have to explain that September is spring in Australia.

1   **a** every spring   **b** once a year
2   **a** kite fliers   **c** people from all over the world
3   **a** make a kite   **c** visit the food stalls
4   **b** by train   **c** by bus

 1.11

F = Fouad, J = Jing

F: Hi, Jing! Do you want to go to the Festival of the Winds next weekend?

J: Festival of the Winds? What is that exactly?

F: It's a kite festival! Look at the poster! It's a festival for people who love kites. It's only once a year, and lasts for one day. I don't want to miss it!

J: I'm not sure. I haven't got a kite.

F: You don't need one! Kite fliers from all over Australia and all over the world come to show their kites and fly them. It's free, too.

J: So we don't pay? That sounds good! When is it?

F: Next Sunday – Sunday the ninth.

J: I like the kites in the poster – lots of different shapes and sizes.

F: They're amazing. There are even kites of huge cartoon characters, and there are even flying trains and flying buildings!

J: So, is the festival just about kites?

F: No it isn't. There is an entertainment programme too, with an art exhibition and different workshops too.

J: Is there a dance workshop?

F: Yes, there is.

J: Fantastic! I love dancing.

F: I don't! I'm a really bad dancer. But there is a kite-making workshop and I really want to go to that. I want to make my own kite and then fly it on the beach! There are also stalls with food and drink from around the world.

J: Mmm! Delicious!

F: Do you want to come with me to the food stalls?

J: Yes, of course I do! You know I love food!

F: How do we get to Bondi beach? I don't want to go by car – it's difficult to park close to the beach.

J: That's true. We can take a train to Bondi Junction and then catch a bus. I'm sure there are buses from Circular Quay.

F: Do you want to check the website and find out? The festival starts at 11am – we don't want to be late.

J: Good idea!

GRAMMAR

PRESENT SIMPLE QUESTIONS AND SHORT ANSWERS

Write this sentence on the board:
I live in Ireland.
Ask students to make it a question:
Do you live in Ireland?
What are the possible answers?
Yes I do. / No I don't.

Ask them to make a statement using *she/he* and elicit *She lives*... Ask them to turn that into a question and elicit *Does she/he*. Ask students to tell you how you form the present simple (*do/does* + base form of the verb). Highlight the pronunciation of *does* /dʌz/. Explain that *do* and *does* are called auxiliary verbs. Highlight the pronunciation of *doesn't* /dʌznt/.

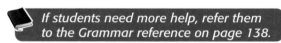 *If students need more help, refer them to the Grammar reference on page 138.*

1   Now ask students to read through the information in the Student's book and choose the right answers.

1 yes	2 comes before

2   Ask students to work alone to complete the sentences with *do* or *does*. Go through the answers by asking individuals.

1 do	2 does	3 do	4 do	5 does

3   Ask students to put the questions in the correct order on their own. Check answers in pairs, then as a class (answers below).

4   Still in their pairs, ask students to match the questions in activity 3 with the short answers.

Answers (3 and 4)
1   Do you speak French? *Yes, I do.*
2   Does she have a car? *No, she doesn't.*
3   Do they want to take the bus? *Yes, they do.*
4   Does the carnival start on Sunday? *Yes, it does.*
5   Do I need some gloves? *No, you don't.*

QUESTION WORDS

Show students how the table works. Then let them look at the table for a minute, reading the possible sentences silently. Ask them for some example sentences.

5   Put students in pairs and ask them to choose the correct words. Feedback by asking individuals for the answer to each question.

1 what	2 Where	3 What time
4 When	5 How much	

6   Ask students to answer the questions in activity 5 so they are true for them. Check their ideas.

ALTERNATIVELY

When they have written their sentences, turn this into a conversation between pairs of students: one of the pair asks the questions and the other answers.

6   Conduct this as a whole class activity. Ask individual students for the sentence completions while the rest of the class write them down.

7   Put students in pairs and designate them A or B. Tell Student A to turn to page 124 and Student B to page 126. Ask them to read their information and then work together to ask and answer the questions without showing each other their text. Student A starts. Then swap.

SPEAKING

A SPECIAL DAY OR EVENT

1   Tell students they are going to talk about special days and events in their country. Put them in pairs to discuss the questions. Conduct quick feedback on what special events or days students celebrate.

ALTERNATIVELY

If students all come from the same country, skip question 1 and ask some individual students questions 2.

2   🔘 1.12 Tell students they're going to hear Leah talking about National Day in Singapore. Ask students to number the pictures in the order they hear them in the recording. Play the recording. Check answers in pairs, then as a class.

C	D	A	B

ALTERNATIVELY

If your class is not strong, get them to discuss what they can see in the photos before they listen.

3 Ask students to read the statements silently and answer any questions. Then play the recording and ask students to listen and choose the correct answer: a, b or c. Check answers in pairs, then as a class.

> **1** a   **2** c   **3** c   **4** b

1.12

> **Leah**: An important day for me? Oh, that's easy! Singapore National Day is really special. It's on the 9th of August. What happens? Well, I spend the day with my family and friends. We watch the National Day parade on a live webcast! It's very colourful! Then we eat delicious chicken rice. I like it very much! I wear national costume too – we call it *Peranakan* dress – it's very beautiful! Why is the day special? Well, it's not just a public holiday to me – it's a day when I can celebrate everything about Singapore and be happy!

Bridge to IELTS

TASK CARDS

Tell students that activity 4 is preparation for the next phase, an IELTS spoken task, which is Task 2, the long turn in the spoken exam. Ask them to read the box. Ask *How long do you have to think about the topic?* (one minute).

4 Tell students that now they will prepare to talk about a day or event that is special for them. Ask them to choose an event and refer them to the bullet points to make a few notes. Move around the class and help with ideas.

5 Ask students to read the topic card and then work in pairs, taking turns to describe their life event. To close the activity, ask one or two pairs to present their description to the class.

WRITING

DESCRIBING A FESTIVAL

1 Ask students to look at the picture and guess the answers to the questions in pairs. Check their ideas. Make the most of disagreements by asking for justifications!

2 Ask students to read the text to check their answers. Conduct whole class feedback.

> **1** a   **2** b

PUNCTUATION

The next exercise looks at basic punctuation. You could check they know the basic terms. Write this on the board:

I live in Beijing.

Circle the capital letters and the full stop. Ask students: *What's the name of a letter like this and this? And what is the name for this?*

3 Ask students to read the text and complete the sentences. Check answers as a class.

> **1** capital letter
> **2** full stop
> **3** months/places (either order)

4 Ask students to rewrite the sentences using the correct punctuation. Move around the class and check they are writing correctly. Ask them to compare in pairs before checking answers.

> **1** My favourite festival takes place in Thailand in April.
> **2** Leah comes from Singapore.
> **3** The festival doesn't happen in Australia.
> **4** He always spends time in Quebec in January.

5 Ask students to spend a short time thinking about a festival they know and to make notes about it using the questions in the table. Monitor as they write.

6 Then ask them to complete the text using their ideas. Move around the class and help them.

When students have finished, ask them to read or show their paragraph to their partner. Conduct brief feedback with the class.

 Communication activities
2B *see Teacher's notes page 128.*

OVERVIEW

It is important for all students to meet 'new' language again and again. This is even more important for students starting at Pre-intermediate level because their language base and ability to deal with skills are not very developed. Reviewing language will help them to consolidate what they are in the process of learning as well as show them which areas they still have not fully understood. With this in mind, it is important that you are positive and supportive if they do not do very well in areas of the Review. Encourage them to see that if they get something wrong, it helps them to see where they should focus their energies. Taking this view will help them to grow in confidence; emphasising failure seldom has the same effect.

The five Reviews revise the language (grammar and vocabulary) that has been covered in previous units. In addition to the natural recycling of language within units, the Grammar reference section at the back of the Student's Book and the language and skills development provided by the Workbook, students should have plenty of opportunities to think about and develop their language and skills work. In the first half of the book, the Reviews are more regular (after every two units). This is because we believe students will need to go over what has been covered more frequently to aid memory and provide further practice. In the second half of the Student's Book, there are just two Reviews (one after every three units).

AIM To revise asking question with *Is / Are there*.

1   This is a controlled speaking activity. Put students in AB pairs. Student A forms and asks questions using the prompts given. Student B answers using the picture on page 126. Remind them not to look at each other's pictures!

Picture A
1   Is there a red sofa? (No, there isn't.)
2   Are there two small windows? (No, there aren't – the windows are not small.)
3   Are there blue walls? (Yes, there are.)
4   Is there a laptop on the desk? (Yes, there is.)
5   Is there a yellow lamp? (No, there isn't.)
6   Are there four bookshelves? (Yes, there are.)
7   Are there two beds? (No, there aren't.)

AIM To revise simple present.

2   Ask students to read the text and choose the correct form to complete the sentences. Check answers in pairs, then as a class.

1 begins	2 don't go	3 take place
4 lives	5 watches	6 do
7 comes	8 spends	9 loves

AIM To revise question forms using *do* or *does*.

3   Tell students to work individually to fill the six sentences with do or *does* and then complete the sentences using the table. Check answers in pairs, then as a class.

to question forms
1   Does Jon speak French?
2   Do they like hot weather?
3   Does Csilla like dogs?
4   Does he live in Canada?
5   Does she drive a black car?
6   Do they study at weekends?

to sentence completion
1   Jon speaks French.
2   He doesn't enjoy sport.
3   Csilla drives a black car.
4   She likes cold weather.
5   They don't study at weekends.
6   He doesn't live in a flat.

4   Put students in pairs to ask each other the questions from activity 3 and give answers which are true for them. Conduct feedback on question and answer forms, and focus on their intonation.

AIM To revise forms of *to be* and *the present simple*.

5   Get students to complete the text on their own and then check in pairs. Monitor as they write.

Conduct feedback, asking individual students for the answers. Draw attention to the present simple in *She comes from Madrid* and to the replacement of *y* with *ie* in *studies*.

1 is	2 comes	3 is	4 lives
5 studies	6 likes	7 enjoys	8 speaks

AIM To practise writing a short text.

6   Tell students to write a text about themselves, using the text about Ana as a model. Students work alone to write their text. Move around and help them.

Ask students to show or read their text to a partner. Feedback by asking a few students to read their text to the class.

ALTERNATIVELY

When students have finished writing, use their texts for a class gallery.

VOCABULARY

AIM To check students remember common adjectives.

1 Ask students to match the opposites to the adjectives on their own, then check in pairs.

1 e	comfortable / uncomfortable
2 c	big / small
3 b	bright / dark
4 a	noisy / quiet
5 d	cold / warm

AIM To revise the verbs for meeting and socialising.

2 Ask students to complete the sentences using the verbs in the box. Check in pairs, then as a class.

1	introduce	2	start
3	go out	4	chat
5	meet	6	say

AIM To revise adjectives for feelings.

3 Ask students to complete the sentences using the words in the box. Check in pairs, then as a class.

1	delicious	2	awful	3	freezing
4	fantastic	5	boring	6	colourful

4 Put students into pairs to spot the two adjectives that work in each sentence. Check their answers as a class.

1	exciting / interesting
2	beautiful / amazing
3	fantastic / delicious
5	colourful / beautiful
6	boring / awful

Bridge to IELTS

TEST PREPARATION

AIM To go over IELTS test preparation.

1 Put students in pairs, and ask them to think about and agree on three things they know about the IELTS exam.

2 Then ask students to read the passage and underline information that is new to them.

3 Now ask students to discuss their answers as a group. Ensure students have correct ideas about IELTS.

4 Put students in pairs to discuss which parts of IELTS they think they are good at and why they would like to take the test. Conduct brief feedback.

Study Skills

LEARNING OUTSIDE CLASS

Tell students how important it is to maximise their exposure to English, especially when students are not living in an English-speaking country or a country where English is spoken as an alternative language. Point out that even in these countries, there are many opportunities to access English, especially through the media and the Internet.

AIM To encourage students to engage with learning outside of the classroom.

1 Put students in pairs to discuss and write a list of ways they can practise their English outside of the classroom, e.g. watching films, reading in English.
Conduct whole class feedback, writing their ideas on the board.

2 Get students to read the text and tick the things they already do, and tell you any new ideas they have got from the list you've created.

3 Ask students to choose just one of the study skills ideas they don't already do and try it for a week. Tell them you will ask them for their experiences in a week.

Make a note to remind yourself in a week to ask your students about the goal they set. You could do this as a warm-up activity at the beginning of the lesson. If you do this regularly, students are more likely to take the goals(s) they set seriously. As a result they will become more effective language learners.

Teamwork

UNIT OVERVIEW

This unit looks at the topic of **teamwork**. The main **speaking** aims are **pronouncing** and using the **strong and weak forms of *can* and *can't*.** The main **grammar** focuses are **adverbs of frequency** and ***can* to talk about ability.** The **vocabulary** focus is on **adjectives to describe character** and **describing people's abilities.** **Writing** covers the use of ***and, also* and *too*** and **writing about a person's abilities.**

WARM UP

Ask students to look at the photograph. Ask *What are the people doing? What does it illustrate?* Point out the people in the photo are all doing the same thing, i.e. illustrating teamwork, working together.

VOCABULARY

ADJECTIVES TO DESCRIBE CHARACTER

1   Ask students to read through the list of adjectives. Check understanding and mime any they don't know. Ask students to work in pairs to match the words with the photos. Drill as you check the answers.

> 1 friendly, happy, warm   2 sad   3 intelligent   4 nervous

Note: 'Nervous' is often seen as 'anxious'. So, for example, contrast feelings before a job interview (*nervous*) with feelings when someone does not phone you to say why they are late (*anxious*).

2   Ask students to work individually to complete the sentences with each adjective. Then check in pairs before conducting feedback.

> 1 hardworking   2 Shy   3 talkative

Ask students to match each word with its opposite. Indicate stress and drill as you check answers.

> hardworking/lazy   shy/confident   talkative/quiet

3   Ask students to circle the correct adjectives in pairs. Check answers.

> 1 intelligent   2 hardworking   3 confident   4 friendly

4   Tell students they are going to use the adjectives in activities 2 and 3 to describe themselves. You might like to model this first. Allow students time to make notes, then put them in pairs to describe themselves to each other. Circulate and check their pronunciation. As feedback, ask some students to read what they have written.

5   In the same pairs, ask students to ask each other the questions in the questionnaire and then turn to page 125 to work out their individual scores. Conduct class feedback.

ALTERNATIVELY

The questionnaire can also be completed individually, then ask students to turn to page 125 to work out their scores. Students then swap questionnaires and read each other's.

LISTENING

1   Tell students they are going to listen to Katrin asking Li Bo the questions on the questionnaire. Ask students to look at the questionnaire and circle Li Bo's answers as they listen. Play the recording. Check answers in pairs, then as a class.

2   Tell students to listen again and choose the correct answers. Ask them to read the questions before they start. Play the recording. Check answers in pairs, then as a class.

> 1 a   2 b   3 a   4 a

1.13

K = Katrin, LB = Li Bo

K: Excuse me, Li Bo? Are you busy?
LB: Not really. I'm trying to write an essay.
K: I'd like to ask you a few questions.
LB: Sure, what about?
K: We're doing some research into new first-year students. It's for Student services. We're asking how new students feel.
LB: Well, that's interesting, but why are you doing it?
K: We want to see if confident students do better in their first year. Then we can help students who are quiet or feel a bit shy.

LB: OK. Let's start.

K: OK, first question. What do you say when friends ask you to go somewhere with them?

LB: Let me think. I like it when they ask me. I usually feel happy.

K: Really? You always say yes?

LB: Yes, I do.

K: OK, next question. What do you do when someone starts a conversation with you? Do you feel happy to talk, do you try to finish the conversation quickly or do you often feel shy?

LB: Hmm. I am often a bit shy and get nervous when someone new talks to me, I think.

K: OK. Let's go to the next question. Where do you usually like working or studying?

LB: Uh, well, I don't like big groups or classes – I sometimes feel a bit shy in them. I don't really like talking in front of a lot of people. I like working at my desk.

K: OK. Now, the next question is … how do other people describe you? What do they say about you?

LB: Ooh – that's a difficult one. Well, they don't think I'm talkative, and they don't think I'm quiet.

K: So they say you're warm and friendly?

LB: Yes, I think so.

K: Right, just one more question. What do you do when someone says something nice to you?

LB: I like it when someone says something nice to me, like when my tutor says my essay is good – I always feel happy then.

K: So, you feel good?

LB: Yes.

K: Thanks very much for your help, Li Bo.

LB: No problem.

 Communication activities

3A see Teacher's notes page 129.

GRAMMAR

ADVERBS OF FREQUENCY

Note: This section only looks at the most common position of adverbs of frequency – before the main verb but after the verb *be*. Mistakes in this are very common, particularly if a learner speaks another European language. It is possible to put adverbs in other places, but at this level focus on the word order covered here.

Write *Adverbs of frequency* on the board. Tell the class that they are words that tell you how often something happens.

Write these incorrect sentences on the whiteboard and ask what the mistakes. Correct them as a class.

We **watch often** TV in the evenings.
(We **often watch** TV in the evenings)
It **rains** in summer **never** in the centre of Australia.
(It **never rains** in summer in the centre of Australia.)
Do they **have sometimes** a barbecue in the garden?
(Do they **sometimes have** a barbecue in the garden?)
She is **late never** for work. (She is **never late** for work.)
Is **always he** lazy? (Is **he always** lazy?)

Ask students to tell you where we usually use adverbs of frequency in a sentence: before the main verb, but after the verb *be*.

Ask them to read the examples in the grammar box.

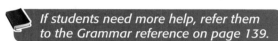 *If students need more help, refer them to the Grammar reference on page 139.*

1   Ask students to count up the adverbs of frequency in the questionnaire and underline them. While they are doing this, move around the class and monitor. Conduct class feedback.

always (once)	sometimes (once)
usually (four times)	often (once)

ALTERNATIVELY

If your class is not strong, first write the most common adverbs of frequency on the board in descending order:
always   usually   often   sometimes   never

2   Ask students to look at the chart and fill in the correct adverbs of frequency. Check answers in pairs, then as a class.

1 always   **2** usually   **3** sometimes   **4** often   **5** never

3   Ask students to work individually to put the underlined words in order. Do the first one as an example. Check answers in pairs, then as a class.

1   Year 3 students *always feel confident* in lectures.
2   Year 2 students *are often confident* about their essays.
3   Students in year 1 *sometimes feel confident* in lectures.
4   My tutor *often asks us to work* in groups.
5   I *am never late for* class.

4   Ask students to work individually to make the sentences true for them using adverbs of frequency. You might like to model this first.

> If the class know each other well, ask them to read one of their sentences aloud to see whether other class members agree. Only do this if you are confident they would feel happy with this.

5   Now ask students to make the sentences into questions. Point out that the verb following *enjoy* is always the *-ing* form and that this form is normally the one used after *like*.

6   Once students have completed their questions, put them in pairs to compare answers. If one pair does not have two answers in common, they move and join another pair (or single student) until every student is with at least one other student. Conduct brief feedback as a class on similarities and differences among them.

ALTERNATIVELY

> Extend the practice by asking students to write or volunteer to the class sentences including adverbs of frequency about themselves, using these (and other) prompts: *at weekends, on holiday, on my birthday, on my own, with friends, when emailing.*

READING

1   Tell students they are going to read about three very different animals. One of them depends on teamwork to stay alive. Ask students to look at the photos in pairs and decide where each animal lives. Check the pronunciation of *meerkat* /ˌmɪəkæt/ as you check answers.

> under the ground = meerkat
> in the air = eagle
> on the ground = snake

2   Ask students to read the passage and match the animals in activity 1 with the paragraphs. This is scan reading, so tell them to look only for the answers to the questions. Stop them after three minutes. Check answers in pairs, then as a class.

> Note: Matching ideas with the pictures is a test of each individual's ability to understand and locate information, which is highly important in IELTS.

> **meerkat:** paragraph A
> **snake:** paragraph B
> **eagle:** paragraph B

Bridge to IELTS

FINDING MAIN POINTS

Point out that many Reading questions in the IELTS exam ask students to understand the main points. Ask students to read the box and ask them how they might find the main points (read the text quickly first and underline the key information in each paragraph).

3   Ask students to work individually to match the ideas with each paragraph. Ask them to underline the sentences that helped them find the answers.

> 1   **Paragraph C:** Teams are small groups of people who work together, but have different skills.
> 2   **Paragraph A:** For them, teamwork is life or death. (Paragraph C is a possibility: Teams usually make better decisions than one person alone.)
> 3   **Paragraph D:** It sometimes takes a long time and it usually needs good preparation.
> 4   **Paragraph B throughout particularly:** Meerkats can't talk like humans, but they can communicate with each other using different sounds.

4   Ask students to match the meanings of the words in the article in pairs. Drill the words as you check the answers.

> 1 survive   2 skill   3 role   4 decision   5 preparation

GRAMMAR

CAN / CAN'T FOR ABILITY

Draw students' attention to the grammar. Write the example on the board:
With more ideas, the group can choose the best answer. They can't survive in the desert alone.

Ask students to tell you when we use *can* and *can't* (to talk about ability).
Ask them what verb follows *can.* Draw attention to and practise the difference in vowel length and quality in *can* and *can't.*

Ask students for examples of things they *can/can't* do then get them to read the examples in the grammar box.

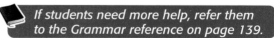

> *If students need more help, refer them to the Grammar reference on page 139.*

1   Ask students to work individually to choose the correct word. Check answers in pairs by asking questions, e.g.: *Can meerkats see long distances?* (Student replies, *Yes, they can.*) etc. In this way, students hear questions with *can,* which is taught later in the unit.

1 can	2 can	3 can't	4 can't	5 can	6 can

2 Ask students to individually complete each sentence using *can* or *can't*.

1 can	2 can't	3 can	4 can

3 Introduce the idea of writing about themselves by modelling the activity. Then ask students to make the sentences true for themselves. Feedback by asking individual students to read out what they can and can't do. Monitor the correct pronunciation of *can't* /kɑːnt/.

4 In pairs, tell students to find out their partner's answers and then the reasons for their answers.

Listening

1 Tell students they are going to listen to a job interview. Ask them to discuss the questions in pairs. Draw the activity to a close by asking individuals to tell the class whether they are good at interviews. *Why/Why not?*

2 Ask students to complete the job advert individually. Check their answers.

1 qualifications	2 experience	3 skills

3 Conduct this as a whole class activity. Ask students to skim-read the job ad to find the answers, then check the answers briefly.

Note: For background, tell students that Glasgow is in Scotland and the Scottish accent is hard to understand at first. Explain that the University of Glasgow was founded in 1451 and is the 4th oldest in the English-speaking world.

4 1.14 Tell students are going to hear Pilar being interviewed for the job in the advert they have just read. Ask them to tick the topics mentioned in the interview. Play the recording. One subject was not discussed. Check what students think this was.

Mentioned: working as a team, language skills, experience abroad, leading a team
Not mentioned: *communication* is not mentioned

5 1.14 Tell students they are going to listen again for more detailed understanding. Ask them to read the statements silently and then mark them true or false as they listen. Answer any questions before playing the recording. They may need to listen more than once. Check answers in pairs, then as a class.

1 F (she has an MBA – a Master's in Business)
2 F (she can)   **3** T   **4** T

🔘 *1.14*

G = Grant, **P** = Pilar

G: Thank you for coming today, Pilar.
P: My pleasure.
G: Well, let's start. So the job is with Student Services – we're part of the university that tries to help the students with any problems.
P: Yes, I looked at Student Services on the Internet.
G: Oh, really – good. Now, you have an MBA ...
P: Yes, from the University of Santiago. I really enjoyed doing it.
G: Yes, Spain is a wonderful country.
P: Chile.
G: Sorry?
P: Chile – Santiago is in Chile.
G: Ah, yes of course. So, do you like learning new things?
P: Yes, I do.
G: Do you think you can learn on the job too?
P: You mean, can I learn things when I'm working on them?
G: Yes – there's a lot to learn in this job. We're looking for someone who can learn quickly.
P: I can do that.
G: Great. And you can speak three languages?
P: Yes, I can speak English and Spanish, of course and my German is quite good too.
G: Why are you interested in the job?
P: Well, I'm interested because I can work with international students. I lived abroad for one year so I know what it's like to study and work in another country. I know what problems international students can have.
G: Like understanding the Scottish accent.
P: Yes, and understanding Scottish weather. So, I can help other international students because I understand their difficulties.
G: Great. And what about working in teams?
P: I'm very good at teamwork. I help the other team members and I can communicate very well with other people.
G: Can you work well under pressure?
P: Yes, I can. I always finish my work on time and I often work at weekends and evenings.
G: So you're very hardworking then?
P: Yes, I am.
G: Do you have experience leading a team?
P: No, I don't. But I do have experience leading projects.
G: So, do you feel that you can manage a team?
P: Yes, I'm sure that I can manage a team well. I have all the skills to do it and I'm sure I can do a good job.
G: OK, well let's talk more about your project management ...

PRONUNCIATION
STRONG AND WEAK FORMS: *CAN* AND *CAN'T*

1   1.15 Draw students' attention to the weak and strong forms of *can* and *can't*. Remind students of the contrast in vowel length and quality here and drill the contrast /kən/ and /kɑːnt/. Play the recording and ask them to write the number of each sentence next to the correct pronunciation.

> 1–3 are the weak form and 4 is the strong form.

Ask students if they can see why only 4 is strong (*can* is not followed by a verb and finishes the sentence).

1.15

1   I can manage a team.
2   Harold can't get a job.
3   Can you speak French?
4   Yes, I can.
5   Pilar can help too.
6   Can you take an IELTS test?

2   1.16 Tell students to listen to each sentence and tick when they hear the strong form of *can*. Play the recording. They may need to listen more than once.

1.16 and answers

1   Can you work well under pressure?
2   Yes, I can do that.
3   I can speak English and Spanish.
4   Yes, I can, too. (strong)

3   1.17 Tell students they are going to listen and answer the questions so they are true for them. Play each question then pause to allow students time to write down their answers. Check answers in pairs, then as a class.

1.17

Can you speak English?
Can you lead a team?
Can you manage people?
Can you finish work on time?
Can you work well under pressure?
Can you listen to people?

Bridge to IELTS

TALKING ABOUT ABILITY

Tell students that talking about ability (what you can do) is an essential function for the IELTS Speaking test. Each of the sentences they are going to hear states what you are good at or can do.

1   1.18 Draw students' attention to weak forms (/ə/ and /ɪ/). Then ask students to listen and repeat the sentences. Drill chorally and individually.

1.18

I'm very good at teamwork.
I'm quite good at teamwork.
I'm not bad at working under pressure.
I'm OK at working under pressure.
I can work well alone.
I can't work well in large groups.

2   Tell students they are going to take turns to interview each other for the job in Listening activity 2. Allow them time to write questions using the prompts given. Move around and help them. Then put them in pairs to interview each other. Go over the points of interest as feedback.

SPEAKING
A PERSON YOU ADMIRE

1   Ask students to work in pairs to match the words and pictures.

> A   Petra Kvitova: sportswoman
> B   Bill Gates: business leader
> C   Aung San Suu Kyi: political leader
> D   Leonardo DiCaprio: actor

ALTERNATIVELY

> Complete the exercise as a class.

2   Put this model question and answers on the board: Q: *What do you know about ...?* A: *He/she's ...,* and model the activity by asking an individual student. Then ask students to ask other students about each person. Keep up the pace as this activity is simply to focus on the task.

3   Ask students to complete the text with the words from activity 2. Ask them to compare answers in pairs. Then play the recording for them to check.

1.19 and answers

Examiner: OK, now can you tell me about a famous person you admire?

Drew: I really admire Leonardo DiCaprio. He's an actor, and he makes really good films. He's hardworking and (1) **funny** – he makes me laugh. I really admire him because he is (2) **generous** – he's rich and he uses his money to help people. He's also (3) **intelligent**. He has a website about the environment and he wants to change the world.

4 **1.20** Tell students they are going to hear Kavitha talking about someone she admires. Ask them to read through the table and complete the answers as they listen. Play the recording. Check answers in pairs, then as a class. Ask students if they agree with Kavitha and if not, why not?

Bill Gates. He's a businessman from America. Because he's very kind and generous.

1.20

Examiner: So, can you talk about a famous person you admire?

Kavitha: I admire Bill Gates. He's a businessman from America. He is the leader of Microsoft and he's very rich. He's intelligent – he wrote a computer program which changed the world. But I admire him because he's very kind and generous – he gives money to help people in poor countries.

Bridge to IELTS

GIVING INFORMATION ABOUT PEOPLE AND THINGS

Remind students that in the IELTS Speaking exam they will have to speak for two minutes on a certain subject. Ask them to read through the box. Model the way you can give information about people or things using *someone who is ...* or *people who are ...* for people, and *something which ...* for things.

5 Ask students to read the topic card and give them time to make notes on a person they admire using the prompts in activity 4.

6 Once students have made notes, put them in pairs to take turns to tell each other about the person they admire. Refer them to the bullet points and tell them to say as much as they can. To close the activity, ask one or two pairs to present their description to the class.

ALTERNATIVELY

The activity can be extended by changing partners, but one change is enough.

WRITING

DESCRIBING A GOOD LEADER

1 Tell students to read through the choices and circle the ideas they agree with. Emphasise that there are no 'right answers'. Ask students to discuss their choices in pairs. Have a class check of their ideas at the end.

2 Ask students to read the list of ideas first, then read the paragraph and tick the ideas mentioned. Check answers in pairs, then as a class.

Note: Point out the comma before *too*.

not mentioned: their home, the person's relationship with the writer

Writing Skills

LINKING IDEAS WITH *AND*, *TOO* AND *ALSO*

3 Ask students to work on their own to complete the paragraph using *and, too* and *also*. Check their answers as a class.

| **1** and | **2** also, and | **3** too, also |

4 Ask students to complete the sentences on their own. Check answers in pairs, then as a class.

| **1** too | **2** also | **3** and | **4** also | **5** too |

5 Ask students to spend a short time thinking of a good leader and his or her qualities and abilities, and to think of an example.

6 Then ask students to complete the text using their ideas. Move around the class and help them. When students have finished, ask them to read or show their paragraph to their partner. Conduct brief feedback.

 Communication activities

3B see Teacher's notes page 129.

Education

UNIT OVERVIEW

This unit looks at the topic of **education**. The main **speaking** aims are to **talk about your studies**, to **interpret a graph** and to **describe trends in writing**. Students also learn how to speed read for information. The main **grammar** focus is on the **present continuous** and the **contrast with the present simple**. The **vocabulary** focus is on **academic subjects** and **higher education**. **Writing** covers some aspects of **describing graphs and trends**.

WARM UP

Ask students to look at the photograph and decide what is being studied. Ask *Does anybody study this?* Ask students to talk more generally about subjects they study/would like to study.

VOCABULARY

1   Ask students to look at the pictures and check they understand all the subjects. Put students in pairs to briefly match the words with the pictures. Check the answers as a class, and explain any subjects which students are unsure about. Don't focus on pronunciation, as this will be covered shortly.

1 history	2 literature	3 languages
4 psychology	5 biology	6 maths
7 computer science	8 business	9 law
10 engineering	11 medicine	12 sociology

ALTERNATIVELY

If your students need more support, brainstorm and build up a list of subjects on the board, before they discuss in pairs.

2   Put students in pairs and ask them to tell each other what they know about each subject.

ALTERNATIVELY

If you think this may take too long or be difficult to structure, ask students to choose three subjects only to talk about with their partner.

3   Ask students to work individually to complete the sentences, and then check in pairs before conducting class feedback.

1 higher education	2 pass	
3 qualification	4 degree	

PRONUNCIATION
SYLLABLE STRESS

1   1.21 Play the listening once. Ask students to listen carefully and underline the stressed syllable in each word. Check answers as a class.

2   1.21 Ask students to listen again and drill chorally and individually. Point out that the stress falls on 'ol' in 'ology'.

1.21 and answers

ge<u>o</u>logy	<u>li</u>terature	<u>la</u>nguages
soci<u>o</u>logy	psych<u>o</u>logy	bi<u>o</u>logy

Communication activities
4A see Teacher's notes page 129.

READING

1   Tell students to read the first paragraph of the text on the webpage to find out about how you can win a competition and tick the right boxes on the list. Check answers in pairs, then as a class.

help other people

2   Tell students to read the webpage for more detailed understanding. Ask them to work individually to complete the phrases. Check answers in pairs, then as a class.

1 win	2 enter	3 study	4 help	5 write

3 Ask students to read the questions and then read the text quickly. This is scan reading, so tell them to look only for the answers to the questions. Give students three minutes and ask them to underline the words that gave them the answers. Check answers in pairs, then as a class.

1 Karl	**2** Atakan	**3** Valli	**4** Atakan and Karl

4 Ask students to read the letter again and choose the correct answer. Check answers in pairs, then as a class.

1 b	**2** b	**3** b

5 Put students in pairs to find the words and phrases in the emails. Point out that the line references are there to help them. Check answers.

1 party	**2** part time	**3** society	**4** community

6 Ask students to match the level, degree and length of course in pairs. There may be some disagreement. Ask students whether this is correct for their country of study, and if not, what are the degree lengths?

Note: Typical degree lengths vary worldwide, usually ranging between 3–4 years. This information is only correct for degree lengths in England and Wales.

1B undergraduate, bachelor's degree	**i** three years
2A postgraduate, master's degree	**ii** one year

GRAMMAR
PRESENT CONTINUOUS

Write the examples on the board:
I'm studying very hard.
I'm teaching Arabic to young children.

Ask students to identify and underline the verb. Ask students what tense this is (present continuous) and if they can tell you the form (present continuous = *be* + verb + *-ing*). Ask students if they know when we use this form. Ask them to check their ideas in the grammar box and read the examples.

ALTERNATIVELY

If your class is able, write the present simple form of the sentence on the board and ask them to make it continuous. Follow with their own examples.

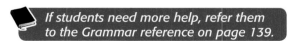
If students need more help, refer them to the Grammar reference on page 139.

1 Ask students to look back at the emails in Reading on page 33 and underline the examples of the present continuous. Ask how many they found in each email.

1 Atakan: 5 examples
1 *I'm studying geology*
2 *I'm having a great time!*
3 *I'm not studying very hard*
4 *Am I enjoying myself?*
5 *Yes, I am!*

2 Karl: 6 examples
1 *I'm really enjoying my time here*
2 *I'm studying biology …*
3 *and working part time*
4 *I'm planning to stay*
5 *… the world is changing*
6 *… the other workers in the supermarket are helping me …*

3 Valli: 4 examples
1 *I'm doing very well*
2 *I'm teaching*
3 *I'm helping*
4 *I'm learning*

2 Ask students to complete Frederika's letter individually with the correct form of the verb, then check in pairs.

1	'm studying
2	'm taking
3	are getting
4	are working
5	are not sleeping
6	'm hoping

3 Ask students to write the questions using the present continuous in pairs. Monitor and help with any problems. In feedback, ask individuals to read each sentence aloud.

1	What are you studying?
2	Which part of the course are you enjoying?
3	What are you working on at the moment?
4	What are you hoping to do after the course?

4 Put students in pairs to ask and answer the questions they've just written. Circulate and monitor. Conduct feedback with examples of good language and correct any problems.

Discussion

This activity gives students a chance to comment on what they've just read. It also helps prepare them for PART 3 of IELTS: the Speaking test (the two-way discussion).

Put the class into groups of three or four; tell them to decide which student in Reading activity 4 should win the prize and why. Move around and monitor. When groups have made their decision check their ideas as a class. Can you come to a class agreement?

READING

1   Put students in pairs to ask and answer the questions about someone they know studying abroad. Feedback by getting some pairs to report who they know and what they are doing.

ALTERNATIVELY

If no one knows anyone studying abroad, ask students if they would like to study abroad: what, where, etc.

2   Tell students this is scan reading and they are looking only for numbers, so they should read the text quickly. Stop them after three minutes and check the answers as a class.

Bridge to IELTS

SCANNING A READING PASSAGE

Explain that the last activity – scan reading – practised skills for the IELTS Reading exam.

Ask students to read the box silently and then ask what the key advice is (you should scan the text quickly to help with the general understanding of a text).

3   Ask students to work on their own to choose the correct answer a, b or c. Ask them to underline any words they don't know as they read. Ask students to compare answers and unknown words with a partner. When checking answers, ask what words were difficult. Suggest the strategy of working out meaning from context.

1 a	2 b	3 b	4 b	5 a

4   Tell students to skim the passage for the words and match them with their definitions. Check answers in pairs, then as a class.

1 campus	2 Western	3 overseas	4 global

GRAMMAR
PRESENT CONTINUOUS AND PRESENT SIMPLE

Tell students they are going to look at the difference between the present continuous and the present simple. Write the examples on the board:

(1) I come from Japan. (use: permanent, unchanging)
(2) I'm studying in New Zealand at the moment.
(use: happening now/temporary)

Ask students to identify which sentence is simple (1) and which is continuous (2). Ask students to suggest ideas for when we choose one form over another (in brackets above) then refer them to the grammar box to check. Ask them to match the sentences to a or b.

a 2, 4	b 1, 3

 If students need more help, refer them to the Grammar reference on page 139.

3   Ask students to work individually to choose the correct form to complete the text. In feedback, ask individuals to read sentences aloud.

1 is	2 is going up	3 costs
4 are doing	5 am eating	

3   Ask students to read through the verbs listed and make the sentences true for their country. Remind them they can make the sentences negative if necessary. Ask them to compare in pairs. Check they are forming the sentences correctly and then ask them to move on to the Discussion.

Discussion

Tell students that the focus of this task is on improving their interaction skills for the IELTS Speaking test.

In new pairs, ask students to discuss how education is changing in their countries. With a multilingual class, get students working in multilingual pairs to compare their ideas.

Conduct brief feedback as a class by asking students to tell you about the education in their country, or, in a monolingual class, to see if they agree on the answers.

 Communication activities
4B *see Teacher's notes page 130.*

Listening

1 Tell students to read through the statements. In pairs, ask them to guess if they are true or false. Check their guesses and move on to activity 2.

2 1.22 Tell students they are going to listen to Esra provide the answers. Ask them to check their guesses and mark the statements true or false as they listen. Play the recording. Check answers as a class.

1	T
2	F (4% more women finish university than men)
3	F (more men than women study science subjects)
4	T

3 1.22 Tell students they are going to listen again. This time they must listen for the percentages and complete the chart. Allow them time to look at the chart first, then play the recording. They may need to listen more than once. Check answers in pairs, then as a class.

1 49.2	**2** 64	**3** 80	**4** 14

1.22

S = Dr Sawyer, E = Esra

S: Good afternoon, everyone. Today Esra is talking about changes in education. Are you ready?

E: Yes, I think so.

S: OK, Esra, let's start.

E: A big change in education in my country is that more women are going to university and colleges. This is happening in many countries. Today I'm talking about the UK …

S: Not your country?

E: No, Dr Sawyer – I'm taking another country as an example.

S: I see.

E: So, some years ago in Britain the number of women in higher education went up until there were more women than men. Today 49.2 per cent of women are now studying at university, with only 37.2 per cent of men at university. There is a 12% difference in the number of men and women at university in the UK. Two other things are important: the kind of qualification women get and the subjects they choose. The percentage of men getting a good degree at university is nearly 60%. But almost 64% of women at university are getting good degrees. Another important thing is that more men leave university early than women. Women students are successfully finishing their courses.

S: So what about the type of course? Is it still true that more men take science subjects than women?

→

E: Well, research shows that there are more women on most courses, especially in law and medicine. But in maths, computer science and engineering there are more men than women. In computer science just under 20% of students are women and 80% are men. In engineering, just 14% of students are women and 86% are men. So more men than women are taking science subjects.

S: And is this just in Britain?

E: No, this is the same in many other countries, and in Arab countries too. So one of the main changes in education is the rising number of women and the fact that women are doing well – this is something we can be proud of.

Pronunciation

Numbers

1 1.24 Tell students they are going to hear three numbers and percentages and to circle the ones they hear. Play the recording. Check answers in pairs, then as a class. They may need to listen more than once.

1.23 and answers

1 39.9 (b)	**2** 80.1 (b)	**3** 12% (a)

2 1.24 Write 39.9 and 18.1 on the whiteboard. Ask individuals if they remember how to read them in English from activity 1. Play the recording straight through.

Repeat the recording and drill the numbers one by one. Focus on the pronunciation of *point* (never *comma*) and % = *per cent* /pə'sent/.

1.24

39	39.9	18.1	80.1	12%	2%

Discussion

Tell students that the focus of this task is on improving their interaction skills for the IELTS Speaking test.

1 Tell students they are going to find out who is interested in which subjects in the class. Ask students to look at the subjects in the table. Then they move around the class and ask others which subjects they are interested in. Tell them to note their answers in the table.

2 Get them to individually complete the sentences using their information about other students. →

3 Ensure this is student led. Conduct a class discussion by asking one student to find out from another student what information they have about interest in each subject. When that student has answered, he/she asks another student about another subject.

SPEAKING

MY STUDIES

1 Tell students they are going to talk about their studies. Put them in pairs to decide which subject the people in the picture are studying. Conduct quick feedback. Answers will vary, ask students to explain their choices.

2 🔘 1.25 Tell students they are going to listen to an IELTS examiner asking three students for information about their studies and that they need to listen and tick the things the students talk about. Play the recording. Check answers in pairs, then as a class.

> **1, 2, 5, 6**
> **Why they are interested in the subject:**
> Adel: I want to understand how life started.
> Yun: … society is changing very quickly in China.
> Esra: I want to find out why there are more women in education. I find it fascinating.

3 🔘 1.25 Ask students to read the statements silently and answer any questions. Then play the recording and ask students to listen and choose the correct answer, a, b or c. Check answers in pairs, then as a class.

> **1** b   **2** b   **3** a   **4** a   **5** b   **6** a

🔘 1.25

> **Ex** = Examiner, **A** = Adel, **Y** =Yun, **Es** = Esra
>
> **Ex:** Can you tell me what you're studying at the moment, Adel?
> **Adel:** At the moment I am an undergraduate student. I'm studying biology at King Saud University in Riyadh in Saudi Arabia. It's a good place to learn and I'm really enjoying my course. Biology is about living things. I'm interested in biology because I want to understand how life started.
> **Ex:** Yun, tell me about your education.
> **Yun:** I'm studying at the University of Wuhan in China. My subject is sociology – that's the study of society. It's a master's degree so it's quite difficult. I'm interested in it because society is changing very quickly in China. I want to understand how these changes affect us. ↵

> **Ex:** Esra, can you tell me about what you're studying?
> **Esra:** I'm from Oman, but I'm studying in Scotland at the University of Glasgow. It's a great place to study. I'm taking a master's in psychology – educational psychology. Educational psychology is the study of how people learn in education. I want to find out why there are more women in education. I find it fascinating.

Living IELTS

TALKING ABOUT YOUR STUDIES

This practises Part 1 of the Speaking test – the introduction and interview between the examiner and one of the candidates. Tell students they are going to practise useful ways to talk about their subject. They have already heard the three students using this language. Play the recording and drill the phrases chorally and individually. Focus on syllable stress and the expression *be interested in, not interesting in.*

1.26

> It's a good place to learn.
> It's a great place to study.
> I'm studying biology.
> My subject is sociology.
> I'm interested in biology.
> I find it fascinating.

4 Ask students to think about a subject they are studying. Refer them to the bullet points and ask them to make notes. Move around the class and help as they write.

5 Put students in pairs. Tell them to read the topic card and take turns to talk about each point, using the notes they made. Move around the class and listen. Conduct brief feedback by asking one or two pairs to tell the class about their discussion.

WRITING

DESCRIBING GRAPHS AND TRENDS

1 Practise the word stress (each word equal stress) and spelling of *bar chart, line graph* and *pie chart.* Then ask students to quickly match these names to the three in the diagram. Ask students to compare their ideas before conducting whole class feedback.

> **left:** line graph   **right:** pie chart   **bottom:** bar chart

2 Get students to read the three groups and put the words into the correct group in pairs. Check answers as a class.

> **A** *getting bigger:* increasing, growing, rising, going up
> **B** *getting smaller:* going down, decreasing, falling
> **C** *no movement:* staying the same

3 Ask students to read the text and choose which chart in activity 1 is being described. Ask them to check in pairs. If necessary, point out that the clue is in the first line of the passage.

> line graph

Writing Skills

PHRASES TO DESCRIBE TRENDS

4 Ask students to read the text on their own and number the questions in the order given. Check in pairs, then as a class.

> b   c   a   d

> 1   line graph   2   On the left
> 3   number of   4   is decreasing
> 5   is becoming

Bridge to IELTS

STRUCTURING INFORMATION ABOUT A CHART

Tell students they are going to write about a graph, which is an important skill in the IELTS Task 1, Written exam. Tell them to read through the box.

6 For this activity students depend entirely on interpreting the graph without a vocabulary list. Tell them they have learnt everything they need to know to complete the task.

Ask students to complete the text individually, then compare with a partner. Monitor and use this as an opportunity to check what students have learnt. Conduct feedback as a class.

5 Get students to study the graph and the vocabulary items. Ask them to work alone to complete the text, then check their answers with a partner.

> 1   line graph
> 2   languages
> 3   number of students
> 4   the time in years
> 5   is increasing
> 6   5 500
> 7   is decreasing
> 8   is staying the same
> 9   French is

OVERVIEW

It is important for all students to meet 'new' language again and again. This is even more important for students starting at Pre-intermediate level because their language base and ability to deal with skills are not very developed. Reviewing language will help them to consolidate what they are in the process of learning as well as show them which areas they still have not fully understood. With this in mind, it is important that you are positive and supportive if they do not do very well in areas of the Review. Encourage them to see that if they get something wrong, it helps them to see where they should focus their energies. Taking this view will help them to grow in confidence; emphasising failure seldom has the same effect.

GRAMMAR AND VOCABULARY

AIM To review *can* for ability.

1 Briefly warm up by asking different students simple questions with *can* (for ability). For example, *Can you play football?*

Ask students to work individually to write the questions with *can*. Briefly check their answers.

> 1 Can you speak two languages?
> 2 Can you remember vocabulary easily?
> 3 Can you do maths well?
> 4 Can you work well in teams?
> 5 student's own answers

2 Tell students to walk around and choose five people to ask their questions and note how many and who can do the things in activity 1.

3 When students have completed activity 2, tell them to write full sentences about the answers they got to their questions, e.g. *Three people can speak two languages. No one can do maths well.* Ask them to compare their sentences in pairs before conducting whole class feedback.

AIM To reinforce the use of *can*.

4 Put students in pairs to correct the mistakes in the sentences. Conduct feedback as a class.

If your class is not strong, you might like to do the first one as an example.

> 1 Lydia ~~cans~~ **can** speak four languages.
> 2 You ~~don't can~~ **can't** study in an Australian University with an IELTS score of 3.
> 3 Pablo ~~no can~~ **can't** do maths.
> 4 ~~You~~ Can **you** play the piano?

AIM To revise adverbs of frequency.

5 Tell students they are going to read a passage about a researcher at a university, Elspeth, and her work habits. Ask students to give you some examples of adverbs of frequency.

Ask students to work on their own to complete the passage. Check answers in pairs, then as a class.

> 1 always   2 often   3 sometimes   4 always

AIM To revise the difference between the present simple and present continuous.

6 Ask students to work on their own to complete the sentences using the correct tense. Ask them to compare answers in pairs before checking as a class.

> 1 are growing   2 are (you) doing   3 learn
> 4 I'm studying   5 drink

7 Ask students to work on their own to complete the sentences using the correct form of the verbs given, and then compare answers in pairs.

> 1 works   2 is studying   3 is learning
> 4 is writing   5 wants

VOCABULARY

AIM To review *can* for ability.

1 Ask students to work in pairs to put the words into three groups: positive, negative, or not positive or negative. Check their ideas as a class, asking if any words were difficult to decide about. Why?

> A **positive:** honest, generous, kind
> B **not positive and not negative:** talkative, shy, quiet
> C **negative:** nervous, lazy, sad

2 Ask students to read the sentences and complete the definitions on their own. Move around and check while they are writing. Check answers in pairs, then as a class.

1 shy	2 talkative	3 lazy
4 honest	5 generous	6 kind

AIM To revise subject names.

3 Ask students to work in pairs to read the course descriptions and decide which subject is being described.

1 literature	2 computer science	3 biology
4 engineering	5 business	

AIM To revise the meanings of nouns associated with jobs and employment.

4 Ask students to work individually to match the words with the definitions. Check answers by asking individuals to write the words on the board.

Bridge to IELTS

LISTENING TEST PREPARATION

AIM To go over the IELTS Listening test.

1 Ask students what they know about the Listening test. Then ask them to read the text carefully and answer the questions.

1 The listening test takes *50 minutes*.
2 The first listening passages are about *general academic subjects*.

2 Put students in pairs and ask them to think of three ways they can practise their listening skills outside class. Conduct whole class feedback, indicating which ideas you think will be helpful.

Suggested answers
CDs of graded readers, with or without the book, listening to English language radio, talking to English speakers, watching English language DVDs (subtitles off), watching English language TV.

OPTIONAL

Ask students to go through the Student's Book in pairs and find examples of Bridge to IELTS tips for the Listening test. Review quickly as a class.

Unit 7 p.51   Unit 11 p.77
Unit 10 p.72

Study Skills

THINKING ABOUT YOUR STUDY HABITS

AIM To encourage students to study more effectively.

1 Put students in pairs and ask them to think of six good study habits. Conduct whole class feedback, writing their ideas on the board.

2 Get students to read the text and check their answers. Ask for extra ideas and list them on the board.

Suggested answers
Check your learning – test yourself, choose carefully where to study, decide how long you are going to study and stick to it, don't study when you are tired, get a friend to test you, plan what you want to achieve, study alone, study in silence (no music), study regularly, turn off your mobile phone.

3 Ask students to read the study habits and choose the answers individually. Get students to compare answers in pairs and discuss any differences. Conduct feedback.

4 Ask students to choose three of the study skills ideas they don't already do and try them for a week. Tell them you will ask them for their experiences in a week.

Make a note to remind yourself in a week to ask your students if they practised their three study habits. You could do this as a warm-up activity at the beginning of the lesson. If you do this regularly, students are more likely to take developing study skills seriously. As a result they will become more effective language learners.

Buildings and cities

UNIT OVERVIEW

This unit looks at the topic of **buildings and cities**. The main **grammar** focus is the **simple past of be** and **regular verbs**. The main **vocabulary** focus is **adjectives to describe buildings and cities**. The **speaking** focus is talking about **a special building and giving your reasons**. The **writing** focus is on **describing a city** and **organising a paragraph**.

WARM UP

Tell students they are going to learn how to talk about buildings and cities. Ask them to work in pairs to find out their partner's favourite building, favourite city and some they don't like. If appropriate, ask them what they think of this school building.

VOCABULARY

ADJECTIVES TO DESCRIBE BUILDINGS

1   Ask students to look at the adjectives in the box and check they understand them. Ask students to work in pairs to describe the three buildings in the photos using the adjectives. Check their ideas as a class.

ALTERNATIVELY

If your students need more support, discuss what they can see in the pictures before they discuss in pairs.

2   As a class, ask students to put the adjectives into four groups: size, age, material, opinion. Put their answers on the board under the four headings. Ask students to write these into their vocabulary notebooks.

size	age	material	opinion
huge	old	stone	ugly
tall	modern	glass	fantastic
small		concrete	wonderful
		brick	

3   Ask students to work in pairs to ask each other what they think of the buildings, which ones they like/ don't like. Encourage them to use the vocabulary from the previous activity and to expand on why they like or don't like the buildings. Conduct whole class feedback.

4   Tell students they are going to hear three students talking about the buildings. Ask them to listen and tick the buildings they hear mentioned. Play the recording. Check answers in pairs, then as a class.

> **1** c   **2** a   **3** b

5   Tell students to read through the questions. Ask them to listen again and choose the correct answers as they listen. Play the recording.

If necessary, pause after each conversation to allow them time to choose their answers. Check answers in pairs, then as a class.

> **1 b** the Business School   **2 c** eat   **3 c** concrete

1.27

Conversation 1
T = Tao, **K** = Karen

T: Sorry, can you help me?
K: Sure.
T: I'm trying to find the Business School.
K: Oh, yes, the Business School. That's easy. You see that big, old building?
T: Yes, it's amazing.
K: That's the Gilbert Scott building. The Business School is in there.
T: Thanks.

Conversation 2
A = Ann, **N** = Nikki

A: Excuse me, I'm looking for the restaurant. Can you tell me where it is?
N: Sure, it's opposite the library. Can you see the modern building made of glass and stone?
A: I think so. The one with green and blue glass?
N: Yes, that's it. That's the Fraser building – you can get sandwiches and hot food there.

Conversation 3
P = Pilar, **L** = Lee

P: Excuse me. Can you help me? I'm looking for the library.
L: The main library?
P: Yes.

L: OK. Look over there at that huge, tall, concrete building. That's the library. It's next to the art gallery.

P: Yes, I can see it.

L: The information desk is at the front door.

P: Thanks.

LISTENING

1 Ask students to work in pairs and to look briefly at the three photos. Ask them to discuss what they think about the building, and if any of them know what/where it is. Check their ideas briefly, but don't tell them what they building is, as they will listen and hear the answer in a moment.

2 In the same pairs, ask students to look at the words and definitions and to match them. If your class is not strong, tell them to begin with the easiest. Any they do not know will then be easier to match.

1 b	2 d	3 a	4 c

3 🔘1.28 Tell students they are going to hear Alan interviewing Professor Gu Ying about the Seed Cathedral. Ask them to listen and number the photos as they hear them mentioned. Play the recording. Ask students to underline the information that gave them the answers.

C	B	A

4 Tell students they are going to listen again for more detail. Ask them to complete the text with just **one** word or number in each gap as they listen. Encourage them to look at the text and think about what could go in the gap before they start. Play the recording. Check answers in pairs, then as a class.

1 building	2 seeds	3 light
4 nature	5 City	6 schools

5 Tell students they are going to listen now for facts and to listen and decide 'yes' or 'no'. Let them read the six questions first, and answer any questions before you start. Then play the recording again. Check answers with the class.

1 N	2 Y	3 Y	4 N	5 N	6 Y

6 Now ask students to listen again and underline the correct information. Play the recording. Check answers in pairs, then as a class.

1 six months	2 clear
3 sixty thousand	4 many times

 1.28

A = Alan, **G** = Gu

A: Good evening and welcome to Great Designs, where we look at some amazing buildings. I'm Alan Davies, and tonight I'm talking to Professor Gu Ying about a building that wasn't here for a long time. In fact it was only here for six months but the ideas for the building are still with us today. Professor Gu Ying works in London, and knows all about the building of the Seed Cathedral – which many people visited in the Shanghai Expo. Professor Gu, welcome to the programme ... How did the project start?

G: Well, the seed bank in London was the starting point. We collected seeds from all over the world for the future. Then in 2010, Thomas Heatherwick decided to use the seeds for the UK building in the Shanghai World Fair in China.

A: It was an amazing building.

G: Yes, it was. It was fantastic. There were thousands of clear plastic rods which were very flexible and moved in the wind. These rods weren't very big – in fact, they were very small – and there were seeds at the end of each rod. So, in the daytime, there was a lot of natural light in the building because sunlight came inside through the rods. And at night the rods lit up, as there was a small light inside each one.

A: How many rods were there?

G: I think there were about 60 000.

A: Was there any special reason for the design?

G: Well, Heatherwick didn't want a lot of high technology in his building. He wanted to show the main idea of the Shanghai World Fair. This was 'Better City, Better Life'.

A: Better City, Better Life? A very simple idea!

G: Yes, it was. He liked all the beautiful parks and gardens in the city of London, and he wanted to show that nature can make a city a better place to live in.

A: Were you at the building when it was in Shanghai?

G: Yes, I was. I was there many times.

A: Was it very special?

G: Yes, it was. It was very peaceful and quiet inside the cathedral. It was very popular – people loved the idea.

A: What happened to all the seeds after the World Fair closed?

G: Well, that's one of the best things about the whole project. After the fair, all the rods were presented to schools in China and the UK to keep. It really was a very great success.

A: That's very good to know. Thank you very much for talking to me about it, Professor Gu.

G: Thank you, Alan.

GRAMMAR
PAST SIMPLE OF *BE*

Put these sentences on the board and ask students if they know the past tense of each:

I am a university student. (I was a university student.)
It is a fantastic building. (It was a fantastic building.)
You are a first year student. (You were a first year student.)

Practise the weak forms of *was* /wəz/ and *were* /wə/ where they are used.

Ask students to look at the grammar box and read the examples there. Draw attention to the strong forms /wɒz/ and /wɜː/ in short answers.

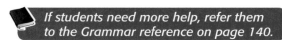

> If students need more help, refer them to the Grammar reference on page 140.

1 Put students into pairs and ask them to choose the correct form of the past tense of *be*. Move around and monitor. Check their answers as a class.

1	was
2	were
3	wasn't
4	were
5	weren't
6	was

2 Ask students to complete the sentences about the Seed Cathedral with the correct form of *be*. Check answers in pairs, then as a class.

Point out that *n't* is more likely in normal conversation and *not* is more likely in writing for a formal audience.

1	wasn't/was not
2	were
3	weren't/were not
4	were
5	was
6	was

3 Ask students to put the words in the correct order to make questions.

Go through the answers by asking individuals. As you check the answers, drill the weak forms.

1	Were /wə/ you at home yesterday?
2	Was /wəz/ she with you last weekend?
3	Were /wə/ they in a blue car?
4	Was /wəz/ it a big party?
5	Was /wəz/ he at the World Fair?

Discussion

This activity helps students prepare for PART 4 of IELTS: the Speaking test.
Put students in pairs to ask and answer the questions. At the end, choose one or two pairs to ask and answer in front of the class.

READING

1 Ask students what – if anything – they know about World Fairs. Then ask them to begin by doing the quiz. Get them to read it and have a go at the questions. Briefly check their ideas. See whether other students agree, disagree or do not know.

2 Then tell them to read the passage about the Eiffel Tower to check their ideas and choose the correct answers. Ask them to note any words they do not know before asking a partner if they know the word(s). Check answers as a class.

1b	London
2b	special buildings from different countries
3a	an entrance to the Paris World Fair

Note: As a point of interest, tell students that French writer Guy de Maupassant (1850–1893) (paragraph C) was a world master of short story writing.

3 Get students to read the passage again to match the four ideas with the right paragraph, A–D. Tell them to underline the words that gave them the answers. Check answers in pairs, then as a class.

1 D	2 A	3 B	4 C

4 Ask students to complete the sentences with words from the text. Tell them to read the paragraph where any unknown words occur before checking answers.

1	advert
2	entrance
3	structure
4	landmark

ALTERNATIVELY

With a strong class, ask students to see how many words they can get without reading again.

 Communication activities
5A *see Teacher's notes page 130.*

GRAMMAR

PAST SIMPLE: REGULAR VERBS

Write these sentences on the board:
We like the food in France.
He visits famous cities for his holidays.

Ask students to put them in the past tense:
(We liked the food in France.)
(He visited famous cities for his holidays.)

Read them out and highlight the difference in pronunciation of -ed: *liked* /laɪkt/ and *visited* /ˈvɪzɪtɪd/. Tell students there are rules for how to pronounce the -ed, which they will learn in the grammar section.

Ask students how we form the negative: *did/didn't* + the infinitive form of the verb. Write the negative form of the above sentences on the board. Follow with students' own examples.

Ask students to read the grammar explanation, and then look back at the reading passage and underline all the verbs ending in -ed and any examples of *did/didn't*.

1   Tell students that if the verb ends in 'e' you just add -d, otherwise add -ed. Ask them how to spell *travelled*. Write it on the board, explaining that final single consonants generally double.

Ask students to write the past forms of the verbs in the box individually, and to look back again at the passage for help. Draw their attention to the spelling of *planned*.

believed	called	designed	enjoyed	hated
needed	planned	travelled		

2   Ask students to work in pairs to complete the sentences with past forms of the verbs. Ask individuals to read the answers aloud to check. Don't focus on pronunciation problems as these will be covered later in the lesson.

1 used	**2** started	**3** completed	**4** liked	**5** decided

3   Ask students to read the sentences and choose the correct answers. Check in pairs, then as a class.

1 enjoyed
2 didn't call
3 didn't use
4 celebrated
5 didn't hate

4   Ask students to complete the sentences with negative past forms of the verbs in brackets. Check answers in pairs, then as a class.

1 didn't want
2 didn't enjoy
3 didn't travel
4 didn't plan
5 didn't design

5   Ask students to work individually to write sentences about themselves. Then ask them to compare in pairs. Move around the class and monitor. Feedback by asking pairs to tell you something interesting they learnt about their partner.

6   Ask students to work in pairs to match the sentence halves. Check answers as a class.

1 b	**2** e	**3** a	**4** d	**5** c

ALTERNATIVELY

With a strong class, set this as a competition. The fastest student says 'Finished' but only wins if all his or her answers are correct!

7   Put students in pairs and designate them A or B. Tell Student A to turn to page 124 and Student B to page 126. Ask them to read their information and answer their partner's questions about 'their' building. Student A starts. Then swap.

PRONUNCIATION

1   ⊙ 1.29 Ask students to listen to the three ways of pronouncing -ed, and to match the words with the ending. Ask students to look at the last consonant of each verb. What is the pronunciation of -ed for each verb? Check answers and drill chorally and individually.

1.29 and answers

1   started /ɪd/
2   designed /d/
3   liked /t/

2 ◎ 1.30 Ask students to listen to the past tense of the verbs and put them in the right column in the table. Play the recording twice. Check answers in pairs, then as a class. Tell students there are three ways to pronounce the final -ed of regular verbs in the simple past tense. The pronunciation depends on the final sound of the verb in the infinitive.

   1 If it is an unvoiced consonant, e.g. /p/, /k/, /f/, /s/, /ʃ/ and /tʃ/, the final -ed is pronounced /t/.

   2 If it is a voiced consonant, e.g. /b/, /g/, /v/, /z/, /ʒ/, /dʒ/, /m/, /n/, /ŋ/, /l/ and /r/, the final -ed is pronounced /d/.

   3 If the final sound is a /d/, or /t/, the -ed is pronounced /tid/. For example: *added* and *wanted*.

◎ 1.30 and answers

/d/	/t/	/ɪd/
designed used believed called	liked finished	started completed celebrated

3 Drill the pronunciation. Either play the audio and ask students to repeat, or ask students to repeat after you.

   Note: The distinction between when to pronounce -ed as /t/ after unvoiced consonants or /d/ after voiced final consonants is hard for speakers of languages which do not have voiced final consonants.

Bridge to IELTS

USING A DICTIONARY

Ask students to read through the box. Go through the dictionary entry with them and ask them to match the parts of the entry with the definitions. Remind them that using a dictionary is an important tool in learning a language.

1 d	2 b	3 c	4 e	5 a

SPEAKING

A SPECIAL BUILDING

1 Ask students to work in pairs to answer the questions.

   Note: In a monolingual class, ask students if they agree on the answers. In a multilingual class, put them in different nationality pairs to compare. If students are from different countries, ask individual students to tell the class what they have learnt about their partner's country. If students are all from the same country, ask them to agree on the 'most special' building, and why.

2 ◎ 1.31 Ask students to look at the pictures and name the place (the Sydney Opera House in Australia). Tell them they are going to listen Kinga talk about the Sydney Opera House. Ask them to number the pictures in the order she talks about them. Check answers as a class.

   Note: This is the kind of task students will have to do in IELTS.

ALTERNATIVELY

If your students need more support, discuss what they can see in the pictures before they listen.

B	**A**	not mentioned: **C**

3 ◎ 1.31 Ask students to read the questions silently. Answer any questions, then play the recording and ask students to listen and choose the correct answer. Check answers in pairs, then as a class.

1 an international	**2** Denmark
3 several times	**4** shape

◎ 1.31

Kinga: A special building? Well, Sydney Opera House is very special for me. It's in Sydney, of course, in the east of Australia. What do I know about it? Well, it's a really spectacular building. The designer was from Denmark. I think his name was Jorn Utzon. He changed his plans for the building many times and the construction work took a long time – fifteen years I think! Why is it special for me? I love the shape of the roof. It's completely unique. It's amazing in daylight and it looks very dramatic at night too. People from all over the world see it as a landmark of Australia. It represents my country and I'm very proud of it.

Living IELTS

BEING POSITIVE

Tell students it's important to sounds positive and enthusiastic in the IELTS exam. Tell them they are going to practise some key expressions, which, if they say them in the right way, will make them sound enthusiastic. Play the recording and drill the expressions.

> It's a really spectacular building.
> It's amazing in daylight.
> It looks very dramatic at night.
> Its definitely my favourite building.

4 Tell students that they are going to talk about a special building. Ask them to choose a building and refer them to the bullet points to make a few notes. Move around the class and help with ideas.

Bridge to IELTS

WHEN YOU DON'T KNOW A WORD

Point out that students may come across a word they don't know in the IELTS Speaking test. Ask them to read the box.

Check comprehension by asking: 'What should you do if you don't know a word in the speaking test?' (Use phrases like *It's similar to …* or *It's like … .*) And 'What will the examiner will think?' (The examiner will think you are keen to express your ideas and get your point across.)

5 Ask students to read the topic card and then work in pairs, taking turns to describe a building using the notes they made. To close the activity, ask one or two pairs to present their description to the class.

WRITING

DESCRIBING A CITY

1 Put students in pairs and ask them to study the two photos and the information. Which facts relate to which city? Conduct whole class feedback.

> Note: As background, you might like to tell students that Liverpool was the birthplace of the Beatles and was the *Titanic's* home port. Santiago was founded in1541 and is named after Santiago in north-west Spain.

photo1 is Liverpool
photo 2 is Santiago

2 In the same pairs, ask students to find the correct vocabulary.

1	central	**2**	port
3	capital	**4**	medium-sized
5	population		

Note: Tell students that some ports, for example Cologne or Montreal, are inland on a river, and many towns are near the sea but are not ports, e.g. a beach resort. The important point is that a port is a trading centre near water.

Writing Skills

ORGANISING A PARAGRAPH

3 Tell students they are going to read a text about Liverpool. Ask them to study the text individually and number the list of ideas in the order they are mentioned.

1 the name of the city and its main characteristics
2 the location of the city
3 the size of the city
4 the main industries
5 when the city was a Capital of Culture

4 Tell students to look at the fact file and complete the text in pairs. Check their answers and conduct feedback as a class.

1 modern and exciting
2 in central Chile
3 large
4 population of 6 million
5 capital
6 industries are finance and mining
7 2004 Santiago was American Capital of Culture

 Communication activities
5B *see Teacher's notes page 131.*

Work

This unit looks at the topic of **work**. The main **speaking** aims of the unit are to talk about a **rewarding experience**. The main **grammar** focus is **past simple questions** and **short answers**, and **irregular verbs (past simple tense)**. The main **vocabulary** focus is on **work and jobs**. The **reading** focus is on **locating specific information**. The **listening** focus is on **exchanging information** and **identifying reasons**. **Writing** covers **describing a job** and the **use of** *so*.

WARM UP

Introduce students to the topic of work. Ask individuals if they have or have had a job. Ask them to look at the photograph and in pairs talk about what the photo shows about work.

VOCABULARY

WORK

1 Ask students to work on their own to match the verbs 1–6 with the words a–f. Check answers in pairs, then as a class.

> **Note:** While students may come up with other grammatically correct alternatives, only one answer will be a correct fit for the next activity.

1	**d** work as a volunteer	**2**	**e** work full time
3	**a** apply for a job	**4**	**c** get experience
5	**f** earn good money	**6**	**b** develop a new skill

2 Ask students to match the phrases from activity 1 with the definitions in 2. Check answers in pairs, then as a class.

1 *work full time:* to work five days a week and eight hours a day

2 *work as a volunteer:* to work because you want to and without being paid

3 *get experience:* to get knowledge from doing something

4 *earn good money:* to get well paid for the work you do

5 *develop new skills:* to learn things you need to do a job well

6 *apply for a job:* to ask for a job in a formal way

3 Ask students to work in pairs to choose the correct answer. Check answers as a class.

1	applied for the job
2	got experience
3	develop new skills
4	work full time
5	work as a volunteer

READING

1 Put students in pairs. Ask them to read and then ask each other the questions. Conduct whole class feedback on who said interesting things.

2 Still in their pairs, ask students to look at the photo and guess three correct things about volunteers at the Student Welcome Centre. Conduct whole class feedback on their guesses, but tell them to read the text to find out the answers.

3 When students have finished reading, check their answers as a class. Ask if there are any words they have a problem with and what the text was for. (They want volunteers at the Student Welcome Centre.)

Volunteers: A, D, F

4 Ask students to work in pairs to discuss whether they would like to work as a volunteer at the centre. Monitor, identifying any language problems worth highlighting. Check their ideas as a class.

ALTERNATIVELY

With a stronger class, extend the activity by putting students in pairs and asking them to interview each other for the job of a volunteer at the centre.

LISTENING

1 🔘 1.33 Tell students they are going to listen to two friends, Sebastien and Monika, talking about the Student Welcome Centre. Tell them to listen and choose the correct answers. Play the recording. If necessary, play the recording again before checking answers.

1 a	**2** c	**3** a	**4** c

2 🔊 1.33 Ask students to read through the questions. Tell them to listen to the recording again and answer 'yes' or 'no' to what Sebastien and Monika talk about. Play the recording. Check answers in pairs, then as a class.

1 no	2 yes	3 no	4 no

🔊 **1.28**

S = Sebastien, M = Monika

S: Hi Monika! You look busy – what are you doing?

M: I AM busy! I want to help as a volunteer in the student welcome centre and I need to apply online.

S: Ah yes! I saw an advertisement in the student union. I'm not surprised they need helpers for the student welcome centre! It's always so busy there. It was really busy when we first arrived as new students. I can't believe that was two years ago!

M: I know – it's amazing! I met you in the queue on the very first day of the semester!

S: That's right! In fact, we waited so long that we got to know each other really well!

M: Yes, we spent an hour in that queue and you told me about your family in Switzerland …

S: And you felt very excited about starting your new life here.

M: I remember! We talked so much that by the time we got to the front of the queue, we didn't remember what we wanted to ask!

S: That's right! I can't believe that we came here two years ago!

M: I know – it's amazing.

S: So do you really want to be a volunteer?

M: Yes, I do.

S: But you don't have any work experience.

M: That's true, but I've got experience of being a student. I understand how new students feel when they leave their own country and arrive in a completely new place. I really missed my family and friends when I left Brazil. I had so many questions, so it was good to talk to the volunteers.

S: That's true. I found them really easy to talk to and they gave me some really useful advice too. But you don't get paid to be a volunteer.

M: I don't care about that. I just want to do something different and help people at the same time. Why don't you apply to become a volunteer too? What do you say?

S: I'm not sure. I'll think about it …

GRAMMAR

PAST SIMPLE QUESTIONS

Introduce the grammar. Write a *wh*-question and a *yes/no* question on the board:
Why did they need to get a job?
Did they enjoy the work at the centre?
Yes, they did./No, they didn't.

Ask students to underline the auxiliary *(did)*. Ask 'Can you see a similarity between these sentences?' They should answer 'yes' (they both use an auxiliary). Check they understand how we form past simple questions *(did + the infinitive form of the verb)*.

Ask students to look at the grammar box and read the examples there. Pay attention to the question form, and ask them to provide more examples.

 If students need more help, refer them to the Grammar reference on page 140.

1 Ask students to work in pairs to put the words in the right order. Do the first one as an example.

> **Answers in brackets are the answers to activity 2**
> 1 Did you feel excited when you arrived?
>   *(4 Yes, I did.)*
> 2 Did we talk about our families? *(5 Yes, we did.)*
> 3 Did he think the volunteers were unfriendly?
>   *(2 No, he didn't.)*
> 4 Did they ask the volunteers for money?
>   *(3 No, they didn't.)*
> 5 Did she see the advertisement? *(1 No, she didn't.)*

2 Still in their pairs, ask students to match the short answers to the questions in activity 1.

3 Tell students they are going to practise *wh*-questions choosing the right *wh*-word. Put them in pairs to make the questions. Do the first one as a class.

> 1 What kind of job did you want when you were a child?
> 2 Why did you decide to learn English?
> 3 When did you last use your mobile phone?
> 4 When did you last talk to your friend?
> 5 Where did you go on holiday last year?

4 Ask students to work individually to answer the questions. Move around and check they are writing correctly. When they've finished, put students in pairs to ask each other the questions and give their own answers. Feedback as a class by asking students what they have learnt about their partner.

5 Tell students to work individually to put the words in the correct order to make questions. Check answers in pairs, then as a class.

> 1 What was your job?
> 2 Where did you work?
> 3 What work did you do?
> 4 How long did you work?
> 5 What did you do?

6 Tell students they are going to ask and answer questions about jobs. Put students in pairs and designate each A or B. Tell Student A to turn to page 124 and Student B to turn to page 126. Ask them to read their information and make sure they understand it. Then ask them to take turns asking the questions in activity 5 about the jobs.

READING

1 Ask students to look at the photographs. Tell students they are going to read about university students doing a job while studying. Tell them they have three minutes to read and to number the photographs in the order they are mentioned in the text. This is scan reading, so they need to read the text carefully but quickly, this is an important skill to develop for IELTS. Encourage them to underline the text where they find the answers. After three minutes, stop them and put them in pairs to discuss their answers. Then conduct a whole class check.

> **c** waiter **a** sports shop **d** museum **b** cinema staff

2 Tell students to read the text again and decide whether each sentence is about Eva (E) or Jun (J). Check answers with the class.

> 1 J   2 J   3 E   4 J   5 E   6 J

3 Ask students to read the text again for more detailed understanding and decide whether the questions are true or false. Check answers in pairs, then check as a class. Ask students what words helped them to decide.

> 1 F (he got a job in a sports shop)
> 2 T
> 3 T
> 4 F (they both learnt a lot)

4 Ask students to work on their own to search for the words to match the definitions. Point out that the paragraph reference is given to help them. Check answers in pairs, then as a class.

> 1 benefits   2 challenging   3 perfect
> 4 valuable   5 rewarding

GRAMMAR
PAST SIMPLE: IRREGULAR VERBS

Explain that many common English verbs are *irregular*. Their simple past is not formed by adding *-ed*. Ask students for examples and write these on the board. Use the following as prompts:

see/saw   *think/thought*
go/went   *come/came*

Ask students to look at the grammar box and read the examples. Ask them where they can find a list of irregular verbs in the Student's Book (page 144).

 *If students need more help, refer them to the Grammar reference on page 140.*

1 Get students to read the list of verbs in the box and then use the text to find the past tenses. Check answers with the class.

> find = found   get = got   give = gave
> learn = learnt   make = made   do = did
> spend = spent   write = wrote

2 Ask students to look back at the text and complete the statements using words from the box. Move around and check they understand, as the technical terms may cause difficulty. Check answers in pairs, then as a class.

> 1 affirmative sentences (e.g. *We found the answer, She gave me a present*)
> 2 infinitive
> 3 auxiliary
> 4 preposition

ALTERNATIVELY

> If your class is not strong, conduct this as a whole class activity.

3 Ask students to complete the sentences individually using the past simple form of the verbs in brackets. Tell them they will find sentence 1 in activity 2 helpful with sentences 3 and 5 here.

> 1 had   2 spent
> 3 didn't feel 4 learnt
> 5 didn't get

4 Put students in pairs to complete the sentences.

1 met
2 didn't tell
3 made
4 didn't find
5 gave

Discussion

Explain that exchanging ideas is an important skill in the IELTS Speaking exam.

Tell students to look at the discussion questions and then look back at the text. Ask them to make a list of the different jobs mentioned to help them with asking questions and giving answers.

Then put them in pairs to discuss the questions. Conduct a whole class vote on the most popular job.

LISTENING

1 Ask students to look at the photos and decide where each person is working and what their job is. (restaurant = waitress, gift shop = shop assistant, beach = lifeguard, bakery = sandwich artist). Then put them in pairs to ask each other the questions. Check their ideas as a class.

ALTERNATIVELY

In a monolingual class, once they have discussed in pairs, conduct this as a whole class discussion. Do they agree on their ideas? In a multilingual class, put students in different nationality pairs, then ask the class to tell each other what they've learnt.

2 [1.34] Tell students they are going to listen to two friends, Jakub and Hiromi, talking about a summer job. Ask them to listen and look at the photos and decide which job Jakub and Hiromi are talking about. Play the recording. Check answers as a class.

photo of the bakery, job = sandwich artist

3 [1.34] Tell students they are going to listen again and tick the things they hear Hiromi and Jakub talk about. Ask them to read the list before they begin. When they are ready, play the recording.

2   4   6

 1.34

J = Jakub, **H** = Hiromi

J: Hi Hiromi! How was your holiday?

H: Hi Jakub! It was great. I didn't go back to Japan though. I didn't have enough money for that so I stayed here. Actually, I spent most of the time working!

J: You worked all holiday? I didn't know. What did you do?

H: I was a sandwich artist.

J: A sandwich artist! What's that? It sounds very important.

H: I made sandwiches in a café!

J: Oh! I'd like to do that. Chicken Caesar is my favourite! Did you eat the sandwiches too?

H: No I didn't! I made so many sandwiches the last thing I wanted to do was eat them! I always had salad for lunch. I didn't just make sandwiches though, I served customers too. I felt very nervous about that at first because I didn't feel confident about my English. But most of the people who came into the shop were really friendly. In fact, I began to really enjoy talking to them. Talking to people became the best part of the job for me! It made me happy. It was a really early start though. I got up at 6am every morning and began work at 7am.

J: You got up at 6am!

H: Yes! I didn't like that – in fact, one morning I slept really late and didn't get to work until 8!

J: So, how many hours did you work?

H: Six hours a day so – 30 hours a week.

J: 30 hours? I thought that students couldn't work more than 20 hours.

H: We can't work more than 20 hours during semester. But you can work as many hours as you want during the holidays. I went to the student centre to check that before I took the job.

J: So did you work Monday to Friday?

H: Yes, weekdays only so I had time to relax on Saturdays and Sundays. In fact, I spent most of my weekends on the beach!

J: I think I need to find a job too.

H: That's a good idea. I found it a really useful experience. I feel much more confident about my English now, and I made some money too! So next mid holiday I can go back to Japan!

J: Do you think I could be a sandwich artist too?

H: Of course you could. After all, you love food!

J: So, can you give me the address of the sandwich shop you worked in?

H: Yes, of course I can. Now, where did I put my pen...?

TALKING ABOUT FEELINGS

 Tell students that the focus of this task is to practise phrases expressing feelings, which will be helpful in the IELTS exam. Ask them to read through the expressions. Then play the recording and drill students. Encourage exaggerated pronunciation.

1.35

I felt very nervous.
I didn't feel confident.
It made me happy.

Put students in pairs and ask them to tell each other about jobs they have done and how they felt. Ask them to use as many descriptive expressions as they can. They can look at the audioscript on page 132 for an example before they start. Conduct brief feedback on anything interesting they talked about.

4 🔘 1.34 Tell students they are going to hear Hiromi and Jakub again and choose the correct answer. Tell them to look at the questions before they listen, then play the recording.

1 a   2 a   3 c

Discussion

This activity gives students a chance to talk about the topic. It also helps prepare them for PART 4 of IELTS: the Speaking test.
Put students in pairs to ask and answer the questions. At the end, ask students to feedback on something interesting their partner said.

SPEAKING

A REWARDING EXPERIENCE

1 Put students in pairs. Ask them to look at the photos and discuss which job they would find the most rewarding. Check their ideas as a class.

2 🔘 1.36 Tell students they are going to listen to Jing and Agnes talking about their rewarding experiences. Ask them to match either Agnes or Jing to each picture. Play the recording. Check answers.

Jing **A**   Agnes **B**

3 🔘 1.36 Tell students they are going to listen again and decide who said what. Tell them to put J or A next to each idea. Check answers in pairs, then as a class.

A made new friends
J had a lot of responsibility
A felt the experience was relevant to her course
A met someone who became special in her life

1.36

J = Jing, A = Agnes

Jing: Last summer I worked as a school holiday assistant. <u>What did I do?</u> Well, I had to think of different activities and games to play with the kids in the morning, and in the afternoons we took them on trips to museums or the zoo. I'm really glad I did it – it was really challenging because I had to think about different ways to keep the children happy and busy! I had to be quite flexible too. Kids can get bored very quickly, you know! The best thing was that it was relevant to my psychology course. I'm so glad I did it!

Agnes: <u>A time when I did something rewarding?</u> Well, I really enjoyed it when I spent a few weeks picking fruit in Tasmania. We began work early in the morning and didn't finish until early evening. Well, it wasn't exactly hard work but it was quite tiring. Why was it so rewarding? Well, the money was good but I also liked the social life. I made some good friends with students from all over the world. In fact, I met my boyfriend there too, so that was an added benefit!

Bridge to IELTS

PLAYING FOR TIME

Point out that students may need time to think in the IELTS Speaking test, so it's a good idea to learn ways of playing for time. Tell them to read through the box.
🔘 1.36 To illustrate, play the opening sentences of what Jing and Agnes say when playing for time (underlined in the audioscript above). Ask students what the question they were asked was: e.g. *What did you do? Talk about a time you did something rewarding.*

4 Tell students they are going to talk about a time when they did something rewarding. Refer them to the bullet points to help them make notes. Move around the class and help with ideas.

5 Ask students to read the topic card and then work in pairs to take turns to talk about their experience, using the notes they made. You might like to give them a time limit (two minutes each). To close the activity, ask one or two pairs to present their ideas to the class.

Communication activities

6A *see Teacher's notes page 131.*

PRONUNCIATION

DIFFERENT PRONUNCIATION WITH THE LETTER e

1 🔘 1.37 Ask students to listen and match the words with the correct pronunciation. Play the recording. Check answers and drill.

💿 1.37 and answers

1	help	**c** /e/
2	answer	**b** /ə/
3	sleep	**a** /iː/

2 🔘 1.38 Ask students to listen and put the words into the correct places in the table. Check answers and drill.

💿 1.38 and answers

/iː/ read, week, meet
/ə/ picture, speaker, confident
/e/ welcome, well paid, friendly

ALTERNATIVELY

If your class is not strong, conduct this as a whole class activity. Drill as you write the answers on the board.

WRITING

DISCUSSING THE BENEFITS OF DOING A PART-TIME JOB

1 Ask students to briefly tell you what jobs the people in the photos have (zoo assistant, bar tender). Ask them to work in pairs to match the jobs in the pictures with the statements.

Picture A 1   **Picture B** 2, 3, 4, 5

2 Ask students to read the question and underline the key words, then compare in pairs.

Suggested answers

students   benefit   part-time job   discuss   examples

3 Ask students to individually rate the importance of the five factors in a job. Ask them to compare with a partner. Can you come to a class agreement?

4 Tell students to read the text and identify which ideas from activity 1 are mentioned.

love animals, spoke to people from different countries

ALTERNATIVELY

Ask student to tell you which ideas from activity 3 are mentioned (earn money, meet people, develop language skills, get work experience).

Writing Skills

LINKING WITH *SO*

5 Write this sentence on the board:
I love animals, so I decided to look for a job where I could work with them.
Underline *so* and ask students to decide whether *so* is used to give a reason or a result (a result). Ask students to underline the two other examples in the text then answer the question.

b give a result (reasons are given by *because, since, as,* etc.)

6 Ask students to match the sentences then rewrite them using *so* in pairs.

1 d I fell very badly, so I went to hospital.
2 a He worked hard at school, so he passed all his exams.
3 b I needed to earn some money, so I applied for the job.
4 c She didn't like the job, so she left it.

7 Ask students to read the question and tick the things that they can write about.

8 Tell students they will now write a short essay answering the question. Ask them to re-read the example text before they begin.

ALTERNATIVELY

If time is short, check students understand how to structure their answer then set as homework.

Communication activities

6B *see Teacher's notes page 121.*

OVERVIEW

It is important for all students to meet 'new' language again and again. This is even more important for students starting at Pre-intermediate level because their language base and ability to deal with skills are not very developed. Reviewing language will help them to consolidate what they are in the process of learning as well as show them which areas they still have not fully understood. With this in mind, it is important that you are positive and supportive if they do not do very well in areas of the Review. Encourage them to see that if they get something wrong, it helps them to see where they should focus their energies. Taking this view will help them to grow in confidence; emphasising failure seldom has the same effect.

GRAMMAR

AIM To review *Wh*-questions.

1 Put students into AB pairs. Tell Student A to form and ask questions using the prompts given. Tell Student B to answer using the information on page 126. Remind them to make complete sentences for their answers, and not to just read the information. Circulate and monitor.

---

1 What's the name of the building?
(It's called the CN Tower.)

2 Where is it?
(It's in Toronto, Canada.)

3 Who built it?
(The Canadian National Railway built it.)

4 When did they construct it?
(It was constructed in 1976.)

5 What materials did they use to construct it?
(It was constructed using / out of concrete and glass.)

6 Why is special?
(It's special because it's a symbol of the city.)

AIM Revision of *was*, *were*, *wasn't* or *weren't*.

2 Ask students to complete the text using the correct words. Check in pairs, then as a class.

1	wasn't	2	was
3	was	4	wasn't
5	were	6	weren't

AIM To review forming verbs in the past simple.

3 Put students in pairs and ask them to decide the correct form of the verbs to complete the sentences. Circulate and monitor.

---

1 designed	2 used	3 constructed
4 didn't like	5 enjoyed	

---

4 In the same pairs, ask students to choose the right verb and form for each sentence. Conduct feedback by asking selected pairs to read whole sentences.

---

1 spent   2 told   3 met   4 didn't find   5 learnt

AIM To practise the use of *so*.

5 Ask students to read the essay question quickly and tell you what the text is about (the importance of protecting old buildings).

Ask students to read through the text and complete it using the correct phrases. Do the first one as a class. Check in pairs, then as a class by asking students to read the whole completed sentences.

---

1 so old, stone and brick designs are special
2 so they link the past and the present
3 so visitors from all over the world come to see it
4 so future generations can enjoy them too

VOCABULARY

AIM To revise vocabulary relating to building materials.

1 Ask students to work individually to match the words with the definitions. Check answers as a class by asking individual students to spell or write the words on the board.

---

1 glass   2 concrete   3 fantastic   4 tall   5 unusual

---

2 Ask students to read the vocabulary list and match the words with the definitions. Check answers as a class.

---

1 unusual   2 modern   3 huge   4 brick   5 wonderful

---

3 Ask students to read through the verb list. Then complete the sentences using the correct verb. Check answers in pairs, then as a class.

---

1 work   2 get   3 earn   4 work   5 apply for

Bridge to IELTS

READING TEST PREPARATION

AIM To go over the IELTS Reading test.

1 Put students into pairs to discuss what they know about the IELTS Reading test. On the whiteboard write: *How long? How many questions? How many reading texts? How long are they? Where do they come from? What types of question?*

Move around and monitor their discussion. Explain that all the information is in the reading text that follows.

2 Ask students to read the text carefully and tick the true sentences. Tell them to correct the information about the incorrect sentences. Conduct whole class feedback.

> 1 true
> 2 false (there are three long reading passages)
> 3 false (there are three reading passages)
> 4 false (the passages are taken from magazines, newspapers and academic articles)
> 5 true

3 Ask students to work in pairs to say how they prepare for the Reading test outside class.

Conduct whole class feedback and make a list of their ideas on the board.

OPTIONAL

Ask students to go through the Student's Book in pairs and find examples of Bridge to IELTS tips for the Reading test. Review quickly as a class.

> Unit 3 p.22
> Unit 4 p.28
> Unit 7 p.51
> Unit 10 p.70
> Unit 12 p.83

KEEPING VOCABULARY RECORDS

It's important for students learning English to regularly revise new vocabulary and create a strategy that works for them to remember new words. Research shows that new vocabulary is lost if not revised after 24 hours.

AIM To encourage students to study more effectively.

1 Put students into pairs to explain to each other how they remember new words. Conduct feedback. Write their ideas on the board.

2 Ask students to read the passage and complete the table with ideas from the passage.

Suggested answers

where to keep new words	how to organise them
notebook	(3) by date: 10 September
(1) cards	alphabetically A, B, C
(2) smartphones	(4) subject: festivals

3 Put students into pairs to discuss which ideas they would like to try. Emphasise that this is a matter of personal opinion. Conduct whole class feedback. Which ideas are the most popular?

4 Ask students to choose one or two ways of recording new words they don't already use and to try them for a week. Ask them to note down five new words over the week. Tell them you will ask them for their experiences in a week.

> Make a note to remind yourself in a week to ask your students to report back on how they kept their five new words. You could do this as a warm-up activity at the beginning of the lesson. If you do this regularly, students are more likely to take developing study skills seriously. As a result they will become more effective language learners.

Urban sports

UNIT OVERVIEW

This unit looks at the topic of **urban sports**. The main **speaking** aims of the unit are to **talk about favourite sports**. The main **grammar** focuses are **the form and use of *have to* for obligation**, *need* for **necessity** and *can for* **permission**. The **vocabulary** focus is on **sports and sports skills**. **Writing** covers **following the subject of a passage**, and some aspects of **linking with *because***.

WARM UP

Write the following questions on the board. Ask students to look at the picture at the top of the page and discuss the questions: *1 What are the people doing? 2 What three adjectives describe how they are feeling? 3 Would you like to skydive? If 'yes', why? If 'no', why not?* Conduct brief feedback. Ask the class to compare their feelings about urban sports (*scared, excited*, etc.).

READING

1   Tell students that they are going to read about an activity called 'Urban Hunt'. Put students in pairs to discuss the questions.

2   Ask students to read the text quickly. This is skim reading, so tell them to look for the answer to the question only *(What do they think an Urban Hunt is?)*. Tell them they have one minute to find the answer, then put them in pairs to compare their ideas. Check the answer as a class.

An Urban Hunt is a team game played in a city, where clues are given and the teams race to find the answers.

3   Tell students they will now read the text again more carefully. Read through the five questions. Explain that these questions are answered by sections of the text called FAQs (Frequently Asked Questions). Refer students to the text and tell them to match the questions to the answers and write the correct letters in the blank spaces. (Number 4 is given as an example.) Check answers in pairs, then as a class.

| 1 b | 2 d | 3 a | 4 (given) | 5 e | 6 c |

4   Tell students to work alone to find words from the text to complete the sentences. Point out that the line references are there to help them and tell them that a word may be in a changed form (e.g. singular/plural). When most of them have finished, stop them and check the answers as a class.

| 1 adventure | 2 puzzle | 3 clue | 4 solve |

GRAMMAR

HAVE TO FOR OBLIGATION: *CAN / CAN'T* FOR PERMISSION

Write these two examples on the board:
Teams have to find answers to 12 questions.
They can phone their friends for help.

Ask students to identify the verb in the first example and underline it. Ask 'Can they choose to answer just ten questions?' Students should answer 'No'. Establish that we use *have to* to talk about obligation.
Then move to the second sentence and underline *can*. Ask 'Can they choose to phone their friends?' Students should answer 'Yes'. Establish that we use *can* to talk about what is allowed.

Ask students to look at the grammar box and read the examples. Pay particular attention to the negative form of *have to*, as students may want to say *'haven't to'*, which is not correct. Ask the group to give you more examples of these two different verbs, using the classroom or school as a context, such as *'We don't have to wear a uniform'*. If their examples are correct, write them on the board under the examples from the book. If they are wrong, ask them questions to guide them to the right answer. For example:
Student: *We don't have to arrive on time.*
You: *Is it a problem if you don't arrive on time?*
Student: *Yes.*
You: *So is it an obligation to arrive on time?*
Student: *Yes.*
You: *So the correct sentence is…*
Student: *We have to arrive on time.*

ALTERNATIVELY

If your class is able, get them to tell you the negative and question forms for each verb. Write these on the board. Follow with their own examples.

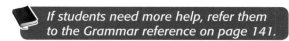 *If students need more help, refer them to the Grammar reference on page 141.*

1 Ask students to look back at the passage, including the FAQs, and underline five examples of verbs with *have to* and seven examples of *can*. They can work in pairs. While they are doing this, move around the class and check they are underlining the whole verb. Conduct quick feedback by reading the text aloud and asking students to call out the verbs.

> You can phone your friends, you can only travel on foot, you can't use private transport, they can watch you, Can I use my smartphone? Yes you can, Can I call friends? (7)
>
> Teams have to find answers You have to answer, them, Do I have to solve the clues in order? You don't have to wear funny clothes, You have to find the quickest route (5)

2 Ask students to work in pairs to choose the correct verb. Do the first one as a class. Tell them that sometimes both verbs are grammatically possible, so they have to choose the verb that makes sense. Go through the answers by asking individuals. As you check the answers, ask students *Is there a choice?*

1 have to	2 can't	3 has to go
4 have to	5 don't have to	

3 Tell students they are now going to practise the verbs in the context of Urban Hunt. Ask students to work alone to complete the text with the correct form of the verb and then to compare their answers. Ask individuals to read the answers aloud to check.

1 have to	2 can't	3 can
4 can	5 can't	6 don't have to

4 This exercise focuses on the form of *have to*. Ask students to work individually to write the questions in their notebook. Move around the class and help them. When they have finished, use Pronunciation to check.

PRONUNCIATION

WEAK AND STRONG FORMS: *HAVE TO*

1 1.39 Ask students to listen and check their answers to activity 4. They may need to listen more than once. Write the correct answers on the board.

2 1.39 Play the recording again. Ask students to choose the correct pronunciation, strong or weak. Go through the answers and asks students what the rule is (*have to* positioned after the verb is weak).

1 W	2 S	3 W	4 S

3 1.39 Play the recording again and ask students to repeat as a group. Ask one or two individuals to repeat for the class.

> #### 1.39
>
> **a** No, I don't have to. I finished it yesterday.
> **b** Yes, I have to start at 7.30.
> **c** No, I don't have to, but I want to see the Manager.
> **d** I have to come to class every day.

Discussion

This activity gives students practice in using the grammar. It also helps prepare them for PART 4 of IELTS: the Speaking test.

Put students in pairs to ask and answer the questions. Listen carefully to their use of *have to* and encourage them to extend their answers if they can. At the end, choose one or two pairs to ask and answer in front of the class.

LISTENING

1 1.40 Tell students they are going to listen to a team taking part in the Urban Hunt. Ask them to look at the map and draw the route as they listen. Give students a minute or two to look at the map and identify key sites before you play the recording. Check answers in pairs, then as a class.

2 1.40 Tell students they are going to listen again for more detailed understanding. Ask them to read the questions silently and answer any questions before playing the recording.

Play the recording and ask students to listen and choose the correct answer, a, b or c.
Check answers in pairs, then as a class. They may need to listen more than once.

1 a	2 c	3 b	4 c	5 c	6 b

> #### 1.40
>
> **B = Bob, D = Dee Dee, J = Joey**
>
> **D:** Hello?
> **B:** Hi, Dee Dee – Bob here, Joey and I need some help.
> **D:** Sure, go ahead.
> **B:** I'm on North Main Street with Joey. We got a clue from City Hunt. Can you help us?
> **D:** What is it?
> **B:** OK. It says: 'Your next challenge is in Japan. Can you find the place where man went into space?'
> **D:** Space. Challenge. Japan? ... It's got to be the Challenger Space Shuttle Memorial statue.
> **B:** Great. But in Japan? ↪

D: It's in Little Tokyo.

B: Great – Joey, there's a taxi, stop it!

D: No, Bob. You can't go by taxi. You have to walk. Go south to East 1st Street and walk for two blocks. It's at the Weller Court building.

J: Hey, Dee Dee. We found the Space Shuttle Memorial.

D: Yes, I can see you on the Internet. You have to take a photo and send it to me. I can put it on the website.

J: OK – I'm sending it now.

D: Send me the next clue too.

J: Right.

D: Got it. 'A mouse and the Lion King come here to play and sing.'

J: That's really difficult.

D: Well, the Lion King is an old cartoon.

J: And the mouse is Mickey Mouse ...

D: Got it! It's the Walt Disney Concert Hall.

J: That's South Grand Avenue. That's near you.

D: Yeah, but I can't go there, it's not allowed. You have to go there, and quickly. I can see the next team is very close to you.

J: How do we get there?

D: Go back to 1st Street. Then take a bus back to Grand Avenue. Hurry!

Discussion

Ask students to read through the questions. Remind them that *would* is about imaginary situations. Put them in pairs to ask and answer the questions. Move around and listen to their discussion and help with vocabulary. At the end, conduct a class vote to see how many students would like to take part in an Urban Hunt.

VOCABULARY

SPORTS AND SPORTS SKILLS

1 Ask students to work in pairs to match the words and pictures.

> 1 climb 2 jump 3 bounce 4 kick 5 balance 6 hit

ALTERNATIVELY

> Complete the exercise as a class. Mime the actions and get students to call out the correct verb. Drill students as you check the answers.

2 Ask students to work in pairs to complete the phrases. Point out that sometimes we can use a variety of verbs if we add a preposition, e.g. *Jump over a building,* but this task asks them just to choose a verb. They should use each verb once only.

> 1 climb 2 jump 3 kick 4 hit 5 balance 6 bounce

3 Ask students to look at the pictures and name the sports they see. Ask them whether they play any of these sports. Put students in pairs to group the sports and write them in the correct space. Check the answers as a class. Drill students' pronunciation as you check the answers.

> 1 karate, judo
> 2 tennis
> 3 basketball, volleyball, golf
> 4 climbing, gymnastics

ALTERNATIVELY

> When students have grouped the sports, ask them to decide which activities we use *go, play* or *do* with and build up a table on the board. Ask students to suggest more sports to add to the table. They then work in pairs to ask and answer about the sports they enjoy, using the correct verb in the present simple. *Do you...*

Go – verb +ing	Play – ball games	Do – other sports
climbing	tennis golf basketball volleyball	judo karate gymnastics

 Communication activities
7A *see Teacher's notes page 132.*

READING

1 Ask students to look at the picture and say what they know about parkour. They may know nothing! If so, tell them they will learn about it when they read the text.

2 Put students in pairs to answer the questions. Tell them you don't expect them to know the answers but they should guess.

Point out that predicting or guessing is part of developing reading skills.

3 Tell students they are now going to read the text to check their ideas. Tell them they have three minutes to read. This is scan reading, so they need to read the text carefully but quickly; this is an important skill to develop for IELTS. Encourage them to underline the text where they find the answers. After three minutes, stop them and put them in pairs to discuss their answers, then conduct a whole class check.

1 b	2 c	3 b	4 c	5 a

5 Tell students they will now read the passage again for overall understanding. Ask students to work alone to match the two halves of each sentence. Point out that they can use grammar clues to help them, such as noticing if verb and subject are singular or plural.

Ask students to compare their answers before checking as a class.

1 b	2 a	3 d	4 e	5 c

Bridge to IELTS

FOLLOWING THE SUBJECT OF A PASSAGE

Point out that part of reading comprehension is following the subject of a text. Refer to the previous task where students used grammar clues to help them match the sentence halves. Read the text in the box and ask students what grammar clues there are (the use of pronouns/other nouns to replace parkour).

GRAMMAR

NEED

Write the two examples on the board:
You <u>need</u> good training shoes.
You <u>don't need</u> specialist equipment.

Ask students to identify the verb in both examples and underline it. Ask 'What follows the verb here?' (*a noun*) and 'What happens when we follow *need* with a verb?' (the verb is an infinitive). Ask 'Is it correct to say *we need going to the park*?' (No, 'we *need to go* to the park'). Ask students to look at the grammar box and read the examples. Pay particular attention to the negative form of *need*, as students may want to say '*needn't*', which is not correct. Ask the students to suggest what they need and don't need to bring for their English class. Add their ideas to the board under the examples from the book.

ALTERNATIVELY

If your class is able, ask them to suggest what they *need/don't need* for Urban Hunt or Parkour without looking at the text.

 If students need more help, refer them to the Grammar reference on page 141.

1 Ask students to look back at the reading text and underline the verbs with *need* and *don't need*. They can work in pairs. While they are doing this, move around the class and check they are underlining the whole phrase. In feedback, ask individual students to read the whole phrase aloud.

You need to be fit and strong
You need to have very good balance
You need to have good concentration
You need to decide on your route quickly
You don't need special equipment

2 Ask students to use the table to write sentences with *need* and *don't need* in their notebook. Move around and check they are writing the sentences correctly.

3 Tell students they are going to describe a sport to their partner and play a guessing game. Put students in pairs and designate them A and B. Tell Student A to turn to page 124 and Student B to turn to page 126. Ask them to read about their sport and make sure they understand it. Students then take turns to describe and guess the sport.

Discussion

Ask students to choose a sport and make a few notes about what they need for it. Point out that they can talk about physical requirements and equipment. Move around and help students with vocabulary if necessary.

Put students in pairs to describe and guess. Monitor their discussion. At the end, choose one or two individuals to repeat their description for the class to guess.

ALTERNATIVELY

You describe a sport to the class and ask them to guess what it is. Then students make up their own description and ask a partner or the class to guess.

LISTENING

1 Ask students to identify the sports and write the words as quickly as they can. Write the words on the board for them to check their spelling as you check answers.

1 cycling	2 swimming	3 walking	4 jogging

2 Put students in pairs to discuss the questions. For feedback, ask one or two students to tell the class about their partner.

Bridge to IELTS

COMPLETING TABLES

Point out that completing tables is often used in IELTS listening tasks. Refer students to the two tables on the page and discuss how they can predict what kind of information is to be completed by reading the headings and looking for grammar clues.

3 Ask students to label the picture. Check answers as a class.

1 lungs	2 heart	3 bone	4 muscle

4 🔘 1.41 Tell students that they will listen to a lecture about the health benefits of these activities. They should tick the box if the speaker says the activity is good for that part of the body. Give them a minute to look over the table, then play the recording. You may like to pause after each sport for students to compare their answers.

Ask individuals to tell the class the answers and confirm them on the board.

	heart	lungs	bones	muscles
Walking	✓	✓	✓	✓
Jogging	✓	✓	✓	✓
Swimming	✓	✓		✓
Cycling	✓	✓		

5 🔘 1.41 Tell students they will now listen again for more detail. Give them time to read through the table and talk about what kinds of words might go in the gaps, e.g. numbers.

Play the recording and tell students to complete the table. When they have finished, ask them to compare their ideas in pairs before conducting feedback.

1 thirty	2 fast	3 10%	4 partner
5 long	6 club	7 300	8 travel

 1.41

Sofia: Hello, everyone. Now, how many people came here by car? That's quite a lot. Think about this – over 70% of car journeys are less than five kilometres. As you know, it's the start of fitness week, so why don't you change your daily routine a little and become healthy too? Let's look at some really easy ways to exercise. These are all activities that don't need special equipment and don't cost a lot of money.

First, walking. We are walking less and less – 20% less than thirty years ago. But walking helps your heart and lungs and improves the strength in your muscles and bones. If you don't do a lot of activity at the moment, you can try walking to the shop instead of going by car, or getting off the bus one stop before your work and walking the extra distance. After a bit of practice, you can try power-walking. Power-walking is walking very fast – almost running. ➡

When your fitness improves, you can try jogging. Jogging is a great way to keep fit – just take it easy at the start. Try to increase your jogging time by 10% each week until you're jogging for 30 minutes three times a week. Like walking, jogging is good for your heart and lungs, your bones and muscles. You can give yourself targets. One day, say that you are jogging to the end of the street. On the next day, say you're jogging to the end of the next street. Find a jogging partner and make a plan together.

Swimming is also a good way to exercise. Although swimming doesn't make your bones strong, it is good for your heart, lungs and your muscles. You can swim as fast or as slow as you like, but the important thing is to keep going. Swimming for long periods is good for burning calories and reducing fat. Again, you can find a partner to swim with or join a club.

Cycling is an excellent way to exercise – just 30 minutes of cycling burns 300 calories. Like swimming, cycling doesn't help to keep your bones strong. But like walking and jogging, cycling can be part of your daily life. For people who travel a short distance to work, cycling can be very good for you. Like swimming, cycling doesn't help to keep our bones strong, but it is very good for our heart and lungs.

So you see we can all make small changes in our lives to help us stay healthy. Now, who wants to sign the Keeping Fit Form?

Discussion

Ask one student to read the task aloud. Discuss what questions they need to ask and write them on the board. If space allows, have students move around and ask each other. To wrap up the exercise, have a quick feedback to see which sport is the most popular.

ALTERNATIVELY

Put students in four groups, one for each sport. Ask students to create a short survey about their sport to ask other members of the class.

SPEAKING
MY FAVOURITE SPORT

1 Ask students to name the sports shown. Then put them in pairs to name the places where these sports are played. In feedback, point out that indoor sports are generally played on a court.

basketball court
golf course
volleyball court
badminton court
football pitch

Conduct this activity as a whole class discussion. Students may be puzzled by the use of different words for the different sports. Assure them that this is just one of those things!

2   Ask students to work in pairs and take turns to describe one of the sports pictured using the phrases given. The student listening should identify the sport described. Move around the class and monitor the students' pronunciation and use of the verbs studied in this unit.

3   Tell students that they are going to listen to someone describing a sport. They should listen and choose one of the sports pictured in activity 1. Play the recording. Check the answer. If students have difficulty, play the first segment of the recording again.

Volleyball

4   Tell students that they are going to listen again for more detail. Give them time to read through the questions and then play the recording. Students check answers in pairs, then as a class.

1 a   **2** b   **3** c   **4** c

1.42

Examiner: OK, Valeria, can you talk about the task card?
Valeria: I like such a lot of sports, but my favourite sport is volleyball. It's absolutely great! You can play it in so many places: inside on a court, or outside in a park. You can even play it on the beach! The rules are really easy. You play in teams of six people. You have to hit a ball over the net. You score a point by hitting the ball onto the ground on the other team's side of the net. You have to use your hands to hit the ball. You can't use your head or feet. It's really easy to learn – anyone can play it. It's my favourite sport because it's very fast and exciting. I really like to get together with friends and play volleyball on the beach. It's such a lot of fun.

5   Ask students to work alone to write about their favourite sport. Refer them to the bullet points and tell them to make notes. Remind students that they need to complete a similar task in the IELTS exam and so they should practise making and working from their own notes. As students write, move around the class and help. Ensure they write notes rather than full sentences.

ALTERNATIVELY

Describe your own favourite sport to the class, and ask them to make notes as you talk. Then ask students to prepare their own notes for a new sport.

6   Ask students to read through the task card. Remind them that this activity will help them prepare for the IELTS Speaking test. Tell students to take turns to describe a sport, using their notes from activity 5 to help them. Before they start, work through the *Living IELTS* exercise.

Living IELTS

ADDING EMPHASIS (1)

 Tell students that the focus of this task is on improving their pronunciation. Point out that when they speak, they need to emphasise key words to sound natural. Play the recording and ask students to underline the key words as they listen. Check answers. Then play the audio again and ask students to listen and repeat chorally.

ALTERNATIVELY

Ask students to underline the key words before they listen and then listen to check their ideas.

1.43

You can **even** play it on the beach.
It's **absolutely** great!
You can play it in **so** many places.
I like **such** a lot of sports.
It's **really** easy to learn.
It's **very** fast.

WRITING

DESCRIBING A CHART

1   Ask students to read through the ideas in the table and then work in pairs to discuss the question. Conduct quick whole class feedback to find out which reason is the most popular.

2   Refer students to the pie chart, which shows why people keep fit. Ask students to describe what the chart tells them, then to read the text silently and tick the ideas from activity 1 if they are mentioned. Students check answers in pairs, then as a class.

The text mentions: it's fun (they enjoy sports), to feel better, for medical reasons, they are part of a club.

Tell students that describing figures in a chart is a very common IELTS writing task. They need to know how to express data in words. Write *one in ten* on the board and ask students to express it as a fraction and a percentage:
One in ten = a tenth = 10%.

If students need more practice, ask them to build a table with further examples:
50% = half = five in ten.

Refer students to the text and ask them to underline sentences with data. Point out that we use *of* when writing complete sentences: *A quarter of people keep fit.*

Writing Skills

LINKING WITH *BECAUSE*

3 Ask students to read the paragraph again and underline the word *because* in the text. Then in pairs, choose the correct option, a or b.

> a

4 Ask students to look at the pie chart about why people don't do sport. Tell them to complete the sentences with the correct reason. Point out that they will need to add more words, such as verbs and prepositions. While they are completing the sentences, move around the class and monitor their writing.

Ask students to compare their ideas before nominating individuals in a whole class feedback. Accept alternative answers if they are grammatically correct.

> 1 they aren't fit
> 2 sport because it is too expensive
> 3 don't do sport because they are too busy
> 4 don't do sport because they don't like it
> 5 of young people don't do sport because they prefer to do other things

ALTERNATIVELY

> Ask students to suggest reasons why young people don't do sport and then look at the pie chart to check their ideas.

5 Ask students to use the table to make notes about the pie chart. This can be done as a whole class activity if you prefer. Build up the information on the board.

Subject	The chart shows	Key information
Why young people don't do sport	5 reasons: expensive/ don't like/too busy/not fit/ prefer other things	Most popular reason: they prefer other things: 40% \n\n Least popular: expensive: 5%

6 Tell students they are now going to write a paragraph using the information and notes they have made. Refer them to the model in activity 2 and point out that the text uses the present simple tense and organisational features such as *finally* to introduce the last point mentioned.

ALTERNATIVELY

> Students write the text for homework.

 Communication activities
   7B *see Teacher's notes page 132.*

The natural world

This unit looks at the topic of **the natural world**. The main **speaking** aims of the unit are to **talk about places of natural beauty**. The main **grammar** focuses are **the form and use of present perfect with *ever* and *never* for experience**, and using the **present simple with *for* and *since*.** The vocabulary focus is on **adjective and noun collocations. Writing** covers some aspects of **presenting an argument.**

WARM UP

Ask students to look at the photographs in pairs and say which continent they think they are in. Don't ask them to describe the picture, as they will see the vocabulary they need for this in the next task. Conduct brief feedback.

VOCABULARY

LANDSCAPE FEATURES

1 Ask students to work in pairs to use the words in the box to label the pictures. Drill and check answers.

A rainforest	B coast	C cliff	D ocean
E beach	F waves	G river	H waterfall

2 Ask students to read the questions and the text quickly. This is scan reading, so tell them to look only for the answers to the questions. Check answers in pairs, then as a class.

1 the Great Ocean Road
2 Australia (the south-eastern coast)
3 soldiers   4 1932   5 It has amazing views

3 Tell students to work alone to find words from the passage to complete the sentences. Point out that a word may be in a changed form (e.g. singular/plural). When most of them have finished, stop them and check the answers as a class. Drill the words as you conduct feedback. Notice the pronunciation of *unique* /juˈniːk/.

1 scenery	2 destination	3 landscape
4 spectacular	5 unique	

LISTENING

1 [2.1] Tell students they are going to hear Leah and Erik talking about the Great Ocean Road. Ask them to read through the statements and write L for Leah or E for Erik as they listen. Play the recording. Check answers in pairs, then as a class.

1 E	2 L	3 E	4 E	5 L	6 L

2 [2.1] Tell students they are going to listen again for more detailed understanding. Ask them to read the statements silently and then mark them true or false as they listen. Answer any questions before playing the recording. They may need to listen more than once. Check answers in pairs, then as a class.

1 F (he went to the south-east coast)
2 F (he nearly got lost)   3 not stated   4 T

2.1

L = Leah, E = Erik

E: Hi Leah! Have you got plans for the holidays?

L: Yeah, I have. I'm going to Australia!

E: Australia? Wow! That sounds great.

L: I know! I'm so excited! I've been online and read quite a lot about it. And I've seen some fantastic photos too – the scenery is very beautiful all along the coastline. Have you ever been to Australia, Erik?

E: Yes, I have! I've only been to the south-east, but it was amazing.

L: When was that?

E: I was there last summer with a few friends. Have you heard of the Great Ocean Road? It's is a very long road that goes along the coast.

L: Yes, I know! I've read that's 234 kilometers long!

E: That's right. Well, we drove along part of the road, as far as Great Otway National Park. It has really thick rainforests. The trees were so close together it was difficult to see where we were going! In fact, we nearly got lost! We saw some spectacular views, too.

L: I've read that there are lots of sandy beaches all along the coastline – I really want to spend some of my holiday relaxing by the sea. I always do that on holiday, and always have! Did you spend any time on the beach? ↳

E: Yes, we did, but it wasn't exactly relaxing! I went surfing. The waves were amazing – I've never seen waves like them. It was really exciting.

L: Surfing! That's exciting. I've never tried surfing. I don't know if I could keep my balance!

E: You never know till you've tried! It only took me a few days to learn how to stand on the board!

L: Em ... I'm not sure. I'd rather stay on dry land and enjoy some wildlife at Tower Hill. Have you heard of Tower Hill?

E: No, I haven't.

L: Tower Hill's an extinct volcano. You can see all kinds of birds and animals there. I've read it's a great place to see kangaroos and koalas. I've seen them in the zoo of course – when I was about five years old! I've never seen them in the wild before.

E: I'm the same. I've only seen them in the zoo. I'd love to see them in their natural habitat.

L: Me too. Have you got any plans for the summer?

E: No.

L: Great! I've just had a brilliant idea ...

Living IELTS

COMMENTING

🔘2.2 Tell students that the focus of this task is on improving their interaction skills for the IELTS Speaking exam. In this section, which is a one-to-one interaction with the examiner, they need to get used to responding to a variety of prompts on different topics.

1 Ask students to read the exchanges. Then play the recording and drill students. Encourage them to exaggerate the pronunciation.

2 Write the following dialogue on the board:
I've been to Jeddah.
Jeddah! That's exciting.

Model the exchange with a strong student. Then put students in pairs. Tell them to choose an activity/ place and tell their partner about it, who comments. Then swap. Ask one or two pairs to demonstrate to the class. Praise exaggerated pronunciation.

VOCABULARY

ADJECTIVE AND NOUN COLLOCATIONS

Write (sandy, golden, thick, beautiful) *beach* on the board and ask students to suggest which adjectives 'go with' the noun.

Establish the fact that *thick* does not go with *beach*. Tell students that this activity practises this feature, called 'collocation'.

1 Ask students to work in pairs to match the adjectives to the correct noun. Check the answers as a class.

1 sandy beach	**2** deep river
3 spectacular view	**4** snowy mountain
5 thick rainforest	**6** extinct volcano

2 Ask students to work alone to complete the sentences with the correct combinations from activity 1. Compare answers in pairs before conducting feedback.

1 thick rainforest	**2** deep river
3 extinct volcano	**4** spectacular view
5 sandy beach	**6** snowy mountain

Discussion

This activity gives students practice in using the vocabulary. It also helps prepare students for PART 4 of IELTS: the Speaking test. Put students in pairs to ask and answer the questions.

 Communication activities
8A *see Teacher's notes page 132.*

GRAMMAR

PRESENT PERFECT SIMPLE + *EVER* AND *NEVER*: PAST SIMPLE

Write the example on the board:
I've been to Australia.

Ask them to identify the verb tense (*present perfect*) and identify the form (*have* + past participle). Ask 'Do we know when he visited Australia?' Students should answer 'No'. Establish that we use this form to talk about past experiences if we don't know when something happened. Ask students which tense we use when we do say the time (*past simple*) and give an example, e.g. *I went to Australia last month.*

Ask students to look at the grammar box and read the examples. Pay attention to the word *ever* in the question, and ask students what meaning it adds (any time in your life).

ALTERNATIVELY

If your class is able, get them to tell you the negative and question forms for the present perfect. (*I've never been to Australia; Have you ever been to Australia?*) Write these up on the board. Follow with students' own examples.

If students need more help, refer them to the Grammar reference on page 141.

1 Ask students to work in pairs to choose the correct verb. Do the first one as a class. Go through the answers by asking individuals. As you check the answers, ask students *Do you know when?*

1 didn't go		**2** has travelled	
3 haven't learned		**4** haven't ever been	
5 made			

2 Ask students to work alone to write the correct question word. Point out that they need to think about the person when choosing *have or has.* Check answers in pairs, then as a class.

1 Have	**2** Did	**3** Have	**4** Did	**5** Has

3 Tell students they are now going to match the answers to the questions from activity 2. Ask students to work alone to complete the task. Check answers in pairs, then as a class.

1 b No, I haven't …
2 c Yes, she did …
3 e Yes, they have …
4 d Yes, they did …
5 a Yes, he has …

4 This exercise focuses on the form of the present perfect and past simple. Ask students to work individually to complete the sentences. Move around the class and help them. When they have finished, ask individuals to read their answers aloud to check.

1 did, do	**2** Did, meet	**3** Have, been
4 did, start	**5** Did, watch	**6** have, read

5 Ask students to write their own answers to activity 4. Move around and check their writing. Then ask students to work in pairs to ask the questions and give their own answers.

ALTERNATIVELY

If you have a strong group, they won't need to write. Ask students for the answers and drill them chorally and individually. Put them in pairs to practise asking and giving their own answers.

6 Ask students to work individually to write the words in the correct order. Check answers as a class and drill.

1 What is it called?		**2** Where is it?
3 Why is it famous?		**4** How has it changed?

7 Put students in pairs and designate them A or B. Tell Student A to turn to page 125 and Student B to page 127. Ask them to read their information and then work together to ask and answer the questions from activity 6 without showing each other their text. Student A starts. Then swap.

 Communication activities

8B *see Teacher's notes page 132.*

READING

1 Ask students to label the pictures. Check answers in pairs, then as a class.

A kangaroo	**B** platypus	**C** dingo	**D** fox
E rabbit	**F** water buffalo	**G** cat	

2 Write on the board:
a) *Native to Australia*
b) *Introduced to Australia*
Put students in pairs to discuss which animals from activity 1 are native to Australia.

3 Ask students to read the text quickly to check their answers. Stop them after three minutes. Ask students to check answers in pairs, then check as a class.

a	Tasmanian tiger, kangaroo, platypus
b	rabbit, water buffalo, fox, cat, dingo

4 Tell students they will now read the text again for more detail. Point out that they need to circle **two** correct answers from the three given. Check answers in pairs, then as a class.

1 b,c	**2** a,b	**3** a,b	**4** b,c

5 Ask students to match the sentence endings and their subject. Check answers in pairs, then as a class.

1 d	**2** c	**3** a	**4** b

6 Ask students to look at the words in context and choose the correct meaning. Check answers in pairs, then as a class.

1 a	**2** a	**3** a	**4** b

GRAMMAR

PRESENT PERFECT WITH *FOR* AND *SINCE*

Tell students they are going to look at another use of the present perfect. Write the example on the board:
He's lived in Australia since 1990.

Ask 'Does he live in Australia now?' Students should answer 'Yes'. 'When did he start living there?' (1990). Establish that we use this form to talk about activities that began in the past and still continue. Underline *since* and ask students if they can make the sentence again, using *for*:
He's lived in Australia for X years.
Write this on the board below the first sentence. Ask students if they can tell you when we use *for* or *since*, then ask them to read the grammar box to check.

> 📕 If students need more help, refer them to the Grammar reference on page 141.

1   Ask students to complete the sentences individually then compare in pairs before checking as a class.

   Ask students to provide their own examples with *for, since* or *how long*.

1 since	2 for	3 how long

2   Ask students to work in pairs to choose the correct form. In feedback, ask individuals to read sentences aloud and drill the class.

1 a long time	2 last year	3 weeks
4 he was a child	5 Friday	

3   Tell students to work individually to read through the sentences and complete them. Conduct whole class feedback.

ALTERNATIVELY

> If your class is strong, conduct this as a whole class activity.

1 for	2 since	3 for	4 since	5 since

PRONUNCIATION

STRONG AND WEAK FORMS: *HAVE* AND *HAS*

1   🔘 2.3 Tell students that *have* and *has* can be pronounced in two ways, depending on their position in the sentence. Play the recording and ask students to mark the strong sound.

ALTERNATIVELY

> Drill the sounds /æ/ (strong) and /ə/ (weak) and ask students if they can hear the difference.

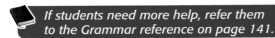
2.3 and answers

1   H<u>a</u>ve you ever been to Australia?
2   Yes, I h<u>a</u>ve.
3   H<u>a</u>s she ever seen a Kangaroo?
4   No, she h<u>a</u>sn't.

2   🔘 2.3 Ask students to listen again and practise saying the sentences.

3   Tell students they are going to ask each other about things they have done, using the correct form of the verbs in the box. Draw their attention to the model sentence. Tell them to write four questions individually, then put them in pairs to ask each other. Monitor and check they are asking and answering correctly.

LISTENING

1   Tell students they are going to listen to and read a blog. Ask them to work in pairs to discuss the questions. Conduct quick feedback and accept any reasonable answers.

1	A blog is short for a weblog, which is a kind of online diary that other people can read.
2 and 3 students' own answers	

2   Ask students to look at the pictures and describe them. Check they know the word *turtle*. Ask them to read the passage quickly and choose the picture that they think best reflects it. Conduct brief whole class feedback.

Picture 1

3   Tell students they are now going to read the blog more carefully to answer some questions. Ask them to work individually to write the answers.

1	Costa Rica
2	worked on a turtle conservation project
3	Sydney
4	excited/happy

4 2.4 Tell students they are going to listen to Caz telling her friend Sergei about the trip and tick the activities she did. Ask them to read through the list then play the recording. Check the answers.

> Caz went to the beach, counted baby turtles, went rafting, visited a volcano, took lots of photographs

5 2.4 Tell students they are going to listen again. Ask them to read through the questions. Check they understand them before you play the recording.
Check answers in pairs before conducting whole class feedback.

> **1** b   **2** a   **3** a   **4** b   **5** a

🔘 2.4

S = Sergei, **C** = Caz

S: Hi, Caz! I haven't seen you for ages! Where have you been?

C: Hi Sergei! I've been in Costa Rica for the last four weeks!

S: Costa Rica? Wow! I've never been to Central America!

C: It was an amazing experience. I worked on a conservation project.

S: Conservation project? What do you mean exactly?

C: Well, I have been interested in animals since I was a child and I've always loved turtles. They are my favourite animals! So, I decided to work as a volunteer on a sea turtle project – to protect sea turtles and their nests on the beach.

S: So, what did you do exactly?

C: Well, I spent a lot of time checking the nests. I counted the baby turtles – that was definitely the best part! I also helped to clean up the beach and we even went on night patrols of the beach – there was a lot to do, but it was very rewarding.

S: So, did you have any free time?

C: Oh yes! It wasn't all about work! One day I went rafting!

S: Rafting? You mean you only had a platform of wood to protect you from the water! I've never done that! It sounds very dangerous!

C: No, it wasn't – it was exciting! It was a great experience to go down the river so fast. I'm so glad that I did it! We also went walking around the base of Arenal Volcano.

S: I've never seen a volcano! Is it extinct?

C: Well, not exactly, but it's not active very often. We had a spectacular view – I took lots of photographs! And another time we went to the rainforest. I've never seen so many different colours in one place – the butterflies were so beautiful and I loved the waterfalls. I'd definitely like to go back one day. It's the best trip I've ever had!

Discussion

This activity gives students a chance to talk about the topic. It also helps prepare them for PART 4 of IELTS: the Speaking test.
Put students in pairs to ask and answer the questions. At the end, conduct a class vote to see how many would like to work on a conservation project.

SPEAKING
A SPECIAL PLACE OF NATURAL BEAUTY

1 Tell students they are going to talk about places of natural beauty in their country. Build up a list of places on the board. Put them in pairs to discuss the questions. Conduct feedback by asking which place most people think is the most important.

2 2.5 Ask students to look at the pictures and name the place (Mount Fuji, in Japan). Tell them they are going to listen to Hiromi talk about Mount Fuji, and ask them to number the pictures in the order she talks about them. Check their answers as a class.

ALTERNATIVELY

> If your students need more support, discuss what they can see in the pictures before they listen.

> **3**   **4**   **2**   **1**

3 2.5 Ask students to read the questions silently. Answer any questions, then play the recording and ask students to listen and choose the correct answer, a, b or c. Check answers in pairs, then as a class. They may need to listen more than once.

> **1** c   **2** c   **3** c   **4** a

🔘 2.5

Hiromi: A special place of natural beauty? Well, Mount Fuji is very special for me. It is in the south-west of Japan. It's the highest mountain in our country – it's nearly four thousand metres high. It's spectacular, so many artists have painted it! I've been to Mount Fuji. I went a long time ago – I think I was six years old. I can still remember it – we went in July. What is special about it for me? That's easy! It's always changing! When we saw it it was light purple in colour but I've also seen photographs where it is snowy and grey! The way it changes colour makes it very special for me. It's also special because it's a symbol of my country – of Japan.

4 Tell students that they will prepare to talk about a special place of beauty. Ask them to choose a place and refer them to the bullet points to help them make a few notes.

Bridge to IELTS

VOCABULARY RANGE

Point out that students may be asked to describe a place or event in the IELTS Speaking test. Ask them to read the box and build a list of adjectives they could use to describe a place.

5 Ask students to read the topic card and then work in pairs, taking turns to describe a place. To close the activity, ask one or two pairs to present their description to the class.

WRITING

THE ADVANTAGES AND DISADVANTAGES OF TOURISM

1 Ask students to look at the picture. Put them in pairs to build a list of advantages and disadvantages that tourism might have on such a place. Check that students understand the prompts in the box and then ask students to use the prompts to help. Conduct whole class feedback, eliciting ideas. Write the ideas onthe board in two columns: advantages and disadvantages.

> **Advantages:**
> more money for local people, job opportunities, etc.
> **Disadvantages:**
> loss of traditional way of life, noise, damage to environment (animals and plants), too crowded, too much pollution, etc.

2 Tell students they are going to read a short text about the effects of tourism and that they should choose the best title. They should ignore the gaps at this point, but read quickly and choose. Check answers in pairs, then as a class.

> c

3 Ask students to read the paragraph again and complete it with the phrases in the box. While they are completing the sentences, move around the class and monitor their writing.

Ask students to compare their ideas before conducting whole class feedback.

> **A** First of all
> **B** However
> **C** For example
> **D** In my opinion

4 Ask students to use the same expressions to complete the sentences. Each expression should be used once only.

> **1** First of all
> **2** For example
> **3** In my opinion
> **4** However

5 Tell students they are now going to think about more advantages and disadvantages of tourism. Ask them to read the ideas and check they understand them. Then ask them to work in pairs to decide whether the ideas are advantages or disadvantages. Elicit the answers as a class.

> **Advantages:** 1   4
> **Disadvantages:** 2   3

6 Ask students to work together to match each sentence with an idea from activity 5. This can be done as a whole class activity.

> **1** d   **2** a   **3** b   **4** c

7 Tell students they will now write a paragraph using the information and notes they have made. Read the title aloud and check that students understand it. Refer them to the model in activity 2 and point out that the text is written in the present simple tense. Ask students to work alone to write their text. Move around and help them.

ALTERNATIVELY

> Use students' completed texts for a class gallery. If time is short, set as homework.

Family

UNIT OVERVIEW

This unit looks at the topic of **families**. The **main speaking aims** of the unit are to **talk about important life events**. The main **grammar** focuses are **the present simple passive** and **the passive and active voice**. The **vocabulary** focus is on **family relationships**. **Writing** covers some aspects of **describing and comparing figures** in a table.

WARM UP

Ask students to look at the photograph and discuss the following questions: *What is the relationship between these people? Where are they? Why? How are they feeling?* Ask students to suggest where the group are from and give reasons.

READING

1 Ask students to read the words in the box and check they understand them. Ask them to work in pairs and to use the words to talk about the picture. Conduct quick feedback.

2 Ask students to read the questions and then read the text quickly. This is scan reading, so tell them to look only for the answers to the questions. Check the answers in pairs, then as a class.

> **1** c   **2** a   **3** a   **4** a

3 Tell students to work alone to find words from the text to complete the sentences. Point out that the line references are there to help them. When most of them have finished, stop them and check the answers as a class. Drill the words as you conduct feedback.

> **1** relatives   **2** guest   **3** lucky   **4** meaning

GRAMMAR

PRESENT SIMPLE PASSIVE

Introduce the grammar. Write the example on the board:
Friends and relatives <u>are invited</u>.

Ask students to identify and underline the verb. Ask students what tense this is (present simple) and whether

they can tell you the form (present simple passive = *to be* + past participle).
Ask students if they know why we use this form. Then ask them to check their ideas in the grammar box and read the examples.

ALTERNATIVELY

> If your class is able, write the active form of the sentence up on the board.
> *People invite friends and relatives.*
>
> Ask students to make it passive. Follow with their own examples.

> *If students need more help, refer them to the Grammar reference on page 142.*

1 Ask students to work individually to write the past participles of the verbs. Do the first one as a class. Go through the answers by asking individuals. Drill students as you check the answers.

> | celebrated | called | coloured | given |
> |---|---|---|---|
> | invited | made | held | worn |

2 Ask students to work alone to complete the sentences. Point out that they need to think about the person when choosing singular or plural, as well as the sense of the sentence. They need to use one verb more than once. Check in pairs, then as a class.

> **1** are   **2** isn't   **3** aren't   **4** is   **5** are

3 Tell students to put the words in order to make sentences. Ask them to work alone to write the sentences and then to compare their answers in pairs. Ask individuals to read the answers aloud to check.

> **1** The baby's parents are given presents by the guests.
> **2** Babies are given lucky envelopes by the guests.
> **3** Each guest is given a red egg by the parents.
> **4** Each egg is coloured red by the parents.

4 This activity focuses on choosing the correct passive form. Point out that students should use the verb participles from activity 1. Ask students to work alone to complete the activity and then to compare in pairs before conducting feedback.

1 is celebrated	2 is called	3 are invited
4 is given	5 are given	

Listening

1   2.6 Tell students they are going to listen to two friends, Jing and Fouad, talking about a red egg and ginger party. Ask them to read through the statements and then choose the correct option as they listen. Play the recording.

Ask students to compare their answers before checking as a class.

1 a	2 b	3 a	4 a

2 2.6 Tell students they are going to listen again. Ask them to work in pairs to match the beginnings and endings to make sentences about Jing's family. Check answers in pairs, then as a class.

1 b	2 a	3 c	4 d	5 e

3 2.6 Tell students they are going to listen again. Ask them to read the statements silently and then underline the correct answer as they listen. Answer any questions before playing the recording. They may need to listen more than once. Check answers in pairs, then as a class.

1 two	2 has	3 many years ago	4 62	5 one month

2.6

F = Fouad, J = Jing

F: Hi Jing! What are you doing?

J: I'm looking at some photos. Do you want to see them?

F: I'd love to! Hey! Is that a red egg? I've never seen an egg that colour before!

J: It's a present from my brother Lee. Look. That's him in that photo. He's older than me. He's twenty-six. And that's his wife Yibo – she's my-sister-in-law. They met before Lee did his military service and they got married when he came back. Yibo is an engineer. We really get on well together. She's like a sister to me.

F: Who's that cute baby? She's adorable.

J: That's Zu. He's a baby boy, actually! He's Lee and Yibo's son. So now I'm an aunt. Zu's really funny – he's always smiling.

F: So, that means Zu is your nephew?

J: That's right. I'm Zu's aunt and Zu is my nephew! This photo was taken at his Red Egg and Ginger party last weekend.

F: Red Egg and Ginger party?

J: Yes, when people have a child, they celebrate a baby's first month birthday with a big party for family and friends. It's a really important event for us. People often have this party in a restaurant but we had our party for Zu at my parents' home in Beijing. Look – there's my father there and there's my mother. They're very proud of their new grandson. My mum's amazing. She's just got her driving licence at the age of 62!

F: Well, you're never too old to learn!

J: That's true! All the guests get presents from the baby's parents when they arrive at the party. Eggs are symbols of change and they are coloured red because in China red means happiness!

F: So, that's why you've got a red egg. What about the babies? Are they given presents too?

J: Oh, yes! They get red envelopes with money inside! But they're given other gifts too. Look at Zu's hat! Do you see the little tiger on it? In China the tiger is a very important animal – the king of all animals. It is believed that the tiger looks after babies and protects them from harm. That's why babies often get presents of tiger hats or tiger shoes. The tiger shoes usually have little eyes on them to guide the baby when they first learn to walk.

F: Who's that old woman standing behind you in the photo? She looks very happy!

J: Oh! That's my grandmother and her husband's standing next to her – he's my grandfather. They got married just after they left school! They're very happy together.

F: She's holding a pair of shoes too.

J: So she is. And what a surprise! There's a tiger at the front of each one!

F: Looks like your nephew's got two tigers looking after him.

Discussion

Tell students that the focus of this task is on improving their interaction skills for the IELTS Speaking test.

1   Ask students to read through the life stages and check they understand them, and then work in pairs to compare their ideas. Encourage them to give reasons for their answers. Conduct a quick class check to see if they agree, then ask students to talk about question 2.

Vocabulary
Family relationships

1   Write three titles on the board – *male, female* and *both* – and ask students to suggest family members for each group. Ask students to work in pairs to add the family members in the box to the correct group.

Check the answers as a class. Indicate stress and drill pronunciation of tricky items such as aunt /ɑːnt/, parents /ˈpeərənts/, son /sʌn/ and nephew /ˈnefjuː/.

Male: father, nephew, brother-in-law, uncle, grandfather, son
Female: aunt, grandmother, mother, niece, daughter, sister-in-law
Both: cousin, parents, children

2 Ask students to find word pairs of male/female words from within the 'both' column. Tell them that one word has no pair.

no pair: cousin

3 The following activities help students confirm the meaning of the vocabulary. Ask students to work individually to complete the sentences, and then check in pairs before conducting feedback.

1 parents	2 nephew
3 aunt	4 grandmother
5 children	6 brother-in-law

4 Ask students to work individually to complete the sentences, and then check in pairs before conducting feedback.

ALTERNATIVELY

If your class are confident with this vocabulary, conduct this activity as a whole class.

1 grandfather	2 uncles	3 cousins	4 niece

5 Ask students to work in pairs to choose the word that is different, and then ask individuals for their answers and reasons.

ALTERNATIVELY

This can be used for a warm up or revision activity in a later class.

1 cousin (not necessarily male) 2 daughter (not plural)
3 brother (not female)   4 son (not plural)

6 Ask students to work in pairs to talk about their own families.

ALTERNATIVELY

If your class are not very strong, let them prepare notes first.

Communication activities
9A see Teacher's notes page 133.

READING

1 Ask students to read through the questions and check they understand them. Put them in pairs to talk about the pictures and questions. Conduct brief feedback to see whether students have similar ideas.

2 Ask students to read the questions and decide on their answers. Emphasise that they are just guessing. Put them in pairs to compare their ideas, then check their ideas as a class.

3 Tell students to read the first paragraph only on page 79. This is scan reading, so tell them to look only for the answers to the questions as quickly as they can, then put them in pairs to compare their ideas. Check the answers as a class.

1 c	2 b	3 b

4 Tell students they will now read the whole text to find out about life in the Hunza Valley. They should look back at activity 1 and tick the things mentioned.

Diet, exercise and positive attitude

5 Ask students to read the text again, then in pairs they should match 1–4 with A–D. Conduct whole class feedback.

1 C	2 B	3 A	4 D

6 Ask students to read the statements and decide whether they are true or false. Remind them to underline the text where they find the answer. Check the answers as a class.

ALTERNATIVELY

If your class are confident readers, conduct this activity as a class.

1 F	2 F	3 T	4 T

7 Ask students to find the words in the text according to the line references and then to use the context to help choose the correct meaning. When most of them have finished, stop them and check the answers as a class.

1 a	2 a	3 a	4 b	5 a

GRAMMAR

PASSIVE AND ACTIVE VERBS

Tell students they are going to look at the difference between active and passive verb forms. Write the examples on the board:
(1) The Hunza people have a simple lifestyle.
(2) Plants are eaten raw.

Ask students to identify which sentence is active (1) and which is passive (2). Ask students to suggest ideas for when we choose one form over another then refer them to the grammar box to check.

1 Ask students to work in pairs and match each sentence with its definition. Point out that in the passive, the object of the sentence (plants) becomes the subject. Ask students to make this sentence active. *(People eat raw plants.)*

> The action is more important than the people (2)
> We are more interested in the people (1)

 If students need more help, refer them to the Grammar reference on page 142.

2 Ask students to rewrite the first sentence and emphasise that the subject and object change places in *passive* constructions. Ask students to continue individually, then compare in pairs before checking. Point out that you only need to use *by* when the person doing the action is specified.

> **1** Fruit is grown in the valley.
> **2** Their lives are spent moving around.
> **3** They were examined by the doctors.
> **4** A lot of vegetables and fruit are eaten.

3 Ask students to work individually to choose the correct form to complete the text. In feedback, ask individuals to read sentences aloud.

1 is located	**2** are known	
3 are picked	**4** (are) eaten	
5 is seen	**6** are given	

Discussion

This activity gives students a chance to comment on the lives of the Hunza. It also helps prepare them for PART 4 of IELTS: the Speaking test.
Put students in pairs to ask and answer the questions.

LISTENING

1 Tell students they are going to learn about a special event in Japan. Ask them to work in pairs to label the picture. Conduct quick feedback.

> **A** kimono **B** belt **C** scarf **D** sleeve **E** sandals

2 Ask students to work individually and use the words from the picture to complete the sentences. Check they know the word *waist.* Conduct quick whole class feedback.

> **1** belt **2** sandals **3** kimono **4** sleeve **5** scarf

3 🔊 2.7 Tell students they are going to listen to Hiromi telling Jakub about a special event in her country. Ask them to read through the statements and then mark them true or false as they listen. Play the recording. Check answers in pairs, then as a class.

> **1** T **2** F **3** F **4** F **5** T

4 🔊 2.7 Tell students they are now going to listen again to answer more detailed questions. Allow them time to read through the statements first, then play the recording. Check answers in pairs, then as a class.

> **1** c **2** a **3** b **4** c **5** b

 2.7

J = Jakub, **H** = Hiromi

J: What an amazing photograph. You look so different in these clothes!

H: Yes, I look very formal! It's my coming-of-age ceremony. It's celebrated by all young people of the age of twenty.

J: Twenty?

H: Yes, twenty is the age we become adults. It's called the age of majority in Japan. Twenty is the age when we get the vote. The ceremony is held every year in January. It's always held on a Monday and it's always the second Monday in January. This day is a national holiday in Japan.

J: Do you all wear special clothes?

H: Girls wear special kimonos. The kimono I'm wearing is the same kimono my mum wore when she was twenty! I'm wearing her white scarf and the same sandals on my feet too! Boys can wear hakama, which is the male version of a kimono, but they usually wear western business suits.

J: Your kimono is so beautiful. I really like the sleeves!

➜

H: They're really long – about one metre long! That's why they are called 'swinging sleeves'. It's the most formal kimono for single women. Older married women wear short-sleeved kimonos.

J: What about the belt? It's very beautiful.

H: Yes, that's an obi. It's a very wide belt which is worn around the waist. It's the most expensive part of the kimono. It's so expensive, in fact, that many families have to hire them.

J: So what happens during the ceremony?

H: Well, the ceremony varies from place to place. Some have performances and speeches, others only have speeches. We listen to government officials talking about what it means to be an adult and the importance of being responsible. We are also given money. It's an important part of the day.

J: What happens after the ceremony?

H: Most people go to parties or bars to celebrate with friends. We eat red bean rice. This is always eaten when there's something to celebrate! Well, you are only twenty once!

J: That's true!

5 Tell students they are going to complete a summary of the ceremony they heard about. Ask them to read through the text and complete each gap with **one** word only. Check answers in pairs, then as a class.

1	twenty
2	Monday
3	belt
4	restaurants

6 Ask students to work individually to write the words in the correct order. Check the answers as a class and drill.

1	Where is it celebrated?
2	Who celebrates it?
3	At what age is it celebrated?
4	What happens at the ceremony?

7 Put students in pairs and designate them A or B. Tell Student A to turn to page 125 and Student B to page 127. Ask them to read their information and then work together to ask and answer the questions from activity 6 without showing each other their text. Student A starts. Then swap.

 Communication activities

9B see *Teacher's notes page 133.*

SPEAKING
AN IMPORTANT LIFE EVENT

1 Tell students they are going to talk about important life events in their country. Put them in pairs to discuss the questions and pictures. Conduct quick feedback by asking which age most people think for each event pictured.

ALTERNATIVELY

If your students need more support, discuss what they can see in the pictures before they discuss in pairs.

2 Tell students they are going to listen to Ana talking about an important life event and that they need to identify the picture she is talking about. Play the recording. Check answers in pairs, then as a class.

the first picture

3 2.8 Ask students to read the statements silently and answer any questions. Then play the recording and ask students to listen and choose the correct answer, a, b or c. Check answers in pairs, then as a class.

1 c   **2** c   **3** a

2.8

Ana: An important life event in my country? Well, I do think that getting a driving licence is a very important life event in Brazil for young people. You can't learn until you're 18. This is the age we become adults – we're no longer children! How do we prepare? Well, it's far from easy. It really does takes a very long time. In fact, I really do think it can be compared to a very long journey! This is because we have to pass several tests. I think there are four altogether – psychological, theoretical, technical and practical. Why is it important? Well, it's important to get your driving licence because it's needed for many jobs in Brazil. What I like most is the independence it brings – the freedom to get in my car and drive where I want. It's a truly fantastic feeling!

Living IELTS

ADDING EMPHASIS 2

1 2.9 Tell students that natural speech has some words that are stressed more than others, to add emphasis. These are usually the important words. Ask students to listen and underline the emphasised words. Compare in pairs then check as a class.

I **do** think that getting a driving licence is a very important life event in Brazil.
It's **far** from easy.
It **really does** take a very long time.
I **really do** think that it can be compared to a very long journey.
What I like most is the independence it brings.
It's a **truly** fantastic feeling!

Ask students to listen again and practise saying the sentences.

2   Ask students to use the examples in the *Living IELTS* box to complete the rules. Make sure students know what an auxiliary verb is (e.g. *do, does).* Do the first one together, then put students in pairs to complete the task. Conduct whole class feedback.

1 far	**2** does, do	**3** really
4 What I like most is	**5** truly	

4   Tell students that now they will prepare to talk about an important life event. Ask them to choose an event and refer them to the bullet points to make a few notes. Move around the class and help with ideas.

Bridge to IELTS

STRUCTURING YOUR TALK

Point out that students may be asked to describe a place or an event in the IELTS Speaking test. Ask them to read the box silently and then ask what the key advice is (that you should turn the prompts into questions).

5   Ask students to read the topic card and then work in pairs to take turns to describe their life event. To close the activity, ask one or two pairs to present their description to the class.

WRITING

DESCRIBING A TABLE

1   Check that students understand the words in the box. Then ask them to look at the pictures and match them to the words. Check answers in pairs, then as a class. Conduct a class discussion on which part of the wedding is the most expensive.

A wedding ceremony	**B** wedding reception
C honeymoon	

2   Ask students to skim read the information in the table and choose the best title. Ask students to compare their ideas before conducting whole class feedback.

---

b

Writing Skills

COMPARING FIGURES IN A TABLE

3   Ask students to use the information in the table to choose the correct words. Compare in pairs, then as a class.

1 reception	**2** thousand
3 honeymoon	**4** flowers
5 wedding cake	**6** presents

4   Tell students they are now going to think about language to compare amounts. Ask them to read the expressions in the box and check they understand them. Tell them that *almost* has the same meaning as *nearly.* Then ask them to work in pairs to complete the sentences, again using the information in the table. Check answers as a class.

1 the most	**2** costs almost
3 the least	**4** almost the same
5 twice the cost	**6** more

5   Ask students to work individually to write sentences. Remind them that they will need to use the present simple of the verb *cost.* Monitor and check their writing. Check answers in pairs, then as a class.

1	The reception costs the most.
2	The reception is twice the cost of the honeymoon.
3	The wedding cake costs almost the same as the presents.
4	The reception costs almost $10 000.
5	The flowers cost more than the wedding dress.
6	The presents cost the least.

6   Tell students they will now write a paragraph using the information and notes they have made. Refer them to the model in activity 3 and point out that the text is written in the present simple tense. Students work alone to write their text. Move around and help them.

ALTERNATIVELY

When students have finished writing, use their texts for a class gallery. If time is short, students can write the text at home.

Review **Units 7, 8 and 9**

OVERVIEW

It is important for all students to meet 'new' language again and again. This is even more important for students starting at Pre-intermediate level because their language base and ability to deal with skills are not very developed. Reviewing language will help them to consolidate what they are in the process of learning as well as show them which areas they still have not fully understood. With this in mind, it is important that you are positive and supportive if they do not do very well in areas of the Review. Encourage them to see that if they get something wrong, it helps them to see where they should focus their energies. Taking this view will help them to grow in confidence; emphasising failure seldom has the same effect.

GRAMMAR

AIM **To revise passive and active verb forms in the present simple.**

1   This is a controlled writing activity. Ask students to work alone to complete the text. Check answers in pairs, then as a class.

1 is celebrated	**2** is called	**3** are invited
4 are placed	**5** include	**6** are added
7 touches		

AIM **To revise phrases for connecting text.**

2   Tell students they are going to read a short text about going to the gym. Ask students to work alone to complete the text with the expressions in the box. Check in pairs, then as a class.

ALTERNATIVELY

Ask students to do the exercise in pairs.

1 because	**2** First of all	**3** for example
4 However	**5** In my opinion	

VOCABULARY

AIM **To revise words used to describe family members.**

1   Ask students to work alone to complete as many words as they can, then put them in pairs to help each other. Check answers as a class by asking individuals to spell or write the words on the board.

1 nephew	**2** sister-in-law	**3** brother
4 cousin	**5** niece	**6** aunt

2   Ask students to place the words on the scale according to age. Check answers as a class.

(Older to younger) grandparent, mother, daughter, grandson

AIM **To check students remember collocations in the context of life events.**

3   Put students in pairs to match the verbs and nouns. Point out that number 4 has been done for them. Check answers as a class.

1 e	**2** c	**3** b	**4** d	**5** a

AIM **To check students recognise collocations in the context of geographical features.**

4   Ask students to work alone to choose the correct adjective for each noun. Check in pairs, then as a class.

Bridge to IELTS

WRITING TEST PREPARATION

AIM **To revise students' knowledge about the IELTS Writing test.**

1   Put students in pairs to write three things they know about how the IELTS Writing test is organised. Remind them you want them to write facts about the exam, not just 'it is hard'. Conduct brief feedback to see how much they know.

2   Ask them to read the passage to check their ideas. Then conduct feedback as a class. Ask students to tell you which part of the writing test they think is hardest and why.

3   Put students into pairs to write one or two ideas on preparing for the writing test. Conduct whole class feedback, indicating which ideas you think will be helpful.

Suggested answers

Ideas for task 1: Get used to writing in short time periods. Choosing a question and underlining the key facts and then spending 15 minutes writing is good practice.

Another important skill is getting used to reading charts and data in table format.

Ideas for task 2: Read as much as possible. Have some pages in your notebook for linking words. Practise planning, paragraphing and organising ideas.

OPTIONAL

Ask students to go through the Student's Book in pairs and find examples of Bridge to IELTS tips for the Writing test. Review quickly as a class.

Unit 4 p.31	Unit 7 p.54
Unit 10 p.74	Unit 12 p.85

ALTERNATIVELY

Ask students to work in groups and prepare a poster with tips for the writing section of the exam, using the ideas mentioned and their own ideas. Display these in the classroom.

Study Skills

USING REFERENCE MATERIALS

It's important for students learning English to maximise their ability to access information about language when not in class. This is particularly important for students who are not living in an English-speaking country or a country where English is spoken as an alternative language. These students have far fewer opportunities to encounter and work with English. Using a dictionary is a key skill for them to develop.

AIM To encourage students to study more effectively.

1 Ask students whether they have dictionaries, and if so whether they are bi-lingual or monolingual, electronic or in book format. Put them in groups to discuss and answer the questions. Monitor their discussion. Point out that question (e) 'if the word is regular or irregular' refers to whether a verb is regular (ending in -ed) when in past simple tense.

2 Ask students to read the text and check their ideas. Conduct whole class feedback. Ask them whether they found any of the information surprising.

a	yes	**b**	yes	**c**	yes	**d**	no
e	yes	**f**	yes	**g**	yes	**h**	no

3 Ask students to work in groups to discuss the features their dictionaries have. Monitor.

Conduct whole class feedback where students decide which kind of dictionary is best and why.

Ask students whether there are any disadvantages to relying on dictionaries and what they can do about it. Ask them whether this section has encouraged them to think of new ways they might use their dictionaries in future. What are they?

ALTERNATIVELY

Build up a list on the board of some of the problems of using dictionaries. Discuss how students can overcome these problems.

Suggested problems and solutions

Problem: Sometimes, several meanings of a word are provided.
Solution: *Check the context carefully. Crosscheck with a bi-lingual dictionary.*

Problem: Looking words up is not memorable.
Solution: *Make a record of words that you want to remember. Create your own examples. Write them in your notebook.*

Problem: Relying on a dictionary makes you lazy.
Solution: *Try and guess the word from context first, then check in a dictionary. Count how often you use a dictionary. Try and limit the number of times.*

Make a note to remind yourself in a week to ask your students if they have changed the way they have been using their dictionaries. You could do this as a warm-up activity at the beginning of the lesson or before students start a reading text. For example, ask half the students to use dictionaries as often as they like and the other half to use context only. When they finish, compare how the use of dictionaries affected their ability and speed in the task. As a result they will become more conscious of the effect of dictionary use as language learners.

Conservation

UNIT OVERVIEW

This unit looks at the topic of **conservation**. The main **speaking** aims of the unit are to **talk about problems.** The main **grammar** focuses are **countable/uncountable nouns** with **the form and use of** *some/any* and *how much/how many*. The **vocabulary** focus is on **word formation. Writing** covers some aspects of **organising a paragraph.**

WARM UP

Introduce the topic of conservation. Ask students to look at the photograph. Ask them why they think the photo of pandas is there and what the unit might be about. Conduct brief feedback and ask students to tell you what they know about conservation. Are there any conservation projects they know about/are involved with?

READING

1 Ask students to read the phrases and check that they understand them by giving their own examples or explanations. Then put them in pairs to look at the picture and talk about Earth Day using the phrases given. Check their ideas as a class.

2 Ask students if they can say where they might see the text on Earth Day (it is a webpage). Then ask them to read it quickly and choose a, b or c. This is skim reading, so tell them to look quickly to get an overall idea. Check answers in pairs, then as a class.

b

3 Check that students understand the words *litter* (paper rubbish, usually on the street) and *campus* (university setting/group of buildings). Tell them to read the text again more carefully and choose true or false. Check answers in pairs, then as a class.

1 T 2 T 3 F (can hold a concert with other students)

4 Tell students to work alone to find words from the passage to complete the sentences. When most of them have finished, stop them and check the answers as a class. Drill the words as you check the answers.

1 event 2 plant 3 celebrate 4 competition

LISTENING

1   2.10 Tell students they are going to listen to three students, Esra, Alex and Carol, planning an Earth Day event. Ask them to match the names with their ideas as they listen. Play the recording. Check answers in pairs, then as a class.

Alex – give out leaflets   Esra – plant trees Carol – organise a clean-up

2 2.10 Tell students they are going to listen again for more detailed understanding. Ask them to read the text silently and complete the gaps as they listen. Point out that they can use a maximum of two words each time. Play the recording.

Check answers in pairs, then as a class. They may need to listen more than once.

1 year 2 two 3 to organise 4 clean up

2.10

E = Esra, **A** = Alex, **C** = Carol

E: OK, so the next thing we're talking about is Earth Day – the day of conservation groups.

A: Yes, we're all in the Ecology Society. Let's organise something this year.

E: That's right, Alex – we didn't do anything last year.

C: We could put up some posters.

E: Or hand out some leaflets.

A: Yes, we could give out some leaflets about Earth Day.

C: That's OK, but what happens then? We put up posters and give out our leaflets, and then what?

A: I see what you mean. Giving out information isn't really celebrating Earth Day. Let's look at some ideas from Earth Day Network.

C: OK.

E: Here's one – planting trees – how about that?

A: It's not a bad idea, but how much time have we got? There are only two months before Earth Day.

E: We could ask students to buy a tree and plant it on campus for Earth Day. ➥

C: Esra, you can't just plant trees around the university. Look at this one – this looks good. What about a concert?

A: Yeah – we can get two or three bands.

E: I can find a speaker to talk about Earth Day.

A: We can hold it at the Student Theatre.

C: It sounds like a good idea, but it could be difficult to organise.

E: What do you mean?

C: Think about bringing the band to the theatre and selling drinks. Have we really got enough time to do this? And there's some money for the Ecology Society, but do we have enough money?

E: Carol's right – it could be too difficult.

A: Yes, it's a good idea, but we can't make a decision today. So Carol, what's your suggestion?

C: How about a campus clean-up? It can't be too difficult to organise and it includes lots of people – staff and students. I'm sure we could get people to do it – we just meet everyone and say where they can collect litter.

E: And there are lots of places to clean up on campus.

A: You bet – we could start with my room!

E: Ugh, yuck.

C: No thanks, Alex.

GRAMMAR

COUNTABLE AND UNCOUNTABLE NOUNS/ *SOME* AND *ANY*

Write the gapped examples on the board:
I have _____ money. Is there _____ water in the bottle? I don't have _____ brothers.

Ask students to complete the sentences (*some, any, any*) and to explain when we use the different forms (*any* for questions/negatives; *some* for uncountable/plural statements).

Ask students to look at the grammar box and read the examples. Ask students to suggest more countable/ uncountable nouns.

ALTERNATIVELY

If your class is not strong, first give them a list of countable/uncountable nouns to categorise. Write these up on the board in two groups. Follow with their own examples.

 If students need more help, refer them to the Grammar reference on page 142.

1 Ask students to work in pairs to decide whether the nouns are countable or uncountable. Do the first one as a class. Go through the answers by asking individuals. As you check the answers, record the nouns in two lists on the board

Countable: problem, idea, month, student, person
Uncountable: music, time, litter

2 Ask students to work alone to choose the correct word. Check answers in pairs, then as a class.

| **1** some | **2** any | **3** some | **4** a | **5** any |

3 Ask students to work alone to complete the sentences. Check answers in pairs, then as a class.

| **1** any | **2** some | **3** Some | **4** any |

ALTERNATIVELY

If your class are confident with this grammar, conduct the activity as a whole class.

4 Put students in pairs and designate them A or B. Tell Student A to turn to page 125 and Student B to page 127. Ask them to write questions and then work together to ask and answer their questions without showing each other their texts. Student A starts. Then swap.

READING

1 Ask students to work in pairs and discuss the questions. Conduct whole class feedback to see what the popular uses of water are.

2 Tell students they are going to read about river life. Ask them to read the text and label the picture with the highlighted words. Check in pairs, then as a class.

| **A** jungles | **B** river | **C** lake | **D** mountains |
| **E** forests | **F** stream | **G** hills | |

3 Refer students to the title of the passage. Ask them to predict which things will be mentioned. Point out that more than one may be mentioned. Don't conduct feedback. They will check their ideas when they read the text.

Bridge to IELTS

USING INFORMATION FOR PREDICTING

Tell students that when they meet a text they need to look at all the information that they have. This includes pictures, headings and layouts. Point out that in an exam they can use these clues to help them before they even read the passage.

4 Ask students to read the passage to check their ideas from activity 3. Check in pairs, then as a class.

a c

5 Ask students to read the passage again and choose the correct answers. Check in pairs, then as a class.

1 c   2 c   3 b   4 b

6 Tell students to work alone to find words from the passage to complete the sentences. Point out that the line references are there to help them. Ask students to compare in pairs, then check as a class.

1 agriculture	2 pollution
3 drill	4 cause

GRAMMAR
HOW MUCH/ HOW MANY

Write the examples on the board:

How _____ water does the country have?

How _____ years do they have?

Ask students to complete the sentences (*much, many*) and to explain when we use the different forms (*How much* for uncountable nouns; *How many* for countable nouns).

Ask students to look at the grammar box and read the examples.

 If students need more help, refer them to the Grammar reference on page 142.

1 Ask students to work alone to choose the correct form. Do the first one as a class. Check in pairs, then as a class.

1 many   2 much   3 many   4 many

2 Ask students to find the answers to these questions in the passage. In feedback, ask pairs to ask and answer the questions in front of the class.

1 30   2 100 mm   3 20   4 10 000

3 Ask students to complete the sentences with *how much* or *how many.* Check in pairs, then as a class.

1 How much	2 How many
3 how much	4 How much

4 Put students in pairs and designate them A or B. Tell Student A to turn to page 125 and Student B to page 127. Ask them to write questions and then work together to ask and answer their questions without showing each other their books. Student A starts. Then swap.

Discussion

Conduct this activity as a class. Ask students to tell you which information surprised or interested them in activity 4.

 Communication activities
10A *see Teacher's notes page 134.*

LISTENING

1 Tell students they are going to listen to some information about animals. Ask them to work in pairs to look at the pictures and discuss the questions. Conduct quick feedback and accept any reasonable answers.

ALTERNATIVELY

With a weaker class, conduct this activity as a class. Name each animal and build up a profile on the board.

2 Ask students to complete the sentences with the words in the box. Check in pairs, then as a class. Drill the answers as you conduct feedback.

1 extinct   2 habitat   3 resource   4 destruction

ALTERNATIVELY

With a weaker class, conduct this activity as a class. Ask students to give examples of *extinct* species (e.g. dodo, dinosaur) and other *resources* (e.g. oil, gas).

3 Ask students to work in pairs to decide what dangers affect the animals in activity 1. Conduct whole class feedback and tell students they will check their answers when they listen.

4 2.11 Tell students they are going to listen to a professor talking about the Red List. Tell them they will learn what this term means as they listen. Tell them to listen and check the dangers to animals they predicted in activity 3.

Polar bear: destroying habitat, climate change
Black rhino: hunting
Dolphin: oil pollution
Mountain gorilla: destroying habitat
Otter: river pollution

5 🔘2.11 Tell students they are going to listen again. Give them time to read through the questions, and then play the recording. Check answers in pairs, then as a class.

1 a	2 c	3 b	4 c	5 a

6 Put students in pairs to choose the correct answers. If necessary, play the recording again. Check answers as a whole class.

> 1 T
> 2 F (sea oil pollution)
> 3 F (cutting down forests)
> 4 F (they're unpopular)

🔘 2.11

Professor Aldred: ... and the next thing to talk about is the Red List. What is the Red List? Well, it is a list of animals in very serious danger. Animal extinction is part of nature, but humans are making this happen between a 100 and 1 000 times faster than happens naturally.

There are many reasons for this. All of them are connected to human activity. Let's look at three threats to animals – pollution, hunting and climate change.

The first part of my talk is about pollution. Some animals are affected badly by water pollution. Let's look at two examples. First, in South America, otters died when chemicals went into their rivers. Second, at sea, oil pollution causes illness in dolphins.

The earth is a big place, but humans are moving into areas where animals live. The problem is that animals need their environment. When we cut down forests we destroy the animals' habitats. Let's look at the mountain gorilla. These animals live in the mountain forests of Africa. But people have cut down their forest homes for farming and there are just under 800 of these beautiful animals in the world now. So, animals are in danger from pollution and destruction of their environment. But others are hunted – we find and kill them to sell them. Let's take an example – the black rhino. Between the 1970s and 80s the number of black rhinos fell by 96% because of hunting. Luckily, people do not want to buy products made from the black rhino anymore. But a much bigger problem is affecting the polar bear. The problem is climate change – the earth becoming warmer. Polar bears live in the Arctic, where effects of climate change can be easily seen. Polar bears hunt on the sea ice. But now the ice is melting earlier, which means that the bears have a shorter time to find food.

So, now let's look at ways of helping these animals ...

72 *Unit 10* **Conservation**

Bridge to IELTS

UNDERSTANDING LONG LISTENING PASSAGES

Ask students to read through the box. Tell them to turn to page 136 and look at the audioscript to find the expressions there. Point out that similar phrases are also useful for organising their writing.

VOCABULARY

WORD FORMATION

1 Write the following words on the board and ask students to identify their grammatical names: *destroy (verb), destruction (noun).*

Establish that recognising certain endings, such as the *-ion* of vision, which indicates a noun, is a useful skill in developing their vocabulary. Ask students to suggest more nouns ending in *-ion.* Point out the two common spellings of *-tion* and *-sion.*

2 Ask students to work alone to write the nouns related to the verbs provided. Compare answers in pairs before conducting feedback. Write the answers on the board. Point out that verbs ending in 'e' drop the 'e' when made into nouns. Ask students if they can think of more examples.

1 pollution	2 conservation	3 extinction

PRONUNCIATION

WORD STRESS IN VERBS AND NOUNS

1 🔘2.12 Ask students to listen and choose the correct stress pattern. Play the recording. Check answers in pairs, then as a class.

c

2 🔘2.12 Ask students to listen again and practise saying the words.

2.12

destruction	conservation	pollution	extinction

Discussion

This activity gives students practice in using the vocabulary of this unit. It also helps prepare them for PART 4 of IELTS: the Speaking test.

Put students into groups of three/four to discuss and agree ways to help animals.

Conduct brief feedback with the class.

ALTERNATIVELY

> If you have a strong class, ask students to discuss in small groups. Each group then presents their ideas to the class.
>
> To finish, have a class vote to see which ways to help animals are the most favoured.

SPEAKING

AN ENVIRONMENTAL PROBLEM

1 Ask students to work alone to name the issues shown in the pictures and then to compare their answers. Conduct a quick whole class check.

> pollution
> global warming
> recycling
> destruction (of forests/habitats)

2 Ask students to read through the words in the box and check they understand them. Then put them in pairs to decide which three are the most important in causing global warming. Conduct brief feedback to see which ideas are popular, then ask students to turn to page 125 to find the answers. Check these as a class.

> Power stations
> Industry
> Transport

3 Ask students how people help the environment in their everyday lives. Check they understand the words in the list and then put them in pairs to discuss. Conduct a quick whole class vote to see which measures are most popular.

ALTERNATIVELY

> If you have a strong group, they may enjoy discussing this as a class.

4 🔘 2.13 Tell students they are going to listen to Veena talking about the environment. Ask them to tick which things in activity 3 she mentions.

> recycle

5 🔘 2.13 Tell students they are going to listen again for more detail. Tell them to look through the box and then complete the gaps as they listen. Point out that they must use a maximum of three words.

> 1 recycling
> 2 latest
> 3 more things
> 4 charity
> 5 online

🔘 2.13

Examiner:	OK. Can you tell me what you think the biggest environmental problem is and the reasons for this?
Veena:	I'm not sure, but I think the main problem is not recycling enough. I guess people always want to buy the latest things – new clothes, a new mobile phone or car. We use them for a short time, then we want the next new thing. I think recycling more can help. By recycling, we don't use up resources and we can use the old things again. I try to help by using things I don't need again. I give things to charity or sell them online, or when they really are not good, I recycle them.

Living IELTS

SAYING YOU'RE NOT SURE

This activity gives students a chance to develop fluency. It also helps prepare them for PART 4 of IELTS: the Speaking test. All students have times when they need to think about language. Knowing which expressions to use when searching for language is a useful strategy.

1 🔘 2.14 Ask students to listen again and complete the sentences with the words provided. Check in pairs, then as a class. Point out that *think* and *guess* are interchangeable.

🔘 2.14 and answers

> 1 I <u>think</u> the main problem is not recycling enough.
> 2 I <u>guess</u> people always want to buy the latest things.
> 3 I'm not <u>sure</u>.

2 🔘 2.14 Ask students to listen and repeat the sentences, chorally and individually.

6 Ask students to work alone to think of an environmental problem. If your students need more support, brainstorm ideas as a class and write them on the board. Ask students to then choose one problem and make their own notes. Monitor and help them.

7 Ask students to read the topic card silently. Answer any questions before putting them in pairs to take turns to talk about it. Remind them to use their notes and the expressions in the *Living IELTS* box.

Move around the class and listen. Make notes of good and incorrect language use, then conduct quick feedback at the end to draw the activity to a close.

WRITING
PROBLEM-SOLVING ESSAY

1 Ask students to look at the pictures and name the environmental problems (oil spills, power station, jet emissions/pollution). Put them in groups of three or four to review the list and decide on the three best ways to protect the environment. Conduct whole class feedback, eliciting ideas on the board.

2 Tell students they are going to read a writing question. Explain they should underline the key words so that they can answer the question in the right way. This is a good strategy for any writing task. Check answers in pairs, then as a class.

> **Students might underline:**
> world's resources too quickly, describe, three ways, stop

3 Ask students to read the paragraph and tick or underline the ideas from activity 1. Ask students to compare their ideas before conducting whole class feedback.

> control/stop pollution
> use less energy

ORGANISING A PARAGRAPH (2)

4 Ask students to read the paragraph again and number the ideas in the order they appear. Check answers in pairs, then as a class. Then ask students to find and underline the three words used to introduce ways of solving the problem.

> **1** the problem
> **2** why the problem exists
> **3** three ways to solve the problem
> *First, Second, Finally*
> **4** conclusion

Bridge to IELTS

LISTING

Ask students to read through the box. Ask them to suggest other words they know that help with listing or organising writing. Suggest they have a page in their notebook for these words, so that they can use them when they have to write.

5 Tell students they are going to work on a new essay title. Ask them to underline the key words and then make notes in the table. Conduct whole class feedback and share ideas on the board. Point out that when planning an essay it can be useful to brainstorm more ideas than you need and then select the best ones.

6 Tell students they will now write a short essay using the information and notes they have made. Refer them to the model in activity 3 and point out that the text is written in the present tense. Ask students to work alone to write their text. Move around and help them.

ALTERNATIVELY

> When students have finished writing, use their texts for a class magazine. If time is short, students can write the text as homework.

Communication activities
10B *see Teacher's notes page 134.*

Design

This unit looks at the topic of **design.** The main **speaking** aims of the unit are to **talk about favourite things.** The main **grammar** focuses are **comparatives** and **superlatives.** The **vocabulary** focus is on **adjectives to describe objects. Writing** covers some aspects of **comparing** and *for* and *against.*

WARM UP

Ask students to describe the photograph and discuss the following questions: *Do you like the car pictured? Who do you think drives a car like that? Would you like this car? Why / Why not?*

VOCABULARY

ADJECTIVES TO DESCRIBE OBJECTS

1   Ask students to read the words in the box and check they understand *efficient* (works well) and *modern* (new). Indicate stress and drill. Ask students to work in pairs to use these words to describe the picture of the car on page 95. Conduct quick class feedback to compare ideas.

2   Ask students to match the words in the box with their opposites in activity 1. Check answers in pairs, then as a class. Indicate stress and drill.

exciting/boring	expensive/cheap
modern/old-fashioned	inefficient/efficient
dangerous/safe	slow/fast
heavy/light	

The following activities help students confirm the meaning of the vocabulary.

3   Ask students to work individually to complete the sentences, and then check in pairs before conducting feedback.

1 boring   **2** safe   **3** efficient   **4** slow   **5** expensive

4   Put students in pairs to describe their (family) car. If they don't have a car, give them some car pictures or names of cars to work with. Or ask them to describe their favourite car.

READING

1   Ask students to read the webpage and choose the best option to describe the kind of competition. Check answers in pairs, then as a class.

c

2   Ask students to read the questions and then read the text quickly. This is scan reading, so tell them to look only for the answers to the questions. Check answers in pairs, then as a class.

1 c   **2** a

3   Tell students they will now read blog entries written by students entering this competition. Ask them to read the two blogs and match two of the headings with gaps 1 and 2. Tell them they just need to read for the main idea and do not need to understand every word.

1 B   **2** C

4   Tell students to read the blogs again and complete the summary. Remind them that each gap can be up to three words only and must be grammatically correct. Check answers in pairs, then as a class.

1 jobs
2 three
3 team leader
4 Pat
5 shape/material
6 material/shape

5   Ask students to work alone to find words from the text to complete the sentences. When most of them have finished, stop them and check the answers as a class. Drill the words as you conduct feedback.

1 project
2 designer
3 mechanic
4 fibreglass
5 carbon fibre

GRAMMAR

COMPARATIVES

Draw students' attention to the grammar. Write the example on the board:
Cars are safer/more safe these days.
Ask them to choose the correct form *(safer)* and underline it. Ask students why this is correct (*safe* is a short adjective). Ask whether they can tell you when we use *more* (with long adjectives).

Ask students to give more examples, then get them to check their ideas in the grammar box and read the examples.

ALTERNATIVELY

With a weaker class, ask the students to stand up in height order and use the following adjectives to compare them: *tall, short.*

Ask students to form a sentence comparing two people in the line. Elicit *X is taller than Y, Y is shorter than X.* Drill. Ask students how we form comparatives (short adjective + -er + than).

Ask students to compare using a longer adjective (*beautiful*). Elicit *X is more beautiful than Y.*

Elicit the rule for longer adjectives (*more* + long adjective + *than*).

Provide more adjectives (*friendly, old*) and get students to compare each other using them. Drill examples.

 If students need more help, refer them to the Grammar reference on page 143.

1   Ask students to look at the blogs again and underline six comparative adjectives. Check answers in pairs, then as a class. Drill chorally and individually.

more experienced	better	lighter
faster	safer	smaller

2   Ask students to work individually to write the comparative form of the adjectives in brackets. Do the first one as a class (*good = better*). Go through the answers by asking individuals. As you check the answers, drill.

1	better	2	more expensive
3	heavier	4	worse
5	smaller	6	thinner
7	lighter	8	faster

3   Ask students to read through the information in the box. Elicit a comparative sentence using the information given and then ask students to write sentences. Check in pairs, then as a class.

Suggested answers

1   The Brackley car is lighter than the Normandin car.
2   The Brackley car is faster than the Normandin car.
3   The Normandin car is more efficient than the Brackley car.
4   The Normandin car is more expensive than the Brackley car.

ALTERNATIVELY

If you feel your class need more speaking practice, conduct this activity orally. Ask them to write the sentences as homework.

PRONUNCIATION

-ER ENDINGS

1   [2.15] Play the recording and ask students to describe how *-er* is pronounced in comparative adjectives.

It is soft/weak. This sound is called schwa /ə/.

2   [2.15] Ask students to underline the weak (*-er*) sounds in the comparative sentences. Play the recording. Ask students to check their answers before checking as a class, then drill with the recording.

 2.16 and answers

It's lighte̲r than this one.
It's faste̲r than the others.
It's much cheape̲r than before.
It lasts longe̲r than the others.

3   [2.16] Ask students to listen and practise saying the sentences.

Communication activities
11A see *Teacher's notes page 134.*

READING

1   Ask students to work in pairs and talk about the pictures and what they know about them. Conduct brief feedback to see whether students have similar ideas. Tell them they will find out the answers by reading the passage.

2   Ask students to read the passage and match each paragraph to a picture. Point out the time frame and stop them after three minutes. Check answers in pairs, then as a class.

Paragraph 1 picture 2	Paragraph 2 picture 1
Paragraph 3 picture 4	Paragraph 4 picture 5
Paragraph 5 picture 3	

1 the tallest	**2** the strongest (the worst)
3 the ugliest (the worst)	**4** longest
5 worst	

3 Tell students to work alone to read the passage again and decide whether the statements are true, false or not given. Tell them this is scan reading, and a typical IELTS - style task. Give them three minutes and remind them to look only for the answers to the questions as quickly as they can, then put them in pairs to compare their ideas. Check the answers as a class.
If the answer is 'No', ask students to tell you the correct answer.

1 Yes
2 Not given
3 No (3% of China's electricity comes from it)
4 Not given
5 Yes

4 Ask students to find the words in the passage and then use the context to help them choose the correct meaning. When most of them have finished, stop them and check the answers as a class.

1 a   **2** b   **3** a   **4** b   **5** a

READING
SUPERLATIVES

Tell students they are going to look at comparing more than two things. Write the examples on the board:
The computer is _____ in the world.

Ask students to complete the sentence with a form of the adjective *large* (the largest). Ask them if they know what this form is called (*the superlative*) and see if they can tell you the superlative for *heavy* (the heaviest) and *beautiful* (the most beautiful), then refer them to the grammar box to check.

 *If students need more help, refer them to the Grammar reference on page 143.*

1 Ask students to look back at the reading passage and find the superlative forms of the adjectives. Check answers in pairs, then as a class. In feedback point out that *the most* must always be used with superlative adjectives.

the greatest	the most beautiful	the heaviest
the tallest	the most expensive	the largest

2 Ask students to complete the sentences, using the adjectives provided in the superlative form.

Discussion

This activity practises the grammar. It also helps students prepare for PART 4 of IELTS: the Speaking test.

3 Put students into groups of three/four to discuss the engineering projects in the unit and decide which is the greatest and why.

4 Ask groups to choose a speaker and then take turns to present their ideas to the class. Conduct a brief class vote.

 Communication activities
11B see Teacher's notes page 135.

LISTENING

1 Ask students to work in pairs to match the old and new products in the pictures.

1+5   2+6   4+3

2 Ask students to talk in pairs about the products they have or would like to have. Conduct brief class feedback to see which products are the most popular.

3 Ask students to read the list and check they understand it. Then tell them to choose three things they think a design engineer does. Put them in pairs to compare their ideas. Do not give them answers, as they will hear these in the Listening.

Bridge to IELTS
CHOOSING FROM A LIST

Ask students to read the information in the box and check they have understood it. Tell them to apply this by underlining the key words in the list in activity 3.

4 2.17 Tell students they are going to listen to a lecture on design engineering and check which of the ideas in activity 3 are correct. If students have any difficulty, ask them to turn to page 136 and listen again while reading the audioscript and underline key sections as they listen.

1   2   5

5 🔘 2.17 Tell students they are now going to listen again for more detailed understanding. Ask them to read the statements silently and then choose the correct answer as they listen. Answer any questions before playing the recording.

Check answers in pairs, then as a class. They may need to listen more than once.

1 b	2 a	3 b	4 b	5 b

 2.17

Professor Findlay: Hello everyone. Welcome to today's talk on modern design. Today Susan Meyer, from German engineering company MET, is talking about design engineering. Susan …

Susan: Thanks, Professor Findlay. Today design engineers work in the top jobs at some of the world's biggest companies. Some of these include Apple's Jonathan Ive, Muji's Naoto Fukasawa, and Dyson's James Dyson. The first part of my talk is about what design engineering is and the skills design engineers need. In the second part, I'm talking about the ideas behind good design engineering.

So first of all, what is a design engineer? A design engineer researches what things or products people like to buy. They also develop ideas for new products. They work in many different areas of industry, from computers to vacuum cleaners. A design engineer manages the process of making something from idea to product. For this reason they work with lots of people. What skills does a design engineer need? Let's look at three things. First, they need to be good at engineering and they may have an education in art and design. Next, they are creative and can think of new ideas. Many engineering projects are answers to questions like 'Can we make this product better?' Third, they are good at solving problems. Design engineers don't just think of ideas, they also think of ways to make their ideas real.

Let me give you some examples of this. James Dyson designed a new vacuum cleaner and made it more efficient. His company takes ordinary machines like hand driers or air fans and uses modern technology to make the product different and work better. In Japan, Naoto Fukasawa looked at CD players and made the design simpler. Fukasawa has also designed mobile phones and other products. He believes good design comes from nature and the environment.

Design engineers need a good understanding of engineering. But design engineers can't do ↪

everything. To make a product in the modern world, we need a team of people. Design engineers need good teamwork skills and need to be good at communicating. Probably the most famous design engineer in the world is Apple's Jonathan Ive. He developed a new way of carrying music around with us in our pocket. Jonathan Ive always says that success is because of his team. He works with a small team in an open office space. All the team work with the same ideas – to keep Apple's products simple and easy to use.

So, we have three sides of the job: firstly, researching products and thinking of good ideas; secondly, working in a team to bring the product to manufacture. And the third thing? A good business mind: design engineers need a good knowledge of business. Design engineers know how to design products that people want to buy. And this is why they have moved into top jobs in business. Now let's turn to the ideas behind good design engineering …

Discussion

Tell students that the focus of this task is on improving their interaction skills for the IELTS Speaking test.

Ask students to work in pairs to discuss the points. Encourage them to give reasons for their answers, and examples if they can. Conduct a quick class check to see whether students agree.

SPEAKING
MY FAVOURITE THING

1 Ask students to work in pairs to ask and answer the questions. Give them a little time to think and make notes before they start.

2 🔘 2.18 Tell students they are going to listen to three people talking about their favourite new thing. Tell them to complete the table as they listen.

1	a few weeks ago	2	shoes
3	designer store	4	smart watch
5	last summer		

3 🔘 2.18 Tell students they are now going to listen again for more detail. Let them read through the sentences. Then play the recording and ask them to complete the gaps while they listen.

1	value, (much) cheaper
2	new, unusual
3	amazing, lighter

2.18

Megumi:	Oh, er. Let me think. Um, my favourite object that I bought recently is probably my new smartphone. I got it a few weeks ago – I bought it online, actually. I needed it because I lost my old one. I'm always losing things! This phone was good value. I'm a student and the most important thing for me is price. I like it a lot because it has the same features as the others but it's much cheaper.
Caroline:	What's my favourite object that I bought recently? It's definitely a pair of shoes. I love them so much. I bought them in a designer store last week. I went to a party on Saturday, and I wanted something new to wear. They are bright red and they look really stylish and unusual. I've never seen anything like them.
Mohammed:	I don't know! I haven't bought anything recently! Let me think … Well, I'm wearing my smart watch. I bought it in Singapore last summer. I got it because it's just so amazing. Look, when you press here it becomes a phone, press here and it plays music. Look, you can even watch videos. Isn't that cool? It's very well designed and it's lighter than a mobile phone. I really like it.

Living IELTS

TALKING ABOUT WHAT YOU LIKE

Ask students to listen and complete the phrases. Play the recording. Check answers in pairs, then as a class. Drill the phrases chorally and individually.

 2.19 and answers

I like it a lot.
I love them so much.
I really like it.

4 Ask students to think of their favourite thing. It doesn't need to be something new. Refer them to the bullet points and ask them to make notes. Tell them they can invent details if they want to.

5 Put students in pairs to describe their favourite object. Tell them to read the topic card and take turns to talk about each point, using the notes they made. Move around the class and listen. Conduct brief feedback by asking one or two pairs to tell the class about their discussion.

WRITING
COMPARISON ESSAY

1 Put students in pairs to discuss the biggest building projects in their country. In a multilingual class, put them in pairs from different countries to compare. In a monolingual class, see if they agree with their partner.

ALTERNATIVELY

> If you think your students will be short of ideas, bring some pictures of famous building projects and discuss the question as a class. Write the ideas on the board.

2 Ask students to read the essay title and underline the key words. Check answers in pairs, then as a class.

> two cities; new transport link; choose; best; transport

3 Ask students to look at the map and discuss what they can see. Tell them to skim read the information in the table quickly and then complete the gaps using the information from the map. Ask students to compare their ideas before conducting whole class feedback. Ask which they think is the best choice of transport.

> **1** tunnel   **2** bridge   **3** 15 minutes   **4** 30 minutes

4 Ask students to read the essay answering this question and find out what the student recommends.

> Road bridge

Writing Skills

FOR AND AGAINST

5 Tell students they are going to look at how the ideas are organised. Ask them to read the essay again and number the paragraphs a, b and c. Check answers in pairs, then as a class.

> **b   c   a**

6 Ask students to work individually to read the essay title and underline the key words. Check answers in pairs, then as a class. Then ask them to underline the most important facts in the table.

> transport system   choose   best

ALTERNATIVELY

> Ask students to write a short essay using the information in the table.

Plans and predictions

This unit looks at the topic of **plans and predictions**. The main **speaking** aims of the unit are to **talk about plans for the future.** The main **grammar** focuses are **the form and use of** *going to* and *will* for future. The **vocabulary** focus is on **collocations.** **Writing** covers some aspects of **giving your opinion.**

WARM UP

Ask students to look at the photograph and, in pairs, to say what they can see. Ask the following prompt questions: *What can you see? How are they feeling? Have you been in this situation? Would you like to be?*

READING

1   Check that students understand the phrases listed. Then put them in pairs and ask them to match the phrases with the pictures. Check the answers and drill.

Ask students to talk about each picture and say what each activity involves. Explain that they will need to expand on the phrases provided.

ALTERNATIVELY

> If your class is not strong, work together as a class to describe the first picture, then let students continue in pairs.

> **first picture:** gap year
> **second picture:** internship
> **third picture:** study abroad

2   Ask students to read the passage quickly and decide where it is from. This is skim reading, so tell them to look only for the overall impression. Check answers in pairs, then as a class.

> b

3   Tell students to read the passage again and match the people with their plans. Tell them that this is scan reading and that they have three minutes. Stop them after three minutes. Check answers in pairs, then as a class.

> 1 c   2 d   3 a   4 b

4   Students will now read the passage again for more detailed understanding. Tell them to read and choose the correct option, a, b or c. Check answers in pairs, then as a class.

> 1 c   2 c   3 c   4 c

VOCABULARY

COLLOCATIONS

1   Ask students to work in pairs to match the verbs with the right nouns. Tell them that sometimes there are several possible matches. Check answers as a class.

ALTERNATIVELY

> Write the four verbs (*make, earn, do, have*) in columns on the board and brainstorm as many matching nouns as students can think of. Encourage them to record these in special pages in their notebooks and to add to them.

> 1   a, d
> 2   a
> 3   b
> 4   a, b, c, d

2   Ask students to complete the sentences with the correct prepositions. Point out that *at* is used twice. Check answers in pairs, then as a class. Point out that there can be other prepositions used, depending on the context. For example: *John works for IBM; He works with Giorgio.*

ALTERNATIVELY

> Ask students to find and underline the collocations in the passage and then complete the exercise.

> 1   at
> 2   for
> 3   at
> 4   about
> 5   around

3 Tell students to match the expressions with their meanings. If they have difficulty, tell them to underline the verbs in the passage and use the context to help them.

| 1 c   2 a   3 b |

4 Put students into pairs to discuss what they think is the best suggestion from the reading passage. Conduct whole class feedback to see which ideas are the most popular.

GRAMMAR
GOING TO

Ask students whether they can remember any of the students' plans from the passage. Build up some prompts on the board.

Patrice/work for an engineering company
Cindy/study in Tokyo

Ask students to complete the sentences with the missing verb *(is going to)* and to identify and underline the verb form *(subject + (not) be going to + verb)*. Ask 'Are we talking about the past or the future?' Students should answer 'Future'. Establish that we use this form to talk about future plans.

Ask students to look at the grammar box and read the examples there. Pay attention to the question form, and ask students to provide more examples.

ALTERNATIVELY

If your class is able, get them to tell you the negative and question forms for 'going to'. *(Are you going to…/ I'm not going to…)* Write these up on the board. Follow with their own examples.

 If students need more help, refer them to the Grammar reference on page 143.

1 Ask students to look at the passage again and underline examples of *going to.* Move around and check they are underlining the whole verb. In feedback, check how many students found.

There are 12. Two are negatives.

2 Ask students to complete the sentences with a form of *going to.* Check answers in pairs, then as a class.

| 1 is going to |
| 2 are (you) going to |
| 3 is going to |
| 4 're not going to |
| 5 'm not going to |

3 Ask students to work in pairs to complete the sentences about Jet. Do the first one as a class. Go through the answers by asking individuals. As you check the answers, drill chorally and individually.

| 1 Jet is going to apply for an internship. |
| 2 He's going to start on September 14. |
| 3 Jet's going to work for AU Engineering. |
| 4 He's going to finish on December 20. |
| 5 Then Jet's going to have a holiday in Turkey. |

4 Ask students to write their own questions using the prompts. Check answers in pairs, then as a class.

| 1 What are you going to do after the course? |
| 2 Where are you going to study? |
| 3 How long are you going to study for? |

5 Put students into groups of four and designate them A, B, C or D. Tell students to turn to the correct pages and read the information about their plans. When they finish, ask them to work as a group to ask and answer the questions and complete the table. Move around and listen to them. When they finish, conduct quick feedback and ask them to say whose plans are the most interesting.

LISTENING

1 Ask students what a gap year is *(a year off between study and work or further study)*. Tell them to read through the list and tick those statements they agree are benefits and put a cross beside those they think are not.

2 Put students into pairs to compare their ideas. Conduct brief feedback.

3 [2.20] Tell students they are going to listen to two friends, Raoul and Izabela, talking about a gap year. Ask them to tick which statements in activity 1 are mentioned as they listen. Play the recording. Check answers in pairs, then as a class.

You have time to think about your future, You become more independent, You develop your confidence

4 [2.20] Tell students they are going to listen again for more detailed understanding. Ask them to read the statements silently and then mark them *Yes, No* or *Not Given* as they listen. Answer any questions before playing the recording. Check answers in pairs, then as a class. They may need to listen more than once.

1 Yes	2 Yes	3 Not Given	4 Not Given

4 Ask students to decide who has each opinion, Raoul or Izabela. Check answers in pairs, then as a class.

1 I	2 I	3 I	4 R	5 R

⊚ 2.20

R = Raoul, I = Izabela

R: Hi there, Izabela! What are you doing?

I: I'm doing research for my gap year.

R: Gap year? Are you going to take a whole year out after university?

I: Yes, I am! It's probably the only time in my life that I'll have that length of time to travel and see the world. And of course it will give me time to think about what I want to do in the future.

R: I suppose it will give you time to think about your options. Where are thinking of going? Somewhere in Europe?

I: Well I've travelled all over France, Germany and Russia, so I feel I know Europe quite well.

R: That's true. And didn't you spend last summer in Sweden and Denmark?

I: Yes, I did, and I really enjoyed it. But the world's a big place and I'd like to see some more of it! I want to go somewhere completely new and different. So, my plan is to spend a few months in Asia and then go on to Australia!

R: Are you sure about that? What about the cost? It will be too expensive.

I: It won't be too bad. And I'm not just going to travel. I'm going to earn some money during the year too. My plan is to look for temporary jobs to help pay my way. I'd love to do fruit picking in Australia!

R: I'm still not sure. It sounds like a complete waste of time to me. And how will a gap year look to a future employer? It will look like you just want to have one long holiday!

I: No, it won't. It will show an employer that I'm independent and can think for myself. And it also shows that I am confident enough to face different challenges. A gap year will make me stand out from other people in a good way. And, you know what they say, Raoul – travel broadens the mind!

Discussion

Put students into pairs to discuss if they would like to take gap year. Why?/Why not? Conduct a class vote to compare ideas. Ask students to say what the challenges and benefits would be.

PRONUNCIATION
GOING TO

1 ⊚ 2.21 Tell students that they are going to work on the pronunciation of *going to.* Play the recording and ask students to match each sentence with the correct pronunciation.

⊚ 2.21 and answers

1 Are you going out this evening? /gəʊɪŋ/

2 Is she going to do a gap year? /gəʊɪŋtə/

2 ⊚ 2.22 Ask students to listen and write 1 if they hear *going* /gəʊɪŋ/ and 2 if they hear *going to* / gəʊɪŋtə/.

3 Ask students to turn to the audioscript on page 137 and practise saying the sentences. Check answers in pairs, then as a class. Drill.

1	going 1, 3, 4, 6
2	going to 2, 5

⊚ 2.22

1 I'm not going! I don't want to.

2 Are you going to take a whole year out of university?

3 Where are you thinking of going?

4 I can't believe she's not going.

5 They're going to go travelling next year.

6 I'll go if you're going.

READING

1 Check that students understand the words in the box and then ask them to use them to talk about the pictures in pairs. Conduct whole class feedback to hear their ideas.

Note: Ask students to read the Bridge to IELTS box before they move on to activity 2.

2 Ask students to read the passage quickly and match the headings with the paragraphs. This is skim reading, so tell them to look only for the overall impression. Point out that they only need four headings. Check answers in pairs, then as a class.

Paragraph A	2
Paragraph B	6
Paragraph C	3
Paragraph D	4

MATCHING HEADINGS AND PARAGRAPHS

Point out that matching headings and paragraphs is a common IELTS reading task. Exercises which are not equal are more difficult than matching an equal number as students cannot so easily guess. Ask students to read the information in the box and then write questions for each of the headings in activity 2.

A What will education be like in 2020?

B What learning equipment will students use? They'll use a small digital tool. This tool will be a library etc.

C What times will people learn? Students will be able to study 24 hours a day, 7 days a week.

D Where will people learn? They'll learn online.

3 Tell students they will now read the passage again for more detailed understanding. Ask them to read the questions silently and then find the answers in the passage. Check answers in pairs, then as a class.

1 a	2 a	3 c	4 a

4 Tell students to work alone to find the words in the passage and then to use the context to match them with their meaning. Check answers in pairs, then as a class.

1 virtual
2 digital
3 tool
4 keyboard
5 headset
6 interactive

GRAMMAR
WILL (NOT)

Tell students they are going to look at another future form. Write the example on the board:
In 2020, students will meet online.

Ask 'Is this a plan?' Students should answer 'No'. Establish that we use this form to talk about predictions about the future. Underline the word *will* and ask students if they can make the sentence negative. *(Students won't meet online.)* Write this on the board below the first sentence. Ask students to read the grammar box to check.

If students need more help, refer them to the Grammar reference on page 143.

1 Ask students to read the passage again, underline examples of *will* and circle examples of *won't*. Move around the class and check they are underlining the whole verb. Check answers in pairs, then as a class by asking them how many they found.

Paragraph A 7	Paragraph B 5
Paragraph C 5	Paragraph D 10

2 Tell students to work individually to read through the paragraph and complete the sentences with *will* or *won't*. Check answers in pairs, then as a class.

ALTERNATIVELY

With a strong class, conduct this activity as a whole class, with students reading aloud.

1 will be
2 won't control
3 will have
4 will work
5 will pay

3 Ask students to work individually to write sentences using the prompts. Move around the class and help them. Check answers in pairs, then as a class. Drill chorally and individually.

1 Students won't go to libraries in 2020.
2 Students won't read books.
3 Students will have meetings online.
4 Students won't take tests.
5 Students will do projects with students in other countries.
6 Students will pay more for education.

Discussion

Put students in pairs to talk about their opinions on the ideas in activity 3. Tell them to give reasons for their ideas and remind them that this will help them prepare for the IELTS Speaking test. Conduct brief feedback to see which ideas are popular.

ALTERNATIVELY

With a stronger class, ask them to write their own ideas and then have a discussion in groups. Revise language for agreeing and disagreeing first.

 Communication activities
12A see Teacher's notes page 135.

Speaking

My plans for the future

1 Tell students they are going to talk about their own plans. Ask students to work alone and choose the statement that they feel describes them. Emphasise that this is not serious.

2 Put students into pairs to compare their answers. Conduct brief feedback.

3 ⊙2.21 Tell students they are going to listen to Lucia, who is talking about her plans for the future. Tell them to read the questions and choose the correct answers as they listen. Play the recording. Check answers in pairs, then as a class.

1 b	2 b	3 b	4 b

4 ⊙2.23 Tell students they are going to listen again for more detail. Ask them to read the sentences. Answer any questions before playing the recording.

Play the recording and ask students to listen and complete each sentence. Check answers in pairs, then as a class.

1	excited
2	amazing
3	wait
4	experience

 2.23

Lucia: I'm going to tell you about my plans for the future. I'm going to study software engineering at university in Umea, a small city in the North of Sweden. I'm going to start next year, in October. I'm extremely excited about it. It's going to be an amazing learning experience. I really can't wait! But I'm slightly nervous too! Why is it important to me? Well, it's rather hard to say. There are so many reasons. Well, let me see. First of all, it's a really good university, so I'm sure I'll learn a lot. But I'm also very interested in living in another country and learning a new language – that's Swedish of course! It's a wonderful opportunity to enjoy myself, make friends and study something I really like. I'm certainly going to make the most of the experience!

5 Tell students they will now prepare to talk about their future plans. Refer them to the bullet points to help them to make a few notes. Move around the class and help students with ideas.

Living IELTS

Giving yourself thinking time

Ask students to read through the box. Ask them if they can add more phrases or sounds for thinking time. (For example: *um, ah, let me think a moment*). Drill them in the expressions.

6 Ask students to read the topic card. Then ask them to work in pairs, taking turns to describe their plans, using the notes they made. To close the activity, ask one or two pairs to present their plans to the class.

Writing

The future of education

1 Ask students to look at the pictures and talk about what they can see. Ask them to work individually and tick the ideas they agree with. Put them in pairs to discuss their answers. Conduct brief feedback to see which ideas are most popular.

2 Ask students to read the question and underline the key words. Check answers in pairs, then as a class.

future; students; educated; outside; classroom; agree or disagree

3 Ask students to read the essay and decide whether the writer agrees or disagrees with the statement. Tell them that they need to underline sections of the text to justify their answer.

Ask students to compare their ideas before conducting whole class feedback.

He disagrees. He thinks the relationship between teacher and learner is the most important part of learning. (He also thinks the relationship between students and classmates is important.)

AGREEING OR DISAGREEING

Ask students to read through the box. Point out that some writing questions ask students to give an opinion and some do not, so it is important they know which kind of question they are answering.

4   Ask students to work individually and choose the correct word to complete each sentence. Check answers in pairs, then as a class.

1   will
2   won't
3   is
4   will

ALTERNATIVELY

With a stronger class, this can be done as a whole class activity. Ask students to say if they agree or disagree with each statement as you check the answer.

Writing Skills

GIVING YOUR OPINION

5   Ask students to read the essay again and underline three phrases for giving an opinion and two for agreeing or disagreeing.

Check answers in pairs, then as a class. Write the answers on the board and ask students to copy them into their notebooks.

Ask students to identify the pattern after the verb *agree* and write it on the board:

(dis)agree + with + noun
(dis)agree + that + clause

> **Giving opinions:** *In my opinion, I (don't) think, I (don't) believe*
> **Agreeing/disagreeing:** *I don't agree that...*
> *I disagree with...*

6   Read the essay question aloud and check that students understand it. Put students into pairs and ask them to make notes on the question. Remind them to underline the key words in the question and to refer to their ideas from activity 1. Monitor and help them with ideas.

7   Tell students they will now write a short essay using the information and notes they have made. Refer them to the model in activity 3 and point out that it is structured into three paragraphs.

Ask students to work alone to write their text. Move around and help them.

ALTERNATIVELY

When students have finished writing, use their texts for a class gallery. If time is short, students can write the text as homework.

 Communication activities
   12B *see Teacher's notes page 135.*

OVERVIEW

It is important for all students to meet 'new' language again and again. This is even more important for students starting at Pre-intermediate level because their language base and ability to deal with skills are not very developed. Reviewing language will help them to consolidate what they are in the process of learning as well as show them which areas they still have not fully understood. With this in mind, it is important that you are positive and supportive if they do not do very well in areas of the Review. Encourage them to see that if they get something wrong, it helps them to see where they should focus their energies. Taking this view will help them to grow in confidence; emphasising failure seldom has the same effect.

GRAMMAR

AIM To revise asking questions with *Is / Are there any… How much* and *How many*.

1   This is a controlled speaking activity. Put students in AB pairs. Student A forms and asks questions using the prompts given. Student B answers using the picture on page 126. Monitor and check they are forming questions correctly. When they have finished, ask them to ask and answer in pairs and to find and circle five differences between the pictures. Remind them not to look at each other's pictures!

Answers picture B:

1   Is there any food? (Yes, there is.)
2   Is there any litter? (No, there isn't.)
3   Is there any music? (Yes, there is.)
4   Are there any people? How many people are there? (Yes, there are many people.)
5   Are there any policemen? How many policemen are there? (Yes, there is one policeman.)
6   Are there any student helpers? How many student helpers are there? (Yes, there are two student helpers.)
7   Are there any posters? How many posters are there? (Yes, there are two posters.)
8   Are there any speakers? How many speakers are there? (Yes, there are two speakers.)
9   Are there any musicians? How many musicians are there? (Yes, there are three musicians.)

Differences: no music picture A, two policemen picture A, no musicians picture A, no litter picture B, no posters picture B

AIM To revise comparative and superlative adjectives.

2   Tell students they are going to read two short texts about a skyscraper and a marathon runner. Check that they know what a skyscraper is (a very tall building). Tell students to work alone and complete the texts with the correct form of the adjectives provided. Check in pairs, then as a class.

ALTERNATIVELY

Ask students to do the exercise in pairs. Complete and check one text before doing the other.

1 tallest	2 bigger	3 higher
4 slowest	5 later	6 heaviest

AIM To revise *going to* future form.

3   Tell students they are going to read a short text about study plans. Ask them to read through the text and then to choose the correct verb form. Check in pairs, then as a class.

1 is going to study	2 is going to fly
3 isn't going to stay	4 is going to travel
5 are going to study	

AIM To revise *will* future form.

4   Tell students they are going to use the information in a graph to complete a short text about university students. Ask them to study the graph. Point out that it refers to the future. Tell students to read through the text and then to complete the gaps with *will* or *won't* and one of the verbs in the box. Check in pairs, then as a class.

ALTERNATIVELY

If your class are not strong, discuss the graph as a class before asking them to complete the text. Ask them to work in pairs to do the exercise.

1 will reach	2 will continue	3 won't go
4 won't be	5 will become	

VOCABULARY

AIM To revise making nouns from verbs.

1   Ask students to work alone to write the nouns. Check answers as a class by asking individuals to spell the words or write them on the board. Drill and mark stress, reminding students that these words are stressed on the syllable before *-tion*.

1 direction	2 information
3 suggestion	4 education

AIM To check students can make the spelling changes to nouns in order to create verbs.

2 Ask students to work alone to write the verbs. Check answers as a class. Drill and mark stress.

1 pollute	2 destroy	3 produce	4 decide

AIM To revise common descriptive adjectives.

3 Put students in pairs to match the words and definitions. Check answers as a class.

1 expensive	2 old-fashioned	3 dangerous
4 inefficient	5 exciting	

AIM To revise collocations in the context of work.

4 Ask students to work alone to choose the correct verb from the box for each noun. Check in pairs, then as a class.

1 do	2 have	3 earn	4 make

Bridge to IELTS

SPEAKING TEST PREPARATION

AIM To go over the IELTS Speaking test.

1 Put students in pairs. Tell students to use the information in the text to complete the table about how the IELTS Speaking test is organised. Conduct brief feedback. Ask them which part of the test they think will be easiest.

1 interview	2 4–5 minutes
3 task card	4 short discussion

2 Put students into pairs to write one or two ideas for practising their speaking skills outside of class. Conduct whole class feedback, indicating which ideas you think will be helpful.

Suggested answers
Practise with a friend who is also studying English. Practise conversations about everyday topics silently in your head. Offer a language exchange to an English speaker.

→

OPTIONAL

Ask students to go through the Student's Book in pairs and find examples of Bridge to IELTS tips for the Speaking test. Review quickly as a class.

Unit 1 p.11   Unit 2 p.17   Unit 3 p.34   Unit 5 p.39
Unit 6 p.44   Unit 8 p.60   Unit 9 p.66

Study Skills

REVISING VOCABULARY

AIM To encourage effective study skills.

1 Put students in pairs to discuss the question briefly and conduct feedback. They may not revise very often! Ask them what methods they use for revising, if any.

2 Ask students to read the text and underline ideas they'd like to try. Conduct whole class feedback. Note which ideas are most popular.

3 Ask students to work alone to choose a vocabulary set from the book.

ALTERNATIVELY

Tell students which set to study.

4 Ask students to create a page in their notebook with three columns, labelled *important / maybe / understand only,* then to write the words from the vocabulary set in the right column. Emphasise that this is a matter of personal opinion. Monitor.

5 Ask students to create another table and put the words from the groups in it, in the left-hand column.

6 Ask students to read through the instructions. Check that they understand that they should use this table to test themselves. Conduct whole class feedback where students decide if this method could be useful. Tell students you will ask them in a week if they tested themselves, and if they remember the words.

Make a note to remind yourself in a week to ask your students if they revised the vocabulary set. You could do this as a warm-up activity at the beginning of the lesson.

1 Home

Writing an email describing accommodation and local amenities (informal)

Tell students that Mohammed (pictured) is going to stay with Ben Fletcher's family in the UK. Read the introductory text and check students know what he's asking about (the accommodation and the area he lives in).

1 Tell students that they are going to read Ben Fletcher's reply and choose the correct option.

Check in pairs, then as a class. Ask students if they would like to stay there.

| 1 a | 2 b | 3 a | 4 a | 5 b |

2 Tell students that Ines is moving to Australia to live in Alice Connor's house. Ask one student to read the email to the class. Then ask students to complete the answer using the information provided. Check in pairs, then as a class.

> The room is **big**. There is a **bed** and there are **bookshelves**. The house is in the city centre. Near the house there is a **park** and there are some **shops**.

3 Tell students that they will now write their own email. Point out how to start and end an informal but friendly email *(Dear…)*. Read through the box and remind students when we use *there is/are* (singular/ plural).

Ask students to write their emails. Move around the class and help them. When they have finished, ask one or two students to read aloud.

> **Suggested answer**
>
> Dear Erica
>
> The room is medium-sized. There is a TV set and there are some DVDs. The house is in the city centre. Near the house there is a museum and there are some shops.

2 Festivals

Completing an online application form for a job (semi-formal)

1 Tell students that they are going to read a job advertisement and apply for a job online. Ask students to read the text and choose the correct answers. Check in pairs, then as a class. Ask students if they think this job is interesting.

| 1 b | 2 c | 3 a |

2 Ask students to rearrange the words to make questions. Do the first one as a class and then monitor students as they write. Check in pairs, then as a class.

> a Where are you from?
> b What do you do?
> c What is your name?
> d What are your interests?
> e How old are you?
> f Are you male or female?

3 Tell students that the questions from activity 2 each have an answer on the online application form. Do the first one as a class. Check in pairs, then as a class.

| 1 c | 2 f | 3 e | 4 a | 5 b | 6 d |

4 Ask students to read about Rhonda and complete the paragraph. Refer them to the paragraph about Alfredo as an example. Check in pairs, then as a class.

> My name is Rhonda Hewson. I am a student. I study business at Harvard University. I like travelling and meeting people. My favourite country is Brazil.

Alternatively

> If your students need more support, complete the text as a class.

5 Now ask students to complete the notes with their own details. Encourage them to invent details if they like. When they finish, ask them to read each other's paragraphs. Draw students' attention to the *Expressing likes and preferences* box. Read through the information in the box and ask students to give their own examples.

3 Teamwork

Completing an evaluation form (semi-formal)

Ask students if they work, or have worked, and how employers check they are working well. Introduce the concept of evaluation *(measuring how good something is)* using numbers.

1 Tell students that they are going to read a short text about this topic and decide what kind of text it is. Check in pairs, then as a class. Ask students if this system is used in their country and what they think of it.

> c

2 Ask students to read the information about Lars and make sure they understand that 0 = the worst score and 4 = the best. Ask them to choose the correct words to complete the paragraph. Check in pairs, then as a class.

1	usually	**2**	never
3	usually	**4**	friendly
5	never	**6**	an excellent

3 Ask them to read the text again and choose true or false for each question, using the information in the chart and the text. Check in pairs, then as a class. Ask students if they think Lars is a good employee.

> **a** true　　**b** true　　**c** false　　**d** false　　**e** true

Draw students' attention to the *Describing appearance* box, and check they understand *sick leave (time off for illness)*.

4 Ask students to read the information on Akemi and use the information in the chart to complete the text. Remind them to use the other texts on this page as models. Check in pairs, then as a class. Ask students if they think Akemi is a good employee.

1	always	**2**	smart
3	always	**4**	time
5	usually	**6**	shy
7	never	**8**	can
9	opinion	**10**	worker

4 Education

Letters asking for and refusing help (informal)

1 Tell students that they are going to read a short letter. Ask them to read the letter quickly and decide what kind of letter it is. Check in pairs, then as a class. Ask students what clues tell them that the letter is personal or informal *(first names, content, closing salutation)*.

> A personal letter

2 Ask students to read the letter again more carefully and answer the questions. Check in pairs, then as a class. Ask students if they think Layla's aunt, Sue, will give her the money.

> **a** New York
> **b** a drama course
> **c** $10 000
> **d** $4 000
> **e** give her the extra $6 000 (she doesn't mention paying it back)

3 Ask students to read the information in Sue's note and then her reply. Check that students understand *accommodation (house* or *flat)*.
>
> Check in pairs, then as a class. Ask students if they think Sue can help.

> No

4 Ask students to read Sue's letter carefully to identify the purpose of each stage. Check they understand *greeting* (hello) and *closing salutation* (goodbye). Check in pairs, then as a class.

> **1** c　　**2** e　　**3** a　　**4** b　　**5** d

5 Ask students to look at the picture of James and his uncle. Then ask students to read James's letter to his uncle and complete the gaps. Point out that they can refer to the model of Layla's letter to help them. Ask a student to read the letter aloud to the class to check answers.

> **1** Dear　　**2** hope　　**3** wondering　　**4** could

ALTERNATIVELY

> If your class is not strong, ask them to find the same sentences in Layla's letter and underline them before completing the gaps as a class.

6 Ask students to write the words in each line in the correct order to reveal Uncle Albert's reply. Check in pairs, then as a class. Point out that *love and best wishes* is a fixed phrase and has to be in this order.

> Dear James
> It's good to hear from you. The biology course sounds fantastic, but I'm afraid I don't have the money. I wish I could help you. Why don't you speak to your parents? I hope you get to Australia.
> Love and best wishes
> Albert

5 BUILDINGS AND CITIES

WRITING A LETTER OF COMPLAINT (SEMI-FORMAL)

1 Ask students to look at the picture and text and identify what kind of text it is. Check as a class. Ask students where they think they might see an advertisement like this (a college noticeboard or café).

> **a**

2 Tell students that they are now going to read the advertisement carefully, for detail, and decide whether the questions are true or false. Check in pairs, then as a class.

> **a** T   **b** T   **c** F

3 Tell students that John answered the advertisement 6 months ago and took the room. He is unhappy and now they are going to read his letter to find out what the problem is. Check in pairs, then as a class. Ask students if they think this problem can be resolved.

> **a**

4 Check students understand *salutation* (greeting). Ask them to work in pairs to number the stages of his letter. The first one has been done for them. Check as a class.

> **1** d   **2** a   **3** e   **4** c   **5** b

5 Tell students that now they will write their own complaint letter, using the notes provided. Before they start, read through the language box and discuss how the sentences could be finished. Students work alone to write the letter.

To close the activity, ask students which of the problems they have read about is the most serious.

ALTERNATIVELY

> If your class is not strong, work together on the letter and write it on the board.

> I am writing in connection with my neighbour, Mrs Alma. The issue is that she doesn't cover her rubbish and it smells bad. I would appreciate it if you could speak to her about it.
> Yours sincerely
> Lisa Khalid

6 WORK

WRITING A LETTER THANKING A FRIEND (INFORMAL)

1 Tell students that they are going to read a short text and identify its purpose. Ask students to read the text and choose the correct answer.

Ask students who is writing (Yves) to who (Jack) and what they think their relationship is (friends).

> **1** c

2 Ask students to read Jack's reply and choose the correct answer. Do the first one as a class and then monitor students as they complete the task. Check in pairs, then as a class.

> **a** away from home
> **b** went on holiday
> **c** good
> **d** Sabine
> **e** the weekend

3 Tell students that they will now read two emails between Ruby and Sam and complete a similar letter. Do the first one as a class. Check in pairs, then as a class.

4   Tell students that Carla came to stay and ask them to read the update. Refer them to the language box and ask them to find and underline examples of each type of phrase in the letters on this page. Ask students to work in pairs to discuss and then write the letter.

Dear Ruby and Sam

How are you? I'm sorry for not writing sooner but I was in hospital for two weeks because I had an accident and broke my leg!

Thank you for the lovely weekend. I really loved the long walk we went on by the sea.

Why don't you come to my place in the mountains for a holiday? I'd love to see you.

I'm looking forward to hearing from you.

Best wishes
Carla

ALTERNATIVELY

If your class is not strong, plan the letter as a class. Write it up on the board as you do so.

7 URBAN SPORTS

DESCRIBING STATISTICS IN A BAR CHART (ACADEMIC)

1   Ask students to look at the chart and description and decide where they would see it. Check in pairs, then as a class.

b

2   Ask students to read the information again and match each paragraph with its description. Check in pairs, then as a class. Ask students if they find any of the information in the text surprising.

a 3   **b** 1   **c** 2

3   Ask students to read the information closely and choose true or false. Check in pairs, then as a class.

a F   **b** T   **c** F   **d** T   **e** T

4   Ask students to read the information and re-write it in the correct order, using full sentences. Check they know the meaning of *gadgets* (small electronic objects). Monitor students as they write. Write the sentences on the board as you check answers, so that students can see the commas.

a The chart shows how men and women spend their money.

b According to the figures, men spend £1 500 a year on gadgets.

c Women spend £50, while men spend much more a year.

d In conclusion, we can see that men spend more than women on gadgets.

5   Ask students to look at the chart and use it to complete the information. Refer them to the other texts on this page for guidance. Monitor students as they write. Check in pairs, then as a class. Write the text on the board.

a The bar chart shows
c 600
e spend only 400 hours / a 100 hours less
g don't spend
b According to the chart
d 500 hours a year
f spend 200 hours doing group sports

ALTERNATIVELY

If your class is not strong, complete the text as a class. Write it up on the board as you do so.

6   Ask students to choose a, b or c to complete the conclusion.

c

Writing bank

8 THE NATURAL WORLD

DESCRIBING WHAT IS HAPPENING IN A GRAPH (ACADEMIC)

1 Check students understand what *deforestation* is (removal of trees so there is no forest any more). Then ask them to look at the graph and text and decide which statement best describes what is said. Check in pairs, then as a class. Ask students if they found the text or the chart more helpful in deciding *(probably the chart).*

> **b**

2 Ask students to read the information closely and match the beginnings and endings of the sentences. Do the first one together.

> **1** b   **2** e   **3** a   **4** c   **5** d

ALTERNATIVELY

> If your class is not strong, talk about what the chart shows as a class. Show students how *steadily* is the opposite of *sharply*. Point out that *decline* and *decrease* are both opposites of *increase*.

3 Ask students to look at the *Key Vocabulary* box and then use the terms there to replace the words in italics. Point out that they may need to change the tense and that there may be more than one option. Check in pairs, then as a class.

> | | | | |
> |---|---|---|---|
> | **a** | rise | **b** | gradual |
> | **c** | rose | **d** | fell / dropped / declined |
> | **e** | steadily | **f** | remained constant |

4 Ask students to write a phrase to describe each graph. Check in pairs, then as a class.

> **1** to remain constant
> **2** a sharp fall / decrease / drop / decline **or** to fall / decrease / drop / decline sharply
> **3** a gradual / steady rise / increase **or** to rise / increase gradually / steadily
> **4** a sharp increase / rise **or** to rise / increase sharply
> **5** a gradual / steady fall / decrease / decline / drop **or** to fall / decrease / decline / drop gradually / steadily

5 Ask students to complete the text in pairs, using the information in the graph. Check as a class.

> The *graph* shows how many holiday flights there were across the world over a 20-year period. According to *the figures*, the number of flights *rose / increased gradually* from 100 million in 1992 to 175 million in 2000. Then there was a *sharp increase / rise* in 2001, to 260 million. That figure *fell / dropped / decreased* to around 225 million in 2002. It continued to *fall / drop / decrease* until 2004, reaching 180 million. But then the number of flights started to *rise / increase* again. The number *rose / increased gradually* to nearly 300 million in 2008 and then *fell / dropped / decreased* once again. It *fell / dropped / decreased gradually* back to 100 million in 2011.

9 FAMILY

COMPARING TWO SETS OF STATISTICS (ACADEMIC)

1 Ask students to look at the diagram and text and identify the best summary, choosing a, b, c or d. Check in pairs, then as a class. Ask students if similar changes have happened in their countries during the same period.

> **d**

2 Ask students to read the information again and choose the correct word to complete each sentence. Check in pairs, then as a class. Ask students if they found any information in the text surprising.

ALTERNATIVELY

> If students have difficulty, point out that *compared to* is followed by a noun whereas *by contrast* is followed by a clause (subject + verb). *While* and *whereas* both indicate contrast and are followed by a clause.

> | | | | |
> |---|---|---|---|
> | **a** | while | **b** | compared to |
> | **c** | whereas | **d** | By contrast |
> | **e** | compared to | **f** | and |

3 Ask students to read through the *comparing and contrasting* box. Answer any questions. Tell them to look carefully at the diagram and choose the correct words to complete the description. Check in pairs, then as a class. Ask students if they found any information in the text surprising.

10 CONSERVATION

DESCRIBING NUMBERS IN A PIE CHART (ACADEMIC)

1 Ask students where you find water in the home (kitchen, bathroom) and check they know what a *tap* and *flush* mean by miming these. Ask them to look at the chart and text and identify its subject matter (how water is used in an average Australian home).

Ask students to complete the sentence with three of the phrases provided and then talk about where to put this sentence in the text.

1 washing clothes
2 toilet use
3 bathing
The sentence could go after the first sentence in the text.

2 Ask students to rearrange the words into correct sentences and write them. Check in pairs, then as a class.

a 30% of water is used for bathing.
b 26% of water is flushed away.
c 22% of water is used in the washing machine.
d 14% of water comes out of the taps.
e 5% of water is used in the dishwasher.
f 3% of water is wasted.

3 Ask students to match each phrase with a percentage from the box.

ALTERNATIVELY

If your students have difficulty, refer to the pie chart and work as a class to express the sections as percentages and fractions before completing this task in pairs.

a 30%   b 26%   c 48%   d 69%   e 19%

4 Tell students that the chart shows how energy is used in an average UK home. Ask them to work in pairs to discuss the data and then write seven sentences using the phrases provided. Check as a class. Ask students if they found any information surprising.

Ask students to link the sentences using linking words. Finally, ask students to complete the description of the pie chart.

ALTERNATIVELY

If your class is not strong, refer to the pie chart and *Describing numbers* box. Ask students to work as a class to express the sections as percentages and fractions before completing this task in pairs.

Nearly two thirds is used to keep the house warm, whereas just under a sixth is used to heat water for showers, baths and washing-up. 6% is used to keep food cold and 6% is used for the laundry. 5% is used on TVs and computers. 4% is used on lights on dark winter nights and 4% is used to heat up food.

11 DESIGN

COMPARING DATA IN A TABLE (ACADEMIC)

1 Ask students to look at the table and decide on the best summary: a, b or c. Check in pairs, then as a class.

c

2 Ask students to use the information in the table and match the questions and answers. Check in pairs, then as a class.

1 b   2 c   3 a

3 Ask students to use the information in the table and answer the questions. Check in pairs, then as a class.

a The Pear UYE21   b 135g
c The Pear UYE21   d 7 hours
e The Pear UYE21   f 11 megapixels

4 Ask students to rearrange the words into correct sentences and write them. Check in pairs, then as a class. Then ask students to write the answers using the information in the table.

ALTERNATIVELY

> If your class need speaking practice, put them in pairs to ask and answer the questions.

> **a** Which is the lightest mobile phone?
> *The Raspberry 8-47 is the lightest mobile phone.*
>
> **b** How much does the lightest phone weigh?
> *The lightest phone weighs 99g.*
>
> **c** Which camera has the lowest resolution?
> *The Raspberry 8-47 has the lowest resolution.*
>
> **d** How high is the lowest resolution?
> *The lowest resolution is 5 megapixels.*
>
> **e** Which battery offers the shortest talk time?
> *The Raspberry 8-47 offers the shortest talk time.*
>
> **f** How long is the shortest talk time?
> *The shortest talk time is 5.5 hours.*

5 Ask students to look at the table and decide what it is about (aeroplanes) and then complete the paragraph. Check in pairs, then as a class.

> The table shows data about three new designs of *aeroplanes / planes*. The table compares the three models in terms of *capacity, weight and noise level*. It is clear that the *heavier planes are better*.

Ask students to use the questions and the information provided to write a detailed comparison. Ask students to compare their paragraphs.

> **Sample answer**
>
> *The heaviest plane is the Aircoach LZ2, which weighs 650 tonnes. It can also carry the most passengers, 555. However, it is the quietest of the three, with a noise level of 8 out of 20. The second heaviest is the Jetstar X440, which weighs 505 tonnes. It can carry the second highest number of passengers, 420, but the noise level on the Jetstar is quite high, 16 out of 20. The Gallant F-290 is the lightest, at 290 tonnes, but it can only carry 340 passengers and it is the noisiest of the three.*

12 PLANS AND PREDICTIONS

DESCRIBING PROPOSED CHANGES IN A DIAGRAM (ACADEMIC)

1 Ask students to look at the plans and decide whether the statement is true or false.

> true

2 Ask students to read the text closely and match the paragraph numbers and questions. Do the first one together. Check in pairs, then as a class.

ALTERNATIVELY

> If your class is not strong, talk about what the plans show as a class, then answer the questions.

> **a** 4 **b** 2 **c** 3 **d** 1

3 Ask students to complete the text with the words in the box. Check in pairs, then as a class.

> **1** present **2** plan **3** extension **4** en suite
> **5** place **6** open-plan **7** utility

4 Ask students to look at the plans and tick the correct column.

	Now	Future
A bedroom with en suite bathroom		✓
A bedroom at each end	✓	
Separate kitchen and dining room	✓	
A bigger living room	✓	
A utility room		✓
An extension		✓
3 bathrooms		✓
An office		✓
An open-plan kitchen / dining area		✓

5 Ask students to read through the language box and work in pairs to apply the phrases to the plans. Then ask them to write a short text similar to that in Exercise 1. Monitor as they write. Check answers in pairs, then as a class.

Grammar reference

Answer Key

UNIT 1
Home

1

a	are	d	are
b	am	e	Are, I am
c	Is		

2

b *'Are there* bookshelves?' 'No, *there aren't.'*
c *'Are there* beds?' 'Yes, *there are* four beds.'
d *'Is there* a park near the house?' 'Yes, *there are* two parks.'

UNIT 2
Festivals

1

a	doesn't	b	don't
c	don't	d	doesn't

2

b does 3
c flies 1
d finishes 2
e goes 3
f watches 2

3

a Does your friend speak Spanish?
b Do you come here often?
c When does the party start?
d What time do you finish work?

UNIT 3
Teamwork

1

a I am always happy.
b She never watches TV.
c Do you usually go out at the weekend?
d Why does he always work so hard?
e What do they usually have problems with?

2

b Can you work well under pressure?
   Yes, I can.
c Can your mother help you with your work?
   No, she can't.
d Can your classmates work well together?
   Yes, they can.
e Can your father speak French?
   No, he can't.

UNIT 4
Education

1

b Are you working hard?
c We're waiting for his answer.
d Are they planning to stay in Oman?
e I'm having a good time at the moment.

2

b It *costs* a lot of money to study in the US.
c *Do you know* the answer?
d Layla? *She's washing* her hair at the moment.
e I'm at the station. *I'm waiting* for you!

Grammar reference
Answer Key

UNIT 5
Buildings and cities

1

> b Was she at school today?
> c Who was at the meeting?
> d How much were those shoes?
> e It wasn't very warm yesterday.

2

> c We married in 2009. Did we marry in 2009?
>   Yes, we did.
> d She wanted a car. Did she want a car?
>   Yes, she did.
> e The police stopped him. Did the police stop him?
>   Yes, they did.
> f You lived in Paris. Did you live in Paris?
>   No, I didn't.

UNIT 6
Work

1

> a Did you meet the volunteers?
> b When did they arrive?
> c Did I speak to you yesterday?
> d What did she do at the weekend?
> e How much did we spend on our last holiday?

2

> a We *had* a terrible holiday.
> b Sorry – I *didn't* see you there.
> c It's okay, I *found* my phone.
> d *Did you meet* at university?
> e He *made* some mistakes, but he *did* well.

UNIT 7
Urban sports

1

> 1 Can   2 can't
> 3 have to   4 have to
> 5 doesn't have to 6 can
> 7 have to

2

> b Does she need
> c You don't need
> d he doesn't need
> e They don't need

UNIT 8
The natural world

1

> b
> A Has he ever tried Korean food?
> B Yes, he has.
> A When did he try it?
>
> c
> A Has she ever met a popstar?
> B Yes she has. She's met Jay-Z.
> A When did she meet him?
>
> d
> A Have you ever done a dangerous sport?
> B No, never.

2

> a for   b since
> c since   d since
> e for

UNIT 9
Family

1

a	is held
b	is given
c	are eaten
d	is considered
e	is celebrated

2

a	Kimonos are usually worn by young women.
b	They spend their lives moving around.
c	People are given more respect as they get older.
d	They eat a lot of fruit and vegetables.
e	They are known for their healthy lifestyle.

UNIT 10
Conservation

1

Countable: people, river, problem, year, poster, tree, idea
Uncountable: water, rain, time, music, food, money, coffee

2

a	any	b	some
c	any	d	some
e	any		

3

a	much	b	much
c	many	d	many
e	much		

UNIT 11
Design

1

a	better, than	b	bigger
c	more expensive than	d	healthier than
e	taller than		

2

a	It is the safest sport I've ever tried.
b	She is the most beautiful woman in the world.
c	Who is the best football team in your country?
d	I'm the fattest person at our gym.
e	They are the friendliest people I've ever met.

UNIT 12
Plans and predictions

1

a	Are you going to stay at home this weekend?
b	She isn't going to finish her course.
c	When are they going to go to Japan?
d	I'm going to travel round Europe for three months.

2

b	Education will be like a business.
c	Private companies will own schools.
d	Governments won't control schools.
e	Students won't have to take exams.

3

b	Will education be like a business? *Yes, it will.*
c	Will private companies own schools? *Yes, they will.*
d	Will governments control schools? *No, they won't.*
e	Will students have to take exams? *No, they won't.*

Introduction to the
Bridge to IELTS Practice Test

THE IELTS TEST

The test is available in two formats: the General Training and the Academic module. The General Training module is for candidates who want to migrate to an English-speaking country, and for those who want to undertake non-academic training or study at below degree level. The Academic module is suitable for those who want to enter an undergraduate or postgraduate study programme in an English-speaking country. The Listening and Speaking tests are the same in both modules, but the modules differ in the Reading and Writing.

The Listening, Reading and Writing are taken on the same day. The Speaking test may be taken on the same day or before or after the other three tests. The tests are outlined in the diagram on the right.

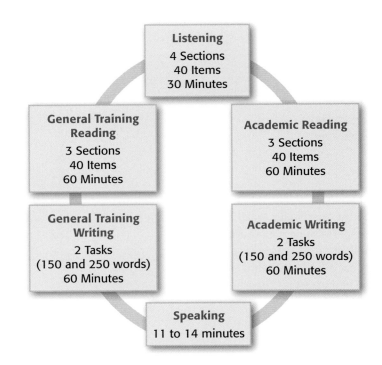

Listening
4 Sections
40 Items
30 Minutes

General Training Reading
3 Sections
40 Items
60 Minutes

Academic Reading
3 Sections
40 Items
60 Minutes

General Training Writing
2 Tasks
(150 and 250 words)
60 Minutes

Academic Writing
2 Tasks
(150 and 250 words)
60 Minutes

Speaking
11 to 14 minutes

THE *BRIDGE TO IELTS* PRACTICE TEST

The *Bridge to IELTS* Practice Test is modelled on the actual IELTS tests so that students can experience something very close to the real test. There are, however, some minor differences.

TEST	IELTS	BRIDGE TO IELTS
Reading	60 minutes: 40 questions	60 minutes: 30 questions
Writing	60 minutes and two tasks: 150 and 250 words	50 minutes and two tasks: 100 and 150 words
Speaking	11 to 14 minutes	Up to nine minutes

These differences between the two tests are deliberate and take into account the level students should have reached by the end of the *Bridge to IELTS* course. For example, students are not asked to write a text that is 250 words long or to speak for 11 to 14 minutes in this practice test because they have not done this during the course. *Bridge to IELTS* is designed to help lower-level students who plan to embark on an IELTS preparatory course in the future.

The practice test is designed to challenge students. It aims to give them the experience of trying an exam in the same format as the IELTS exam and is close to the actual exam in terms of challenge. It is crucial that students are told that the practice exam is similar to the real exam but not the same. If students are not told this, there is a real risk of setting up false expectations about their readiness to take the actual IELTS exam.

ADMINISTERING THE PRACTICE TEST

We suggest that students do the Listening, Reading and Writing Tests back-to-back so they experience what the actual exam is like. The Speaking Test can be done on the same day or a week before or after the other tests. If this would not be practical in your institution, the test can be broken up to suit your teaching context. If there are two or more groups taking the Practice Test, it is important that they take the tests at the same time to avoid the possibility of students sharing information about the tests with each other.

Before the Listening and Reading Tests, make enough photocopies of the answer sheets so that each student has one copy of each. The Answer sheets are on page pages 126–127 of the Teacher's Book.

Make sure that students arrive at least five minutes before the exam; it can be very distracting to test-takers when latecomers enter the room. Tell students to bring a pen, preferably black, a pencil and a rubber. They will need the pencil to write their answers on the answer sheet.

Certain rules should be enforced during the exams. There should be no talking, no looking at other people's answer sheets and no passing of papers between the test-takers. Remember that no dictionaries, reference books or mobile phones should be used. Ask all students to turn off their phones before the tests start.

PART 1: LISTENING

Time: **40 minutes in total:** 30 minutes to complete three sections and 40 questions, plus 10 minutes to transfer answers.

Try to find a quiet room to take the test in so that students are not distracted by noise. Check the volume of the CD player before the test so that all students will be able to hear the recordings easily.

- Make enough photocopies of the Listening test material on pages 102–108 and the Listening answer sheet on page 126 before the test.

- Hand out the answer sheets plus a piece of blank paper for students to write their answers on. Ideally, they should write the numbers 1–40 on the paper before they start the Listening. Alternatively, you can provide a piece of paper with the numbers already printed on them.

- Tell them that at the end of the Listening they will have 10 minutes to transfer their answers onto the answer sheet. Then ask students to write their name at the top of the answer sheet. They can ignore the other information required.

- Tell students that they will **only hear the recording once**. Then play the recording through without stopping.

- When the recording is finished, tell students they have 10 minutes to transfer their answers onto the answer sheet. Tell them to be careful they put the right answer next to the correct number. Remind them that correct spelling is important as well as observing any word limits for certain questions.

- After five and then nine minutes, tell them how long they have left.

- At the end of 10 minutes, ask students to put down their pencils and collect in the answer sheets.

PART 2: READING

Time: **60 minutes** to complete three sections and 30 questions; note: **no time to transfer answers**.

- Make enough photocopies of the test material on pages 109–115 and the Reading answer sheet on page 127 before the test.

- Ask students not to look at the Reading test material and then put it face down on the students' desks. Then hand out the answer sheets. Tell students they need to write their answers directly on to the answer sheet and then ask them to write their names on the answer sheet.

- Tell students they have 60 minutes to complete the test. Write the start and finish time on the board so they can all see the times. Then get them to turn over the text material and start the exam.

- Tell students when they only have five minutes left. When the time is up, collect in the answer sheets as well as all the test material.

PART 3: WRITING

Time: **50 minutes** to complete two tasks of 100 and 150 words.

- Make enough photocopies of the test material on pages 116–117. Make sure students have enough writing paper and that you have spare paper if needed.

- Put the test material face down on the students' desks and tell the students they have 50 minutes to write two texts. Remind them they have approximately 20 minutes to write at least 100 words for Task One and approximately 30 minutes to write at least 150 words for Task Two.

- Tell students when they only have five minutes left. When their time is up, tell them to put down their pens and collect in the answer sheets as well as all the test material.

PART 4: SPEAKING

Time: **Up to nine minutes** to complete three speaking tasks. Allow for approximately 10 minutes to test each student.

- Photocopy the Speaking test material on page 118 and cut out the two topic cards for Part 2 of the Speaking test on page 119. You have two different cards so that you can alternate them with every two students.

- Go through the three parts of the test following the instructions for each part of the test. Give students a mark out of 10 for each of the four categories listed in the *Marking the test* section below.

MARKING THE TEST

There is no pass or fail in IELTS. Each part of the test is scored on a scale from 0–9. Candidates' results show how well they did in each part of the test as well as an Overall Band Score. This is calculated as an average of the four scores, for example:

Listening: 7, Reading: 7.5, Writing: 5.5, Speaking: 6 = a total of 26 ÷ 4.

So the Overall Band Score is 6.5.

LISTENING AND READING

Use the answer key on pages 124–125 to mark the answer sheets. Answers are either right or wrong. Misspelt words are considered incorrect. In the Listening test there are 40 questions; one mark for each correct answer. In the Reading test there are 30 questions and each correct question receives 1.333 marks. Add up the total number of correct answers and multiply them by 1.333. Round up the number, for example: 21 correct answers: 18 x 1.333 = 23.994 rounded up becomes a total of 24 points.

The way that test-takers' scores are converted into an IELTS band score is confidential. Below is an approximate guide to help you convert your students' results.

THE LISTENING TEST

Band Score	7	6.5	6	5.5	5	4.5	4	3.5	3	2.5
Score / 40	30–31	26–29	23–25	18–22	16–17	13–15	10–12	8–10	6–7	4–5

THE READING TEST

As the Reading practice test combines elements of the Academic and the General Training, the table below reflects an approximate balance between the two tests.

Band Score	7	6.5	6	5.5	5	4.5	4	3.5	3	2.5
Score / 40	32–35	29–31	26–28	23–25	19–22	16–18	12–15	10–11	7–9	5–6

THE WRITING TEST

Model writing answers are provided on page 125. This is a difficult test to mark and IELTS examiners complete extensive training before they are ready to accurately assess candidates' marks. The marking system below provides a rough guide to help you establish your students' results.

Give each student a mark out of 10 for each of the following criteria:

Task achievement in Task One and Task response in Task Two	/10
Coherence and cohesion	/10
Lexical resource	/10
Grammatical range and accuracy	/10

Add up the marks and see which Band score the student has according to this table.

Band Score	8	7.5	7	6.5	6	5.5	5	4.5	4	3.5	3	2.5
Score / 40	35–36	32–34	30–31	26–29	23–25	18–22	16–17	13–15	10–12	8–10	6–7	4–5

THE SPEAKING TEST

As with the Writing Test, this is a difficult test to mark without extensive training. The marking system below provides a rough guide to help you establish your students' results.

Give each student a mark out of 10 for each of the following criteria:

Fluency and coherence	/10
Lexical resource	/10
Grammatical range and accuracy	/10
Pronunciation	/10

Add up the marks and see which Band score the student has according to this table.

Band Score	8	7.5	7	6.5	6	5.5	5	4.5	4	3.5	3	2.5
Score / 40	35–36	32–34	30–31	26–29	23–25	18–22	16–17	13–15	10–12	8–10	6–7	4–5

Listening

SECTION 1

QUESTIONS 1–10

Complete the notes below.

Write **NO MORE THAN ONE WORD OR A NUMBER** for each answer.

TOP FASHIONS – WORK ENQUIRY FORM

PERSONAL INFORMATION

PHONE NUMBER: **1** _____

ADDRESS: **2** 54 _____ Street, New Farm

CURRENT WORK / STUDIES: part-time job in a shoe shop
studies **3** _____ part-time at college

REASON FOR WANTING A JOB: likes the quality of the clothing and the reasonable
4 _____

OTHER WORK EXPERIENCE: worked in a **5** _____ for two years

SKILLS: able to work well with people
able to work in a **6** _____

WORK PREFERENCES

DAYS: not able to work on **7** _____

START DATE: after the **8** _____ of this month

TYPE OF WORK WANTED: at the beginning, wants to be an **9** _____
in the future, wants to be a **10** _____

OTHER INFORMATION

BEST WAY TO SEND DOCUMENTS?: by post

SECTION 2

QUESTIONS 11–15

*Choose the correct letter, **A**, **B**, or **C**.*

Gardens and Parks

11 The City Centre Gardens were first made for
    A rich people
    B school children
    C farmers

12 What are visitors still able to see in the City Centre Gardens?
    A a fountain
    B a zoo
    C a tea house

13 Which section of the Mount Rising Gardens won an award last year?
    A the Herb Garden
    B the Australian Rainforest
    C the Bamboo Grove

14 Which facility is closed for repairs at the moment?
    A the Library
    B the Lecture Room
    C the Sky Dome

15 What is the best way to get to the Mount Rising Gardens?
    A by car
    B by bus
    C by bike

QUESTIONS 16–20

What feature does each of the following places in the Parkland have?

*Choose **FIVE** answers from the box and write the correct letter, **A–G**, next to questions **16–20**.*

Features visitors can see:

A   an outdoor art collection
B   lots of rocks
C   a small waterfall
D   a statue
E   many types of birds
F   bright colours
G   a boardwalk

Places:

16 The Lake   _____

17 The Forest   _____

18 The Headland   _____

19 The Fern Garden   _____

20 The Spectacle Garden   _____

SECTION 3

QUESTIONS 21–25

*Choose the correct letter, **A**, **B**, or **C**.*

Design Course

21 What do Jenny and Paul agree is the most difficult part of their course?
  A The number of assignments.
  B The amount of reading.
  C The number of presentations.

22 Why does Paul want Jenny to look at his assignment?
  A To check he has answered the question.
  B To check his diagrams are clear.
  C To check for spelling mistakes.

23 Why do Jenny and Paul think yesterday's lecture was so good?
  A Because of the lecture theatre.
  B Because of Professor Skinner.
  C Because of the topic.

24 What do Jenny and Paul like about the article by Jenkins and Smith?
  A It was easy to understand.
  B It had good examples in it.
  C It was written recently.

25 How do Jenny and Paul feel about the Design course?
  A They're happy they chose it.
  B They would recommend it to others.
  C They want to study it overseas.

Listening

QUESTIONS 26–30

What opinions do Jenny and Paul have about each of the following presentation topics?

*Choose **FIVE** answers from the box and write the correct letter, **A–G**, next to questions **26–30**.*

Opinion of the topic:
A it's a very important topic
B it's been done before
C lots of pictures are available
D it's too difficult to explain
E it will be studied next year
F the Professor would like it
G lots of books are available

Presentation Topics:

26 Watch design   _____

27 Car design   _____

28 Telephone design   _____

29 Bridge design   _____

30 Building design   _____

SECTION 4

QUESTIONS 31 – 34

*Choose the correct letter, **A**, **B** or **C**.*

31 Where is Earthwatch's head office?
   A Tokyo
   B Boston
   C Melbourne

32 What is Earthwatch focusing on this year?
   A climate change
   B oceans
   C conservation

33 Who is able to volunteer with Earthwatch?
   A only people interested in the environment
   B only people who have had special training
   C only people with particular skills

34 Are there any limitations on the age of volunteers?
   A You can't be more than 60.
   B You have to be over 16.
   C There is no age limit.

QUESTIONS 35–40

Complete the notes below.

Write **NO MORE THAN TWO WORDS OR A NUMBER** for each answer.

The Earthwatch Turtle Project

Leatherback turtles are the **35** _____ reptiles in the world.

Length: over 1.75 metres

Weight: usually about **36** _____ kilograms

Colour: Black with lighter spots. They also have a pink spot on their head.

Their shell is **37** _____ than other turtle shells.

The leatherback turtle is in danger of becoming **38** _____.

Currently, there are only about **39** _____ leatherback turtles in the world.

Reasons for their declining numbers:
- too many buildings along the beach
- they get caught in **40** _____.

Earthwatch volunteers can help in many ways. For example, they can:
- count the turtles, and
- measure the turtles.

Reading

SECTION 1: PART 1

QUESTIONS 1–6

*The reading passage has six sections, **A–F**.*

*Choose the correct heading for sections **A–F** from the list of headings below.*

*Write the correct number, **i–viii**, in boxes **1–6** on your answer sheet.*

List of headings
i Taking photos
ii Winning a Brownie
iii Naming the Brownie
iv Early success of the Brownie
v Why the Brownie is important
vi Selling the Brownie
vii Describing the Brownie
viii A design problem

1 Section **A**

2 Section **B**

3 Section **C**

4 Section **D**

5 Section **E**

6 Section **F**

The Box Brownie camera

Section A
In 1900, the Eastman Kodak company started selling a cheap hand-held camera called the Brownie. It was immediately successful because it was so easy to use. It came in a simple black cardboard box. The outside had an expensive-looking leather cover. In those days, cameras needed photographic film to take photos. To put the film into the Brownie camera, you just opened the camera box, put the film inside and then closed it up again. Easy!

Section B
When the photographer saw something he wanted to photograph, he simply held the camera, looked through the viewfinder, aimed and pressed the shutter. (The shutter was a kind of button.) After he finished taking photos, he removed the film from the camera, took it to the camera shop and came back later to collect the photos.

Section C
In the first year, the Eastman Kodak company sold a quarter of a million Brownies. However, the first 15 000 Brownies had something wrong with them. They didn't close properly after you put the film in. Most of them had to be replaced later. In mid-March, 1900, the Eastman Kodak Company finished manufacturing a new version. It was a lot better, so the same problem didn't happen again.

Section D
The Brownie is considered by experts to be the most important camera ever manufactured. This is because it was produced so cheaply that anyone, not just professionals or rich people, could own it. And also because it was so simple to use – you didn't need special training.

Section E
Eastman wanted a special word to describe his new invention. He knew it was important to create a word that would be short, easy to remember, and pronounceable in any language (he was thinking about a worldwide market). He chose "Brownie" for two reasons – there was a popular children's book of cartoons of the same name, and the camera was manufactured for Eastman by Frank Brownell of Rochester, New York.

Section F
George Eastman was very clever. He knew children were important in marketing. He promoted the camera to children so they would ask their parents for one. The Brownie advertisements used small, cute creatures. Children loved them. He also encouraged children under the age of 16 to join the Brownie Camera Club. This was a free club – children could get prizes for good photos and receive a special book.

PART 2

In the diagram, you can see that the original Box Brownie was a large rectangular box with a handle on top. People used the handle to carry it, like a bag. You could open the camera box and put the film inside. After you put the film in, you shut the box carefully. There was a lock on each side of the box to stop it opening. There was a small key called a Film Advance on the side that connected to the film inside. You had to use the key to roll the film forward inside the camera box after you took a photo. There were two small square holes called viewfinders. You looked through those when you wanted to take the photo. On the front of the box, there were three holes. The larger one was the lens. In the later Brownies, they used plastic to make the lens; in earlier models like this one, it was glass. To take the photo, you simply pressed the shutter down slowly. The shutter was on the side of the box just under the viewfinder.

QUESTIONS 7–10

Label the diagram below with the words from the box.

Write your answers in boxes 7–10 on your answer sheet.

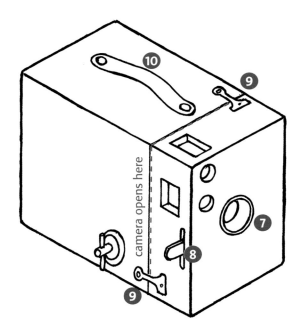

camera opens here

Parts of the Brownie	
lens	shutter
handle	film advance key
viewfinders	lock

The History of Lighthouses

The light in a lighthouse helps the captain of a ship to sail in the dark when he cannot see the coast properly. The light is also useful if there are dangerous rocks or similar hazards. From very early times, lighthouse lights were made by burning wood to create fires. To make the fires large enough and bright enough, the man in the lighthouse had to burn a lot of wood. It was hard work to keep the fire burning because the wood always burnt very, very quickly. During the early 1500s, they used coal for fires in lighthouses. Coal was better than wood in making fires because it burned more slowly and produced a very bright light – much brighter than wood. However, the lighthouse man had to work harder to keep its fire bright, especially when the weather was bad. They tried putting glass windows into the lighthouse so they could keep the fire burning more easily, but dirt and ash from the fire stuck to the glass and made the light less bright and harder to see. Some lighthouses used many candles to make the light easier to see, but in bad weather, they needed still-brighter lights because the candlelight was often quite dull. The next thing they tried was lamps with burning oil. They used special oil, but in cold weather, the oil became hard and lighthouse men had to warm it up before they could use it. Warming the oil helped it to flow properly. Experiments in lighting lighthouses with electricity began in England in 1859 and in France several years later. It took a long time for it to be used though, because many lighthouses weren't close to power lines. It was not until the 1920s that lighthouses could be connected properly and cheaply to a source of electricity. Since around 1950, further developments in technology have made lighthouses less important to sailors. One of these developments is the use of radio signals to help ships keep away from danger.

QUESTIONS 11–15

Complete the summary below using words from the box.

Write your answers in boxes 11–15 on your answer sheet.

radio signals	wood fires	bright	hot
oil	flow	lamps	electricity
coal	steady	dull	slow

The earliest lighthouses used **11**_____ to light up the nearby area and stop ships sailing into rocks. Years later, they started burning coal – the light from burning coal was very **12** _____ , but it needed lots of work to keep it burning. Candles worked quite well, but candlelight was often **13** _____ particularly in bad weather. Later on, they used lamps that contained **14** _____ . They started to use **15** _____ in the early 1900s – that's when they were able to connect the lighthouses to power.

The Pharos Lighthouse

When Ptolemy Soter became the ruler of Egypt in 323 BC, he decided that the city of Alexandria needed a lighthouse. The city was getting bigger and bigger because many people from far away came to sell their goods. The city needed a lighthouse to help the many trade ships to sail safely into Alexandria's busy harbour. They decided to construct the lighthouse on Pharos Island in the middle of the harbour.

When they finished building it about twenty years later, it was the first lighthouse in the world and the tallest building at that time except for the Great Pyramid, which was slightly taller. Experts think that the construction cost 800 talents, the same as about three million dollars today.

The design was unlike most modern lighthouses, but more similar to the design and shape of an early twentieth-century skyscraper. There were three stages, each built on top of the other. The building material was stone blocks stuck together with mortar, and the lighthouse was decorated with small statues and other artwork.

The lighthouse was a tourist attraction. There was a small balcony at the top of the tower for people wanting to make the climb to see the view. At around 300 feet above the sea, the view from there was very beautiful. In the ancient world, it must have been very exciting for people to be able to climb a man-made tower like the Pharos.

The Pharos Lighthouse stood for over 1500 years, surviving a very bad storm that hit the eastern Mediterranean in 365 AD. The storm caused cracks in the walls of the lighthouse, and some of the blocks started to fall off. This made the whole building much weaker. In 1303 AD, a major earthquake shook the region, causing the Pharos Lighthouse to fall down forever.

QUESTIONS 16–20

Do the following statements agree with the information given in the reading passage?

In boxes 16–20 on your answer sheet, write

YES   *if the statement agrees with the information*
NO   *if the information contradicts the information*
NOT GIVEN   *if there is no information on this*

16   The Pharos Lighthouse was built on an island.

17   When it was built, the Pharos Lighthouse was the tallest building in the world.

18   The Pharos Lighthouse looked like lighthouses we have today.

19   The stairs to the top of the lighthouse were hard to climb.

20   Bad weather caused the Pharos lighthouse to become weaker.

SECTION 3

The Statue of Liberty

The Statue of Liberty is the famous statue that stands on Liberty Island in New York Harbour. At a height of 151 feet (46m), it is extremely tall. The statue was a gift to the United States from the people of France, and over the years it has become a symbol of freedom. Many people think an American designed it, but it was in fact created by a French artist, Frédéric Bartholdi.

The designer tried many designs and models, including children and animals, before he chose a female figure, wearing a gown and cloak, holding a torch high above her head. The statue's body looks like a Greek goddess. In the early drawings, the statue's face was going to look like the president's wife, but Bartholdi decided to copy the face of Charlotte Beysser, Bartholdi's mother.

Bartholdi decided to make the skin from copper sheets. This was a good choice because the workmen were able to lift and work with the sheets with no difficulty. He considered other cheaper metals but thought they might be too hard to work with because of their weight.

On October 28th 1886, the President of the United States opened the Statue of Liberty in a ceremony in front of a huge, excited crowd. The President gave a long speech, and Bartholdi was asked to give one too but he refused because he was a shy man. A fireworks display was delayed until November 1 because of poor weather, but the parade went ahead as planned.

Members of the general public – people like you and me – were not allowed on the island during the ceremony – just officials and important people. The only females at the ceremony were the President's wife and the designer's granddaughter, who was only ten.

After the ceremony, they lit the statue's torch, but the light was very faint and no one could see it from far away. Despite this disappointment, the enormous pale statue quickly became a landmark. Many immigrants who sailed into New York Harbour believed that the statue was a welcoming sight and it became a popular tourist attraction.

In 1982, engineers looked at the statue and saw that it needed repairs and money spent on it. The first examination showed that the right arm wasn't attached to the body properly. When strong winds blew, the arm was rubbing against the side of the statue, creating a hole. They also replaced about two per cent of the copper on the outside of the statue because they could see an orange-coloured stain – they thought this was caused by the rain. Although they noticed this "orange problem" as early as 1936, the workers doing early repair work just covered it in layers of paint. That did not solve the problem though.

The statue was closed to the public so they could make repairs. It took many years because it was in worse condition than people first thought. Getting materials to and from the site was not too difficult due to modern engineering knowledge, but the whole exterior had to be cleaned with strong dangerous cleaners. Because of this, the repairers had to wear special clothing and gloves.

The statue closed again in October 2011 so they could install new lifts and staircases, and improve the facilities, like bathrooms. When it opened again, visitors had to pay for the ferry service to get to the island, as private boats were no longer allowed to stop there. This money will help pay for future work on the statue and Liberty Island.

QUESTIONS 21–30

*Choose the correct letters **A, B, C** or **D**.*

Write your answers in boxes 21–30 on your answer sheet.

21 Who designed the Statue of Liberty?
   A an American
   B a Frenchman
   C American and French designers
   D a French designer living in New York

22 The statue's face looks like
   A the designer's mother.
   B the American President's wife.
   C a Greek goddess.
   D a child.

23 The designer made the statue using copper because
   A it was the colour of skin.
   B it was cheaper than other metals.
   C it was heavy.
   D it was easy to work with.

24 When they finished the statue, they celebrated with
   A a parade.
   B a speech by the designer.
   C fireworks.
   D special music.

25 Who weren't allowed on the island during the celebrations?
   A women
   B old people
   C children
   D ordinary people

26 At first, people were disappointed with the statue because
   A it was too big.
   B it was a dull colour.
   C its light wasn't strong enough.
   D it was too difficult to visit.

27 In 1982, engineers discovered
   A early repairers covered problems with paint.
   B the statue's arm was nearly falling off.
   C there were holes everywhere.
   D they had to replace most of the copper.

28 It took a long time to repair the statue because
   A there was bad weather.
   B they needed to make special equipment to fix it.
   C they had to use dangerous materials to clean the outside.
   D it was difficult to get there every day.

29 When the statue opened again,
   A entry was free.
   B the bathrooms were nicer.
   C people weren't allowed to use the stairs any more.
   D you could sail your boat right up to the island.

30 The main purpose of this article is to
   A explain how statues are made.
   B criticise the way the statue was built.
   C advertise the Statue of Liberty.
   D give facts about the Statue of Liberty.

Writing

WRITING TASK 1

You should spend about 20 minutes on this task.

> **The bar chart below shows the percentage of adults and the kinds of electronic devices they own.**
>
> **Summarise the information by selecting and reporting the main features, and make comparisons where relevant.**

Write at least 100 words.

Electronic devices owned by adults in the US

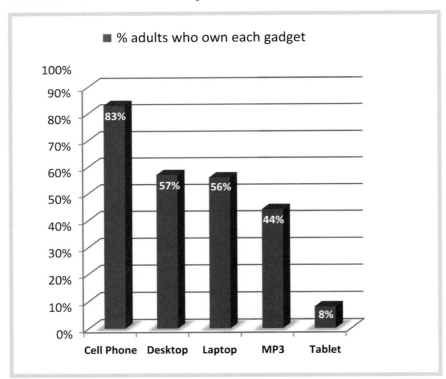

WRITING TASK 2

You should spend about 30 minutes on this task.

Write about the following topic.

> **What are the advantages and disadvantages of living in a big city?**

Give reasons for your answer and include examples from your own knowledge or experience.

Write at least 150 words.

Practice Test

Speaking

THE SPEAKING TEST

The IELTS Speaking test is 11 to 14 minutes long. In this mock IELTS test, the students are asked to speak for a shorter period of time. There are three parts to the test: in Part 1 the candidate answers questions about themselves and their family or everyday life. In Part 2 the examiner gives the candidate a card with prompts on a topic. In this case the topic is holidays. You will need to make a few photocopies of the card below before the interview. The candidate has sixty seconds to prepare themselves and then they have to talk for one to two minutes. In Part 3 the examiner asks the candidate some discussion questions linked to the topic in Part 2.

The instructions below tell you what to do and say to the candidate in each of the three parts of the test.

PART 1

Start the conversation by talking about the questions in the first box. After that select ONE of the two topics (sport or festivals), and continue the conversation. This section of the test should take two to three minutes.

Examiner: *Now, in this first part, I'd like to ask you some questions about yourself, OK? Let's talk about where you are living now.*

- Do you live in a house or an apartment at the moment?
- What do you like about the place you live in now?
- Is there anything you don't like about where you live?
- What kind of house or apartment would you like in the future?

Examiner: *Alright, let's talk about sport now.*

- What sports do you like to do or to watch?
- Which sports are popular in your country?
- Do you think people do enough exercise these days?
- Do you think it's important for children to play sports?

OR ...

Examiner: *OK, I'd like to talk about festivals now.*

- Which festivals are important in your country?
- What do people do during an important festival in your country?
- What was your favourite festival when you were a child?
- Do you think festivals will still be important in the future?

PART 2

Examiner: *OK. I'm going to give you a card on the topic of holidays and you have to talk about the topic for one to two minutes. First you have a minute to think about what you're going to say. Make notes if you want to.*

Hand the candidate the card below and give them sixty seconds to think about / make notes on the topic. When the time is up say:

Alright? Remember you have one to two minutes for this, so don't worry if I stop you. I'll tell you when the time is up.

- -

Candidate test card

Talk about a holiday that you enjoyed.
You should say:
- Where you went on holiday
- Who you went on holiday with
- How long the holiday was for and explain why you enjoyed the holiday so much.

- -

PART 3

This part of the test should last no more than two or three minutes. Make sure that you ask the candidate to give you back the Candidate test card.

Examiner: *Can you give me back the test card, please? Thank you. Now I'm going to ask you a few questions about holidays. Let's consider how important holidays are for people.*

- Why do you think people need to have holidays?
- Do you think people should have more or fewer holidays?
- Are holidays different now to how they were in the past? In what way?
- Do you think holidays will change in the future? Why? / Why not?

Examiner: *OK, that's the end of the Speaking test. Thank you.*

Listening test audioscripts

NARRATOR: THE LISTENING TEST

There are four sections in the test.
There are ten questions in each section.
You will only hear the recordings once.
The test takes approximately 30 minutes.
At the end of the test you will have time to transfer
your answers on to the answer sheet.

SECTION ONE

You will hear a telephone conversation between a man
in a shop and a woman who is interested in working in
the shop. Before you listen, look at questions 1 to 10.

Now listen and answer questions 1 to 10.

PETER: Hello, Top Fashions, Peter speaking. How can I help you?

CLAIRE: Oh hello. I'm looking for some part-time work and I'm ringing to find out if you have anything available.

PETER: Well we don't have any jobs at the moment, but let me take a few details from you in case something comes up in the next few months. OK, the first thing I'll need is your name.

CLAIRE: Yes, it's Claire Brown.

PETER: Great, and your phone number?

CLAIRE: My mobile is 042 879 5361.

PETER: 042 879 5361. Correct?

CLAIRE: Yes, that's right

PETER: OK, got that. And what's your address, Claire, in case we want to send something out to you?

CLAIRE: My address is 54 Taylor Street.

PETER: Can I just check the spelling of that? Is it T.A.Y.L.O.R?

CLAIRE: Yes, it is. And the suburb is New Farm.

PETER: Great. So what are you doing at the moment, Claire? Are you working, or studying?

CLAIRE: A bit of both actually, Peter. I work part time in a shoe shop in the city. I've been doing that for a few years now.

PETER: Well that's good experience. You must be used to dealing with customers by now!

CLAIRE: I sure am. It's really busy. I also study part time. I'm doing a fashion course at the local college. I'm really enjoying it.

PETER: That's wonderful Claire, and is that why you want to work with us?

CLAIRE: Yes, I've always loved clothes, but the reason I want to work at your shop in particular is that I've always been impressed with the quality of your clothing and the cost is always really reasonable.

PETER: That's good to hear. Now, have you had any other work experience that you think might be relevant to working with us?

CLAIRE: Mm, let me think. I worked in a bar for a couple of years. That job taught me a lot about dealing with customers in a busy environment.

PETER: Well from what you've told me so far, you certainly have some of the skills that we would look for in our sales staff. You sound like you're good at dealing with people.

CLAIRE: Yes that's true. I really enjoy helping people.

PETER: And from what you've told me about your other jobs, I'd like to write down that you've got experience at working in a team.

CLAIRE: That's right. I wouldn't like to work on my own – I think I'd get bored.

PETER: Well, you wouldn't get bored working here. There's no time for that, it's such a busy shop.

CLAIRE: Sounds great.

PETER: OK, if a job did become available, what days are you able to work?

CLAIRE: Well I'm lucky that my course at the college is mainly in the evening, so I can work any day. Oh, actually no, I have to study on Friday, so I can't work on that day.

PETER: Mm, that's a pity. We're pretty busy on that day, but as long as you could work on a Saturday, that's obviously the busiest day for us.

CLAIRE: Of course, yes, that shouldn't be a problem.

PETER: And when would you be available to start work, Claire?

CLAIRE: Well I'd have to tell my current employer that I wanted to leave, so that would take a couple of weeks …

PETER: So shall we say some time after the 20th of the month?

CLAIRE: Yes that sounds about right. I should be free then.

PETER: And Claire, what kind of work are you interested in doing exactly?

CLAIRE: Well at the start, I guess I would be happy having quite a simple role, you know, as an assistant. That would give me chance to learn more about how the shop works in general.

PETER: And after that?

CLAIRE:	Eventually I would like to have a more senior job. One thing I've always wanted to do is to be a manager. I think that would be a challenging job but an exciting one.
PETER:	Well you're certainly ambitious. Look, I've got lots of details off you and we'll certainly be in touch if anything comes up. Actually, I've got some general information about working for the company that I could send you. How would you like me to send it, by email?
CLAIRE:	Actually, could you send it by post please? I'm having a bit of trouble with my computer at the moment and I can't always open things properly.
PETER:	Sure, that's fine. Well, thanks for the call Claire, it was lovely to talk to you and …

NARRATOR:

That is the end of Section one. You now have some time to check your answers.

NARRATOR: SECTION TWO

You will hear a talk at an Australian Tourist Information Office given to visitors who want to find out about gardens and parks in the local area. Before you listen, look at questions 11 to 15.

Now listen and answer questions 11 to 15.

PAM:

Hello everyone. My name's Pam and I work here at the Tourist Information Office. Welcome to today's talk, which is about the gardens and parks we have in our beautiful city.

I'll start by talking about the City Centre Gardens. They were first created many years ago, in 1855, mainly as a kind of farm. The people coming to Australia in those early days had to be fed, so it was here that plants were tested by farmers to find out which ones would grow best. The Gardens were also for people to walk around and relax in, so they weren't just for wealthy people, but for everyone. The City Centre Gardens have always been popular with families, and more recently with school groups.

Over the years the Gardens have changed. It's hard to believe now, but there used to be a small zoo in the Gardens where visitors could even see an elephant! That's not possible today of course, and sadly it isn't possible either to visit the beautiful tea house that used to stand in the middle of the Gardens. But if you visit the café, you can see photographs of the old tea house. The café, by the way, is next to a beautiful fountain that has survived from the early days. We are lucky to still have it today.

OK, I'll move on now to talk about another beautiful area of our city, the Mount Rising Gardens. There are lots of different sections in the Mount Rising Gardens such as the Bamboo Grove where you can see different types of bamboo growing, or the Herb Garden which has a lovely smell as you walk through it. The Australian Rainforest section has the world's largest collection of Australian rainforest trees. It was actually awarded first prize in an International Parks and Gardens competition last year!

There are many other facilities on offer at the Gardens. There's a Library, which is a very comfortable, quiet place to sit and read. There's also a Lecture Room, where community lectures are held every week. This room has recently been renovated and now has all the latest technology to help make the talks more interesting. I'd normally recommend visiting the Sky Dome where you can see the stars and planets at night, but, unfortunately, it'll be closed for the next few weeks whilst some problems with the telescopes are fixed.

OK, how to get to Mount Rising Gardens? I wouldn't recommend taking your car – parking can be a real problem there. The best idea is to catch the bus. Several services leave from the city so you won't have to wait long, and you'll be dropped off right at the front entrance. If you're thinking of cycling, then just be careful, the roads can be very busy, so make sure you cycle safely.

NARRATOR:

You now have time to look at questions 16 to 20. Now listen and answer questions 16 to 20.

Finally I'll talk about our beautiful Parkland. This area is right next to Central Station, so it's really easy to get to and once you're there you can walk around and enjoy the different features. There's the Lake, for example, which is home to lots of fish as well as a wide variety of birds.

The Forest area is quite new. Subtropical rainforest trees have recently been planted there and a fantastic boardwalk winds through the forest. This is a perfect place to walk through and look at trees that are native to this area.

The Headland is a good place for the more adventurous to go! As you climb over large rocks you'll be able to imagine what real headlands on the Australian coast are like.

The Fern Garden. The Fern Garden is a beautiful area to sit in and relax for a while. There's a little waterfall in one corner, and it can be very peaceful to sit there and just listen to the water – you'd never know you were so close to the city!

Finally, The Spectacle Garden is at the heart of the Parkland and here you'll see some of the world's most colourful and unique subtropical plants. Don't forget your camera when you go!

OK I think that's about it. If anyone has any questions …

Listening test audioscripts

NARRATOR:
That is the end of Section two. You now have some time to check your answers.

NARRATOR: SECTION THREE
You will hear two students, Jenny and Paul, discussing their Design course at University. Before you listen, look at questions 21 to 25.
Now listen and answer questions 21 to 25.

JENNY:	Hi Paul. How are you?
PAUL:	Hi Jenny. I'm OK thanks, but I've just got so much study to do.
JENNY:	Yes, I know. I've been studying really hard too.
PAUL:	There's so much reading to do. That's the thing that's making it all so hard for me.
JENNY:	I agree. I feel like I read all day long and there's still more to do! But at least we've only been given one assignment so far.
PAUL:	Yes, I've nearly finished my assignment, so I'm not worried about that. And we only have one presentation this semester, so that's fine.
JENNY:	Yes, I'm not too worried about the presentation either.
PAUL:	Actually Jenny, would you mind looking through my assignment? I'd love to get your opinion on something.
JENNY:	Oh Paul, you're not worried about spelling mistakes are you!
PAUL:	No, of course not. And I won't make you look at all the diagrams to make sure they're clear either!
JENNY:	Thank goodness for that!
PAUL:	No, what I really need your help with is whether I've actually answered the question properly. I'm worried I've missed something out.
JENNY:	You worry too much Paul, but of course I'll look through it. I'm sure it'll be fine. So, what did you think about the lecture yesterday?
PAUL:	I really enjoyed it, but I always enjoy Professor Skinner's lectures. Don't you?
JENNY:	Mm, sometimes I do, but I don't think that's what made it so good yesterday. I think it was the topic, 'The future of design'. I was just so interested in it.

PAUL:	Me too. It's the best topic we've had for a while.
JENNY:	But that lecture theatre was so hot and uncomfortable. I hope we don't use it again.
PAUL:	No, it was pretty bad. I was glad to get out into the fresh air. Oh, by the way, have you managed to read the article the Professor gave us?
JENNY:	The one by Jenkins and Smith? Yes I have. I enjoyed it. I thought it was written really clearly and simply.
PAUL:	Yes it was. I didn't find it difficult to understand at all. Although some of the examples of designs were a bit out of date.
JENNY:	Yes, like the development of vacuum cleaners.
PAUL:	Mm, it would be more interesting if they'd used computers or music players as their examples. But it was written some time ago wasn't it?
JENNY:	About ten years ago I think. Paul?
PAUL:	Yes?
JENNY:	Are you glad you chose the course?
PAUL:	Well, for me it's been really good, but I'm not sure I'd recommend it to anyone else because there's so much work to do!
JENNY:	I agree. You'd have to be really interested in design and be willing to work hard. But I'm so glad I'm doing it.
PAUL:	Me too. Are you thinking of studying overseas next year?
JENNY:	No way! I think this university is great. I wouldn't go anywhere else.
PAUL:	I feel the same. I think we definitely chose the right place.

NARRATOR:
You now have time to look at questions 26 to 30.
Now listen and answer questions 26 to 30.

JENNY:	Have you chosen a topic for your presentation yet?
PAUL:	Well, I thought about watch design.
JENNY:	Oh yes?
PAUL:	Yes, I like it because I could use lots of visuals, you know pictures, to show different designs and styles. There's lots of them on the Internet.
JENNY:	Good idea. I thought you would choose car design.

PAUL: I'd like to, but someone else did it last week, remember?

JENNY: Oh yes. I'm thinking about telephone design. I think Professor Skinner would be interested in it. He's always talking about his latest mobile phone!

PAUL: That's true. I was surprised to see fridge design on the list. To me that's such a boring topic.

JENNY: I agree, but someone else might like it. What about bridge design?

PAUL: Well, there are just so many types of bridges to talk about, I thought it would be too hard to explain them all in ten minutes.

JENNY: That's true. I was thinking about building design, but we're actually going to study that in more detail next year, so I thought I'd leave it.

PAUL: Good idea. Well, we'd better get some more study done. Shall we go to the library?

NARRATOR:

That is the end of Section three. You now have some time to check your answers.

NARRATOR: SECTION FOUR

You will hear a talk by someone from Earthwatch, an international environmental charity. Before you listen, look at questions 31 to 34.

Now listen and answer questions 31 to 34.

Good morning everyone. I am here to talk to you about Earthwatch, an international organisation which was set up in 1971 to help protect the natural environment. Earthwatch has offices in major cities around the world like Tokyo and Melbourne; its headquarters are in Boston.

Earthwatch supports more than 50 essential research projects around the world. We mainly work in the areas of conservation, climate change, oceans and cultural heritage. Our main focus each year changes depending on what we consider to be the greatest need – this year it's on the area of conservation.

Since 1971, we have recruited more than 90 000 volunteers. These volunteers have joined scientists and researchers in working on projects in 28 countries around the globe. Earthwatch volunteers are people like you! They're students, teachers, families and professionals who are committed to the environment and want to be involved in saving it. No prior skills are needed; you don't have to be trained in anything specific. We do say, though, that you should have a real commitment to the environment. We need people who are passionate and interested in making the world a better place for our children's children. By volunteering, you will feel like you are doing something positive. Volunteers range in age from 16 years on our family teams to quite a few who're over 60; there is no upper age limit!

NARRATOR:

You now have time to look at questions 35 to 40. Now listen and answer questions 35 to 40.

OK, I'd like to tell you about a project that Earthwatch is currently involved in, to do with leatherback turtles in Trinidad in the Caribbean. Leatherback turtles are the world's largest living reptile. Scientists have done a lot of research into these strange and fascinating animals. We know, for example, that they can grow to more than 1.75 metres long! And the heaviest leatherback ever found was more than 500 kilograms, although most of them grow to approximately 350 kilograms! They have an unusual appearance compared with other turtles. For example, they are a different colour to other marine turtles. They are mostly black, but covered in lighter patches or large spots all over their body and shell. And they all have a spot on top of their heads that's pink. Another thing that makes them different to other marine turtles is their shell – all other marine turtles have a very hard shell, but leatherback turtles are different. The shell on their back is softer.

Unfortunately, the leatherback is in very serious danger of becoming extinct. The global population for this species was estimated to be 120 000 adult animals in 1982. Initially it was thought that numbers were halved to around 60 000. Unfortunately, recent studies have shown numbers are now down to about 30 000.

There are two main reasons for the decline in the number of leatherback turtles in the world today. The first reason is that a lot of building is being done along the beaches. This makes it hard for the leatherbacks to find places to dig their nests and lay their eggs. The second reason is that many of them get caught accidentally in fishing nets every year. A lot of research is currently being done to stop this happening.

Data collected recently by Earthwatch volunteers gives us important information on the number of turtles making nests at the site. The volunteers are able to help the researchers by, say, counting the number of turtles on the beach, or measuring the turtles, so accurate records can be kept.

NARRATOR:

That is the end of Section four. You will now have time to transfer your answers to the answer sheet.

Practice Test
Answer Key

LISTENING

SECTION 1

1	042 879 5361
2	Taylor
3	fashion
4	cost / price
5	bar
6	team
7	Fridays / Friday / a Friday
8	20th / 20 / twentieth
9	assistant / Assistant
10	manager / Manager

SECTION 2

11	C	**16**	E
12	A	**17**	G
13	B	**18**	B
14	C	**19**	C
15	B	**20**	F

SECTION 3

21	B	**26**	C
22	A	**27**	B
23	C	**28**	F
24	A	**29**	D
25	A	**30**	E

SECTION 4

31	B
32	C
33	A
34	B
35	largest / biggest
36	350
37	softer
38	extinct
39	30 000 / 30 thousand / thirty thousand
40	(fishing) nets

READING

SECTION 1
The box brownie camera

Part 1
1 vii
2 i
3 viii
4 v
5 iii
6 vi

Part 2
7 lens
8 shutter
9 lock
10 handle

Section 2
Lighthouses

Part 1
11 wood fires
12 bright
13 dull
14 oil
15 electricity

Part 2
16 T
17 F
18 F
19 NG
20 T

Section 3
The Statue of Liberty

21 B
22 A
23 D
24 A
25 D
26 C
27 A
28 C
29 B
30 D

Writing

Sample answers

TASK 1
The bar chart shows the number of adults by percentage and the electronic devices they own. According to the figures, the most popular electronic device is the cell phone. It is owned by 83% of the adults asked. The tablet is owned by only 8% of the adults asked, so it is the least popular device. The desktop and the laptop are owned by a similar percentage of adults, while the MP3 is owned by 44% of adults. In conclusion, we can see that the cell phone is owned by many more adults compared to the other devices, and very few adults prefer the tablet.
(**104** words)

TASK 2
There are many big cities in the world. Some famous cities are London, Sydney and Tokyo. Living in these cities has many advantages. For example, they are lively places and full of interesting things to do. You can play sport, visit tourist attractions and eat in all the restaurants. Large cities are full of beautiful buildings, parks and gardens. There are more universities, so students can find a course to study and it is often easier for students to find a job. However, it is difficult to live in a big city. Big cities can be very dirty and there is more pollution because there are lots of cars. Often buses and trains in cities are crowded and noisy. There are many rich people in large cities, but there are also many poor people. In conclusion, I think that big cities are good places to visit, but I prefer to live in a smaller place.
(**155** words)

BRITISH COUNCIL

UNIVERSITY of CAMBRIDGE
ESOL Examinations

IELTS Listening and Reading Answer Sheet

Centre number:

Pencil must be used to complete this sheet.

Please write your **full name** in CAPITAL letters on the line below:

_____

Then write your six digit Candidate number in the boxes and shade the number in the grid on the right.

| 0 1 2 3 4 5 6 7 8 9 |
| 0 1 2 3 4 5 6 7 8 9 |
| 0 1 2 3 4 5 6 7 8 9 |
| 0 1 2 3 4 5 6 7 8 9 |
| 0 1 2 3 4 5 6 7 8 9 |
| 0 1 2 3 4 5 6 7 8 9 |

Test date (shade ONE box for the day, ONE box for the month and ONE box for the year):

Day: 01 02 03 04 05 06 07 08 09 10 11 12 13 14 15 16 17 18 19 20 21 22 23 24 25 26 27 28 29 30 31

Month: 01 02 03 04 05 06 07 08 09 10 11 12   **Year** (last 2 digits): 09 10 11 12 13 14 15 16 17 18

Listening	Listening	Listening		Listening	Listening	Listening	
			Marker use only				Marker use only
1			✓ 1 ✗	**21**			✓ 21 ✗
2			✓ 2 ✗	**22**			✓ 22 ✗
3			✓ 3 ✗	**23**			✓ 23 ✗
4			✓ 4 ✗	**24**			✓ 24 ✗
5			✓ 5 ✗	**25**			✓ 25 ✗
6			✓ 6 ✗	**26**			✓ 26 ✗
7			✓ 7 ✗	**27**			✓ 27 ✗
8			✓ 8 ✗	**28**			✓ 28 ✗
9			✓ 9 ✗	**29**			✓ 29 ✗
10			✓ 10 ✗	**30**			✓ 30 ✗
11			✓ 11 ✗	**31**			✓ 31 ✗
12			✓ 12 ✗	**32**			✓ 32 ✗
13			✓ 13 ✗	**33**			✓ 33 ✗
14			✓ 14 ✗	**34**			✓ 34 ✗
15			✓ 15 ✗	**35**			✓ 35 ✗
16			✓ 16 ✗	**36**			✓ 36 ✗
17			✓ 17 ✗	**37**			✓ 37 ✗
18			✓ 18 ✗	**38**			✓ 38 ✗
19			✓ 19 ✗	**39**			✓ 39 ✗
20			✓ 20 ✗	**40**			✓ 40 ✗

Marker 2 Initials		Marker 1 Initials		Band Score		Listening Total	

IELTS L-R v4.0

denote Print Limited 0121 520 5100

DP650/394

Please write your **full name** in CAPITAL letters on the line below:

_____

Please write your Candidate number on the line below:

_____

Please write your three digit language code in the boxes and shade the numbers in the grid on the right.

0 1 2 3 4 5 6 7 8 9
0 1 2 3 4 5 6 7 8 9
0 1 2 3 4 5 6 7 8 9

Are you: Female? ▭   Male? ▭

Reading   Reading   Reading   Reading   Reading   Reading

Module taken (shade one box):   Academic ▭   General Training ▭

#		Marker use only	#		Marker use only
1		✓ 1 ✗	21		✓ 21 ✗
2		✓ 2 ✗	22		✓ 22 ✗
3		✓ 3 ✗	23		✓ 23 ✗
4		✓ 4 ✗	24		✓ 24 ✗
5		✓ 5 ✗	25		✓ 25 ✗
6		✓ 6 ✗	26		✓ 26 ✗
7		✓ 7 ✗	27		✓ 27 ✗
8		✓ 8 ✗	28		✓ 28 ✗
9		✓ 9 ✗	29		✓ 29 ✗
10		✓ 10 ✗	30		✓ 30 ✗
11		✓ 11 ✗	31		✓ 31 ✗
12		✓ 12 ✗	32		✓ 32 ✗
13		✓ 13 ✗	33		✓ 33 ✗
14		✓ 14 ✗	34		✓ 34 ✗
15		✓ 15 ✗	35		✓ 35 ✗
16		✓ 16 ✗	36		✓ 36 ✗
17		✓ 17 ✗	37		✓ 37 ✗
18		✓ 18 ✗	38		✓ 38 ✗
19		✓ 19 ✗	39		✓ 39 ✗
20		✓ 20 ✗	40		✓ 40 ✗

Marker 2 Initials		Marker 1 Initials		Band Score		Reading Total	

1A BINGO!

AIM To practise forming questions using the present simple tense.

Before class
Make one copy for each student.

In class
A Tell students they are going to play bingo. Explain that they need to form questions correctly and ask other students in the class.

B Give each student a Bingo! sheet and practise with the class using the first box in the table. Explain that when students hear a 'Yes' response to their question, they write the name of that student down under the question in the box. If they hear a 'No' response, they ask other students until they hear a 'Yes'. When a student has two rows of names (across, down or diagonally), they shout 'Bingo'.

C Note down any questions that students had difficulty with. Put students into pairs so they can discuss and correct the errors.

1B PRONUNCIATION PELMANISM

AIM To give further practice of the vowel sounds /ɒ//eɪ//aɪ/ in vocabulary from Unit 1.

Before class
Make one copy for each pair/small groups of students.
Note: Vowel sounds and words should be copied on different coloured paper in order to identify them.

In class
A Remind the class of vowel sounds by writing /ɒ//eɪ/ /aɪ/ on the whiteboard. Elicit any words students can remember with these sounds from the unit.

B Explain the pelmanism game – students will have two groups of cards spread out lying face down on the table. One group is of words from the unit, the other group is the vowel sounds /ɒ//eɪ//aɪ/. One student begins by turning over a word then a vowel. If the vowel sound matches the one underlined in the word, the student wins that pair and keeps them, then they can have another turn. Play continues around the group until all the pairs have been won.

C Monitor and help with any pronunciation difficulties.

2A WHISPERS

AIM To consolidate new vocabulary and give practice in listening.

Before class
Copy enough sentences for each team. The game works best with about five or six students per team. Divide the board into one column for each team. Head each column with 'Team 1', Team 2' … etc.

In class
A Tell the class they are going to play a team game of 'whispers'. Explain that each team will have to stand in a line facing the front of the class, with the first person in the team standing at the board in front of his/her team's column, ready to write. Tell students that you are going to give the last person in each team a strip of paper with a short sentence on it. When you say 'GO!' this person will whisper the sentence to the teammate in front. Explain that this student will need to listen carefully and repeat that sentence to the teammate in front of him/her, who will then repeats it to the teammate in front, and so on. Explain that when the teammate at the board hears the sentence, he/she writes it down on the board in the team's column.

B The first team to write the sentence correctly on the board wins that round. If the first team's finished sentence has errors, go to the next team and keep looking until a sentence has been written that is error free.

C When the first sentence is finished, the student in the front goes to the back of the line and the student who is second in line becomes the writer. The game continues in this way until all the sentences have been written correctly.

2B RUNNING DICTATION

AIM To consolidate vocabulary and give practice in punctuation, using full stops and capital letters.

Before class
Copy the worksheet and cut up the sentences.
Note: For large classes, each sentence may need to be copied twice.

In class
A Stick the sentences in random order on the walls around the room, making sure they are spaced out. Divide students into pairs. Student A is the writer, Student B is the runner.

B Explain that when you say 'GO', Student B must run to the nearest sentence, memorise it and then run back to his/her partner, who writes it down. Tell students that Student B is not allowed to touch the paper, take the paper back to Student A or shout the sentence across the room. Student B does this for each of the sentences. Explain that if Student B forgets part of a sentence, he/she can go back and re-read it.

C When all the sentences have been recorded, each pair sits down together and checks spelling, numbers the sentences in the correct order, and then punctuates the paragraph.

> **Note:** This can be done as a competition: the pair that is the most accurate wins.

> (13 errors)
>
> 1 For many **A**ustralians, the biggest and most exciting celebration of the year is **N**ew **Y**ear's **E**ve.
>
> 2 **D**uring the day and night, there is amazing entertainment everywhere as people wait for the new year.
>
> 3 **A**t midnight there is usually a massive fireworks display.
>
> 4 **E**veryone then goes home to bed and wakes up on January 1ˢᵗ.

3A ADJECTIVES CROSSWORD

AIM To recycle and consolidate character adjectives.

Before class
Make enough copies of the crossword for each student in the class – half the class needs crossword A, half needs crossword B.

In class
A Tell students that the crossword contains character adjectives and elicit a few examples on the board. Explain that the crosswords are different and that students will work in pairs to help each other to complete their crosswords.

B Demonstrate how to ask for a clue, e.g. 'What's the clue for 1 across?', 'What's the clue for 3 down?'. Tell students they can give each other hints if a word is hard for them, e.g. 'It begins with 'c'.' Then hand out the crosswords.

C Fast finishers could talk about which adjectives describe them, or people they know, and why.

Across	Down
1 shy	1 sad
2 friendly	3 intelligent
4 nervous	6 quiet
5 talkative	8 lazy
7 confident	
9 hardworking	

3B ADVERB CIRCLES

AIM To provide further practice of adverbs of frequency.

Before class
Make one copy for each student.

In class
A Revise the five adverbs of frequency studied on page 26: *often, sometimes, never, usually, always.*

B Give out the photocopies and tell students to complete the five sentences with adverbs of frequency so that the sentences are true for them.

C Tell students they need to write the five adverbs they chose randomly in the circles at the bottom of the handout. They then need to fold over the paper so they can only see the circles with the adverbs written in them.

D Ask students to swap papers with a partner. They now have to find out why their partner wrote these adverbs by guessing what they refer to and asking follow-up questions to extend the discussion. Model the activity:

> **S1:** *I think you wrote 'sometimes' because you are sometimes late for class!*
> **S2:** *You're right.*
> **S2:** *Why are you sometimes late?*
> **S1:** *Because I come here after work and the traffic is very bad.*

E Conduct brief feedback at the end.

4A ACADEMIC SUBJECTS WORDSEARCH

AIM To recycle vocabulary related to academic subjects and higher education.

Before class
Make one copy for each pair of students.

In class
A Tell students they're going to do a wordsearch in pairs. Explain that they have to find the academic subjects and higher education words they studied in a previous lesson.

Note: If you want to increase the challenge, ask students to cover up the words they're searching for. Tell them there are 18 words in the wordsearch and see how many they can remember from the previous lesson. Words go across or down.

B Put students in pairs and give out the wordsearch.

C Fast finishers can check their answers then practise the pronunciation (syllable stress) of each word or test each other on the spelling of the words.

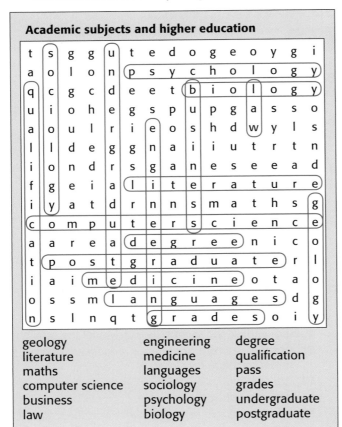

Academic subjects and higher education

geology	engineering	degree
literature	medicine	qualification
maths	languages	pass
computer science	sociology	grades
business	psychology	undergraduate
law	biology	postgraduate

4B DINNER PARTY

 (10min)

AIM To provide further practice of the present simple and present continuous.

Before class
Make one copy for each student.

In class
A Introduce the idea of hosting a dinner party (inviting people to your home for a meal and good conversation).

B Put students in pairs. Draw a plan of the dinner table on the board:

Tell students they will get a handout with descriptions of six guests. Their task is to decide where each guest will sit.

C Give out the photocopy and allow students a few minutes to read through the information.

D Model the language they will need in order to do the task, e.g. *'I think Eva should sit next to Fazia because Eva's learning to play the guitar and Fazia plays the guitar most evenings to help her relax.'*

E Extend the activity by getting pairs to compare their seating arrangements to see how similar or different they are.

Note: There are no correct answers, but students should be able to explain why they sat each guest where they did. This could be used as a springboard for drama, e.g. set groups up as if at a dinner party and assign each student a role from the worksheet. Let them use their imagination to act out their part, but remind them of the importance of using correct present tenses!

5A THE RUNNING GAME

 (10min)

AIM To consolidate new vocabulary from the Reading text.

Before class
Copy the vocabulary list three times – one for each team. Divide the board into three columns and head each one with 'Team A', 'Team B' and 'Team C'.

In class
A Tell students that they are going to play a vocabulary game that's related to 'the Eiffel Tower' Reading. Give them five minutes to look through the reading text. After five minutes, divide students into three teams – Team A, Team B and Team C. Tell students that each team will be asked to line up two metres from the board in front of their column. (It is useful to put something on the floor that the teams can stand behind, like a ruler or a piece of scrap paper).

B Explain that you are going to give the first person in line a list of scrambled words from Unit 5. You are going to shout out a number. The first person in each team must look at the scrambled word next to that number. With the team's help, he/she must unscramble the word and run up to the board and write the word quickly. The first team to write the word correctly wins one point.

C Explain that the person who has just run should give the list to the person behind and then go to the end of the line. The next student steps up and the process is repeated again until all the numbers/words have been unscrambled.

1	advertise	6	tower
2	culture	7	impact
3	engineer	8	structure
4	landmark	9	metal
5	design	10	communication

5B GUESS THAT WORD

 (10min)

AIM To consolidate all new vocabulary from Unit 5.

Before class
Photocopy and cut up the words so that you have two sets of cards.

In class
A Tell students that they are going to play a vocabulary game. Before you begin, give everyone five minutes to look through the vocabulary in Unit 5.

B Put students into two teams. Explain that you are going to choose a student from each team and show them a word from Unit 5. The two chosen students will then have to turn to their team (with their backs to each other) and mime the word for their teammates. Explain that they will have only one minute to act out the word. Tell them they cannot point at any object or use words or sounds.

C The first team to correctly guess the word wins one point. After each word is guessed, a new student is chosen from each team to act out the next word.

    Note: Students will need to be reasonably familiar with the words from the unit for this game to work as some of the vocabulary requires creative guessing – but this is what makes it fun!

6A QUESTION TIME

 (10min)

AIM To revise yes/no questions and vocabulary associated with jobs.

Before class
Photocopy and cut up the words so that you have one set of cards for each group of three.

In class
A Tell students they are going to revise vocabulary to do with jobs. To warm up, brainstorm job vocabulary and write it up on the board. Briefly discuss and then erase.

B Explain to students that they will be placed into groups of three. One student will select a card, without showing his/her partners. The two partners will then have to guess the job on the card by asking yes/no questions. The first person to guess the job correctly gets one point.

C Before you begin, briefly revise asking closed questions using *do* by writing on the board: *Do + you +* base form of verb. To model the activity, ask one student to come to the front and quietly tell him he is a nurse. Elicit yes/no questions from students – encourage them to use *do*. You can start the questions by asking *Do you wear a uniform?, etc.*

D When you feel students understand the game, tell them to take it in turns to be the 'guessers' and the one turning over the cards. The student with the most points wins.

6B STRIP STORY

 (10min)

AIM To consolidate the use of the past simple tense, and practise using new vocabulary introduced in Unit 6.

Before class
Make one copy of each story for every pair of students. Cut up each story into strips and place the strips into an envelope.

Note: The story is in the correct order, so you will need to jumble it.

In class
A Divide students into pairs. Tell students you are going to give them a story that has been cut up into strips. They have to put the strips into the correct order. Each strip forms part of a complete story. Explain that the first pair to correctly sequence their story wins.

B Give each pair an envelope.

C Say, 'GO! ' Make sure everyone finishes the activity. Early finishers can read the story to each other. With a strong class, make this a race. (For the correct order, see page 147, as the story isn't jumbled.)

7A What am I doing?

AIM To recycle vocabulary from Unit 7 related to sport and verb/noun collocations.

Before class
Make one copy for each group of three/four students and cut the activities into one set.

In class
A Introduce the activity by miming an action, e.g. *go climbing*. Ask *What am I doing?* Get students to guess. Make sure students use a verb and noun as all the examples on the slips follow this pattern.

B Put students in groups of three/four and give out the slips. Students then take turns miming. The student who guesses correctly gets one point. They play until all the slips have been won.

C Fast finishers can review Unit 7 grammar by choosing a sport from the slips (e.g. *play tennis, golf*) and talk about what you *(don't) have to, can, can't, (don't) need to* do when you play this sport.

7B Sport – Talk Topic

AIM To practise the IELTS Speaking test, Part 2 by talking about sport and to review the grammar from Unit 7.

Before class
Make one copy for each student.

In class
A Remind students that in Part 2 of the IELTS Speaking test they have to talk about a topic. Tell students they are going to talk about a sport they like to watch. Give students the handout and ask them to look at the task and to underline key words, e.g. *sport, watch, what, where played, rules, why like*.

B First, ask students to look at sentences a–h and match each sentence to a numbered part of the task. Conduct brief feedback.

1 = b	2 = d, h	3 = e, f	4 = a, c, g

C Remind students about adding emphasis (page 66 Student's Book) and do some controlled practice of this with the tennis sentences.

D Students now prepare to talk about the topic using their own ideas. Put them into small groups and give each student two minutes to talk. Give the other students in the group a reason to listen each: e.g. they can time the speaker, listen in order to ask a follow-up question, or give the speaker feedback on what they did well.

8A Pictionary

AIM To revise vocabulary studied in Unit 8.

Before class
Make enough copies so each group of three students has an A, B or C card.

In class
A Explain to students they are going to play pictionary using words studied in Unit 8. Do an example on the board to check students know how to play, e.g. draw a person surfing to elicit *'(go) surfing'*. Make sure students know that the person drawing can't speak, only draw, and the person who guesses correctly gets a point. Tell them they also win a bonus point if they get the word in brackets.

B Put students into groups of three and give them their words (they can't show them to the others!). Make sure they have paper for drawing on, and allocate a score keeper.

C Fast finishers could test each other on the spelling.

8B Have you ever … ?

AIM To practise present perfect simple + *ever* and past simple.

Before class
Make one copy for each student.

In class
A Review the grammar studied in this unit: present perfect simple for past experience (the emphasis is on the experience, not the time) and past simple for specifics (detail such as *when, why, who, what* is emphasised). Write a present perfect simple question on the whiteboard: *Have you ever been to another country? Yes I have. /No I haven't.* Then elicit follow-up questions for *yes* and *no* e.g. *Which country did you go to?* or *How long did you stay?*

B Tell students they are going to ask a partner four questions about their past experience. But first they have to form *Have you ever* questions, and prepare two follow-up questions in case the answer is *yes* or *no*. Tell them they also have to make up their own *Have you ever* question.

C Hand out the photocopies and give students time alone to form the questions. When ready, put them in pairs to ask and answer. Tell students they have to report back on the most interesting thing they found out about their partner – this gives them a reason to listen.

9A Hot Seat

AIM To provide free practice in discussing family relationships (IELTS Speaking test, Part 2).

Before class
Make one copy of the questions for each group of three. Organise coloured counters (about 20 per group).

In class
A Tell students they will work in groups of three. Each group will receive a set of question cards, and a pile of counters. In each group, one person will be chosen to sit in the Hot Seat. Explain that the student in the Hot Seat will have to turn over a question card and answer the question/s on it as fully as possible in 30 seconds – but the answer can be the truth or a lie. The other students in the group have to decide whether the answer is the truth or a lie and give reasons why.

B Explain that if students guess correctly (i.e. whether the student in the Hot Seat has told the truth or if they have lied), they can take a counter from the pile in the middle. But if they guess incorrectly, they have to give one of their counters to the student in the Hot Seat.

C When you are sure students understand, put them into groups of three. Place a set of question cards (face down) and a pile of counters in the middle of the group. Each student in the group also receives five additional counters. Each student should have a turn at sitting in the Hot Seat and answering a question. The student with the most counters at the end wins.

9B Passive voice race

AIM To provide practice in recognising and using the passive and active voice.

Before class
Copy the worksheet three times and cut into strips. Place each of the three identical sentences into one envelope so you end up with 12 envelopes. (To shorten the activity, just reduce the number of sentences.) Divide the board into three columns and give each column a heading: 'Team 1', 'Team 2', 'Team 3'.

In class
A Tell students they are going to work in teams to change sentences from the active voice to the passive voice, and from the passive voice to the active voice.

B Put students into three teams – Team 1, Team 2, Team 3. In each team, give every student a number. Explain that when you call out a number, the three students who have been given that number have to run up to you, take a strip of paper and run back to their team.

  Note: Each team gets a strip of paper with the same sentence.

C Tell students that they then have to work together as a team to decide if the sentence is in the passive or active voice. If it is a passive sentence, they have to change it to the active voice; if it is an active sentence, they have to change it to the passive voice. They must do this without writing anything down, just discussion.

  Note: Remind students that they should use *by* where necessary.

D When the teams think they have the correct answer, the student who ran to get the strip of paper must run to the board and write the correct sentence there in his/her team's column. The first team to write the sentence correctly wins one point.

  Note: Where there are fewer or more than 12 students in a team, students may need to have more than one turn – or you can choose to use fewer sentences.

Active to Passive

1 They hold a party on the baby's first birthday. =
A party is held on the baby's first birthday.

2 Brides wear white dresses in Australia. =
In Australia white dresses are worn. /
White dresses are worn in Australia by brides.

3 Many farmers grow rice in China. =
Rice is grown by many farmers in China. /
In China rice is grown by many farmers.

4 They pick vegetables from the garden. =
Vegetables are picked from the garden.

5 They give the bride money. =
Money is given to the bride.

6 We celebrate special events at home. =
Special events are celebrated at home.

Passive to Active

7 A speech is given by the bride's father. =
The bride's father gives a speech.

8 Wedding cake is eaten by all the guests. =
All the guests eat wedding cake.

9 Fruit is grown by the Hunza people. =
The Hunza people grow fruit.

11 Fish are caught in that river by fishermen. =
Fishermen catch fish in that river.

10 Their lives are spent moving around. =
They spend their lives moving around.

12 A special kimono is worn by Japanese brides. =
Japanese brides wear a special kimono.

10A NOUGHTS AND CROSSES

AIM To revise countable and uncountable nouns.

Before class
Make one copy for each group of three students.

In class
A Model noughts and crosses by putting a 3 x 3 grid on the board. One student is 'O', the other is 'X'. The aim of the game is to achieve a row of three O's or three X's in any direction. Demonstrate the activity by writing a word in one square and get students to make a sentence using that word. E.g. *there are = There are six people in my family.*

B Put students into teams of three – two players and one 'judge'. Explain that the players must choose a particular square and make up a sentence using the word/s in that square. The judge's role is to decide whether each player's sentence is correct. If the sentence is correct, the player can mark the square with a chosen 'O' or 'X'. If it's incorrect, the original

words are left in the square and it is the other player's turn. The first player with a row of three X's or three O's wins the game.

C Put students into groups of three and allocate roles. Hand out the photocopies. At the end of each game, the students swap roles, so that each student has a chance to play and judge.

10B VOCABULARY RACE

AIM To revise vocabulary studied in Unit 10.

Before class
Make one copy of each set for each group of three/four students. Cut up each set.

In class
A Divide the class into groups of three/four. Give each group a set of cards and ask them to place them in a pile face down. They should take turns to look at a word without showing it to the other students. They should define the word, but not say it, and the others should guess the word. The student who guesses correctly keeps the card. The one with the most cards at the end is the winner.

B At the end, check meaning and pronunciation as a class.

11A WHICH IS ... ?

AIM To practise comparative structures.

Before class
Make enough copies so that each student has one topic strip.

In class
A Put a topic on the board, e.g. *pets*. Elicit two types, e.g. *1 a cat 2 a dog*. Ask students for an adjective to compare the two e.g. *good*. Ask students how to complete the question stem *Which is… ?* using the chosen adjective in a comparative structure, e.g. *Which is better, a cat or a dog?* Elicit an example answer: *I think a dog is better than a cat because you can play games with it.* You can encourage an extended answer by asking students for more information or examples: *You can throw a ball to a dog, or run with it in the park. When I was a child I had a dog and … etc.*

B Give each student a slip of paper with a topic. They have to think of two categories, an adjective, then make a question. Monitor and give help.

C Ask students to stand up, mingle and ask and answer their questions. Tell them to remember/note down any interesting answers and to report back on the most interesting one at the end.

    Extension: For a stronger group, get them to memorise their question before they mingle.

11B FOUR OF THE BEST

AIM To practise the IELTS Speaking test, Part 2.

Before class
Make one copy for each group of four students.

In class
A Tell students they are going to practise Part 2 of the IELTS Speaking test – the individual long turn. Remind students they have 1 minute to underline the key words in the task and make notes, then they have 1–2 minutes to talk. Tell students they should try to use adjectives, comparatives and superlatives to talk about the topic.

B Put students into pairs and place the four topic cards face down between them. Student A is the time-keeper, and Student B is the candidate. Ask Student B to choose a topic from the pile and start to prepare to talk about it; ask Student A to time 1 minute. Student A then asks Student B to start talking and times 1–2 minutes. When the time is up, they swap roles.

C Fast finishers move on to the next two topics. They could also practise asking follow-up questions to extend the discussion further.

12A WILL THINGS BE DIFFERENT?

AIM To practise future forms *will* and *won't*.

Before class
Make enough copies so that students have one question strip each.

In class
A Put an example on the board, e.g. *In the future will classrooms be different?* Elicit possible answers using *will* and *won't* e.g. *Yes they will, they'll have more*

technology in them or *No they won't, there'll be tables, chairs and a board like now.* Drill question and answers so students become familiar with the forms and the intonation patterns.

B Give one question to each student. Ask them to practise saying their question until they know it without looking at the paper. Monitor and help with meaning or pronunciation problems.

C Ask students to stand up. Tell them they have to mingle and talk to four other students. Give them a reason for listening e.g. *find the most interesting* or *funniest* or *most unusual answer.* Encourage students to add more information and detail to their answers if they can.

D Conduct feedback by asking a few students to share some of their answers with you.

12B LOTTERY WINNERS!

AIM To practise future forms *going to* and *Are you going to…? What are you going to…?*

Before class
Make one copy for each student.

In class
A Tell students to imagine they have all just won a share in a huge lottery (decide on an amount that is a fortune in your country). Put these topic words on the board and ask students to plan what they're going to do with their fortune: *home, work, study, car, holidays, buy, give to family, friends, charity.* Model first, e.g. *I'm going to buy a big house near the beach. I'm going to stop work and have a long holiday.*

B Give out the questions and ask pairs of students to work together to form them.

> Where are you going to live?
> What car are you going to drive?
> What holidays are you going to have?
> What are you going to buy?
> Are you going to give any money to friends or family?
> Are you going to give any money to charity?
> Are you going to continue to work or study?

B Drill questions. Then ask students to stand up and mingle/put two pairs together. Tell them to ask each other some of the questions. Give them a reason for listening e.g. *Find out who has the most surprising/ funny/interesting idea to report back.*

C Conduct feedback as a class on some of the best answers they heard.

Communication activities

1A Bingo!

Find someone who ...

reads a lot Name: _____	worries a lot Name: _____
is a calm person Name: _____	owns more than six T-shirts Name: _____
likes to go to the cinema Name: _____	likes very hot weather Name: _____
enjoys eating at expensive restaurants Name: _____	is happy most of the time Name: _____
is from a capital city Name: _____	is the youngest in the family Name: _____
spends a lot of time online Name: _____	likes playing computer games Name: _____
cries in sad movies Name: _____	watches too much TV Name: _____
is interested in sport Name: _____	has a noisy family Name: _____

Find someone who ...

reads a lot Name: _____	worries a lot Name: _____
is a calm person Name: _____	owns more than six T-shirts Name: _____
likes to go to the cinema Name: _____	likes very hot weather Name: _____
enjoys eating at expensive restaurants Name: _____	is happy most of the time Name: _____
is from a capital city Name: _____	is the youngest in the family Name: _____
spends a lot of time online Name: _____	likes playing computer games Name: _____
cries in sad movies Name: _____	watches too much TV Name: _____
is interested in sport Name: _____	has a noisy family Name: _____

Find someone who ...

reads a lot Name: _____	worries a lot Name: _____
is a calm person Name: _____	owns more than six T-shirts Name: _____
likes to go to the cinema Name: _____	likes very hot weather Name: _____
enjoys eating at expensive restaurants Name: _____	is happy most of the time Name: _____
is from a capital city Name: _____	is the youngest in the family Name: _____
spends a lot of time online Name: _____	likes playing computer games Name: _____
cries in sad movies Name: _____	watches too much TV Name: _____
is interested in sport Name: _____	has a noisy family Name: _____

Find someone who ...

reads a lot Name: _____	worries a lot Name: _____
is a calm person Name: _____	owns more than six T-shirts Name: _____
likes to go to the cinema Name: _____	likes very hot weather Name: _____
enjoys eating at expensive restaurants Name: _____	is happy most of the time Name: _____
is from a capital city Name: _____	is the youngest in the family Name: _____
spends a lot of time online Name: _____	likes playing computer games Name: _____
cries in sad movies Name: _____	watches too much TV Name: _____
is interested in sport Name: _____	has a noisy family Name: _____

1B PRONUNCIATION PELMANISM

/aɪ/	n<u>i</u>ce
/aɪ/	f<u>i</u>ne
/aɪ/	sc<u>i</u>ence
/aɪ/	Fr<u>i</u>day
/aɪ/	Ch<u>i</u>na
/aɪ/	<u>I</u>
/aɪ/	sm<u>i</u>le
/aɪ/	<u>eye</u>
/eɪ/	Austr<u>a</u>lia
/eɪ/	m<u>a</u>ke
/eɪ/	n<u>a</u>me
/ɒ/	wh<u>a</u>t
/ɒ/	fr<u>o</u>m
/ɒ/	c<u>o</u>nversation
/ɒ/	c<u>o</u>ntact
/ɒ/	sh<u>o</u>pping

Communication activities

2A WHISPERS

1 He thinks this cake is delicious.

2 This carnival is really interesting.

3 He likes to paint colourful pictures.

4 Watching the fireworks is fantastic.

5 I think that's an awful idea.

6 This class is never boring.

---

1 He thinks this cake is delicious.

2 This carnival is really interesting.

3 He likes to paint colourful pictures.

4 Watching the fireworks is fantastic.

5 I think that's an awful idea.

6 This class is never boring.

---

1 He thinks this cake is delicious.

2 This carnival is really interesting.

3 He likes to paint colourful pictures.

4 Watching the fireworks is fantastic.

5 I think that's an awful idea.

6 This class is never boring.

---

1 He thinks this cake is delicious.

2 This carnival is really interesting.

3 He likes to paint colourful pictures.

4 Watching the fireworks is fantastic.

5 I think that's an awful idea.

6 This class is never boring.

2B RUNNING DICTATION

1 for many australians, the biggest and most exciting celebration of the year is new year's eve

2 during the day and night, there is amazing entertainment everywhere as people wait for the new year

3 at midnight there is usually a massive fireworks display

4 everyone then goes home to bed and wakes up on january 1st

1 for many australians, the biggest and most exciting celebration of the year is new year's eve

2 during the day and night, there is amazing entertainment everywhere as people wait for the new year

3 at midnight there is usually a massive fireworks display

4 everyone then goes home to bed and wakes up on january 1st

3A ADJECTIVES CROSSWORD

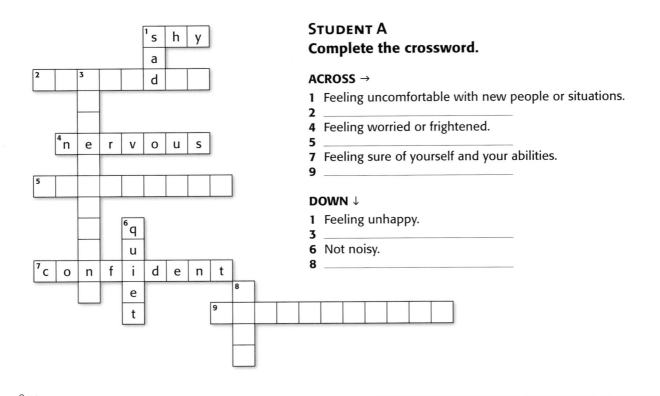

STUDENT A
Complete the crossword.

ACROSS →
1 Feeling uncomfortable with new people or situations.
2 _____
4 Feeling worried or frightened.
5 _____
7 Feeling sure of yourself and your abilities.
9 _____

DOWN ↓
1 Feeling unhappy.
3 _____
6 Not noisy.
8 _____

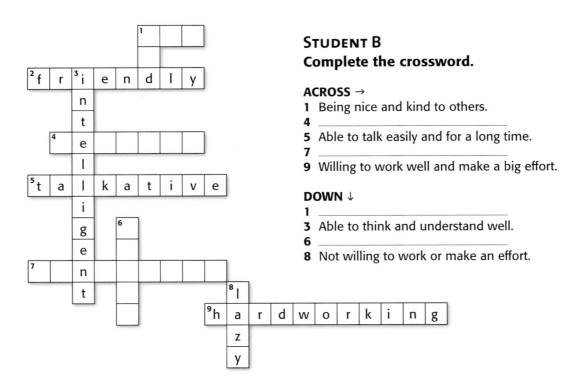

STUDENT B
Complete the crossword.

ACROSS →
1 Being nice and kind to others.
4 _____
5 Able to talk easily and for a long time.
7 _____
9 Willing to work well and make a big effort.

DOWN ↓
1 _____
3 Able to think and understand well.
6 _____
8 Not willing to work or make an effort.

3B ADVERB CIRCLES

Complete the sentences with your own ideas.

often   sometimes   never   usually   always

1 I _____ forget to do my homework.
2 I am _____ quiet in class.
3 I am _____ late for class.
4 I _____ enjoy working in a group.
5 I _____ feel confident when I speak English.

- - - - - - - - - - - - - - - - -

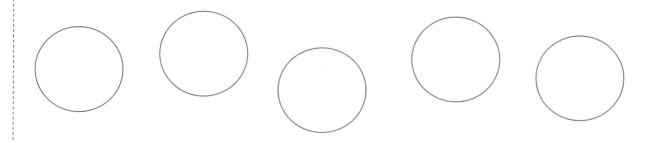

Complete the sentences with your own ideas.

often   sometimes   never   usually   always

1 I _____ forget to do my homework.
2 I am _____ quiet in class.
3 I am _____ late for class.
4 I _____ enjoy working in a group.
5 I _____ feel confident when I speak English.

- - - - - - - - - - - - - - - - -

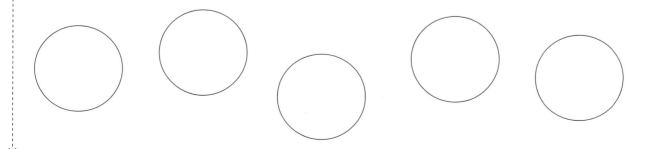

4A ACADEMIC SUBJECTS WORDSEARCH

Academic subjects and higher education

```
t s g g u t e d o g e o y g i
a o l o n p s y c h o l o g y
q c g c d e e t b i o l o g y
u i o h e g s p u p g a s s o
a o u l r i e o s h d w y l s
l l d e g g n a i i u t r t n
i o n d r s g a n e s e e a d
f g e i a l i t e r a t u r e
i y a t d r n n s m a t h s g
c o m p u t e r s c i e n c e
a a r e a d e g r e e n i c o
t p o s t g r a d u a t e r l
i a i m e d i c i n e o t a o
o s s m l a n g u a g e s d g
n s l n q t g r a d e s o i y
```

geology   engineering   degree
literature   medicine   qualification
maths   languages   pass
computer science   sociology   grades
business   psychology   undergraduate
law   biology   postgraduate

Academic subjects and higher education

```
t s g g u t e d o g e o y g i
a o l o n p s y c h o l o g y
q c g c d e e t b i o l o g y
u i o h e g s p u p g a s s o
a o u l r i e o s h d w y l s
l l d e g g n a i i u t r t n
i o n d r s g a n e s e e a d
f g e i a l i t e r a t u r e
i y a t d r n n s m a t h s g
c o m p u t e r s c i e n c e
a a r e a d e g r e e n i c o
t p o s t g r a d u a t e r l
i a i m e d i c i n e o t a o
o s s m l a n g u a g e s d g
n s l n q t g r a d e s o i y
```

geology   engineering   degree
literature   medicine   qualification
maths   languages   pass
computer science   sociology   grades
business   psychology   undergraduate
law   biology   postgraduate

Academic subjects and higher education

```
t s g g u t e d o g e o y g i
a o l o n p s y c h o l o g y
q c g c d e e t b i o l o g y
u i o h e g s p u p g a s s o
a o u l r i e o s h d w y l s
l l d e g g n a i i u t r t n
i o n d r s g a n e s e e a d
f g e i a l i t e r a t u r e
i y a t d r n n s m a t h s g
c o m p u t e r s c i e n c e
a a r e a d e g r e e n i c o
t p o s t g r a d u a t e r l
i a i m e d i c i n e o t a o
o s s m l a n g u a g e s d g
n s l n q t g r a d e s o i y
```

geology   engineering   degree
literature   medicine   qualification
maths   languages   pass
computer science   sociology   grades
business   psychology   undergraduate
law   biology   postgraduate

Academic subjects and higher education

```
t s g g u t e d o g e o y g i
a o l o n p s y c h o l o g y
q c g c d e e t b i o l o g y
u i o h e g s p u p g a s s o
a o u l r i e o s h d w y l s
l l d e g g n a i i u t r t n
i o n d r s g a n e s e e a d
f g e i a l i t e r a t u r e
i y a t d r n n s m a t h s g
c o m p u t e r s c i e n c e
a a r e a d e g r e e n i c o
t p o s t g r a d u a t e r l
i a i m e d i c i n e o t a o
o s s m l a n g u a g e s d g
n s l n q t g r a d e s o i y
```

geology   engineering   degree
literature   medicine   qualification
maths   languages   pass
computer science   sociology   grades
business   psychology   undergraduate
law   biology   postgraduate

4B DINNER PARTY

A Eva:

A musician, *(play)* piano and violin, *(teach)* music at a high school

Other interests:
(play) in a jazz festival at the moment, *(learn)* to play the guitar

---

B Fazia:

An architect, usually *(design)* office buildings and shopping centres, often *(travel)* overseas to look at architecture in other countries

Other interests:
(play) the guitar most evenings to help her relax, *(read)* a lot of history books, *(research)* her family tree at the moment

---

C Vicky:

A doctor, *(work with)* babies and children, *(lecture)* to medical students at a university

Other interests:
(love) travel, *(visit)* somewhere different every year, *(plan)* a trip to Italy at the moment

---

D Jean-Paul:

A chef, *(work)* in a local Italian restaurant, *(be)* very proud of his herb garden at the restaurant

Other interests:
(grow) his own fruit and vegetables at home, at the moment he *(think)* about buying chickens to keep in his garden

---

E Tomas:

A vet, mainly *(look after)* domestic animals and farm animals, he often *(do)* charity work to raise money for animals

Other interests:
Sport! *(play)* tennis and cricket every week, *(train)* for a 42km marathon at the moment

---

F Phillip:

A history teacher, *(work)* in a local high school, regularly *(take)* students on trips to historical cities, e.g. Rome in Italy

Other interests:
Food! *(love)* cooking and eating, *(learn)* Italian cooking at the moment

---

Communication activities

5A THE RUNNING GAME

1	detsavrie	6	oetwr
2	utrclue	7	matipc
3	nieregne	8	tutrsrcue
4	adaklnmr	9	eamtl
5	eindsg	10	cmnctoomuiain

✂ -

1	detsavrie	6	oetwr
2	utrclue	7	matipc
3	nieregne	8	tutrsrcue
4	adaklnmr	9	eamtl
5	eindsg	10	cmnctoomuiain

✂ -

1	detsavrie	6	oetwr
2	utrclue	7	matipc
3	nieregne	8	tutrsrcue
4	adaklnmr	9	eamtl
5	eindsg	10	cmnctoomuiain

5B GUESS THAT WORD

old	old
huge	huge
glass	glass
ugly	ugly
modern	modern
concrete	concrete
brick	brick
famous	famous
sunlight	sunlight
seed	seed
market	market
tourist	tourist
engineer	engineer
port	port
lively	lively
industry	industry
building	building
mining	mining
population	population
library	library

6A QUESTION TIME

VOLUNTEER	CINEMA STAFF	BUILDER	CASHIER
ZOO ASSISTANT	SHOP ASSISTANT	TEACHER	GARDENER
DOCTOR	MUSEUM WORKER	LAWYER	PAINTER
WAITER/WAITRESS	DENTIST	CLEANER	POLICE OFFICER

VOLUNTEER	CINEMA STAFF	BUILDER	CASHIER
ZOO ASSISTANT	SHOP ASSISTANT	TEACHER	GARDENER
DOCTOR	MUSEUM WORKER	LAWYER	PAINTER
WAITER/WAITRESS	DENTIST	CLEANER	POLICE OFFICER

VOLUNTEER	CINEMA STAFF	BUILDER	CASHIER
ZOO ASSISTANT	SHOP ASSISTANT	TEACHER	GARDENER
DOCTOR	MUSEUM WORKER	LAWYER	PAINTER
WAITER/WAITRESS	DENTIST	CLEANER	POLICE OFFICER

VOLUNTEER	CINEMA STAFF	BUILDER	CASHIER
ZOO ASSISTANT	SHOP ASSISTANT	TEACHER	GARDENER
DOCTOR	MUSEUM WORKER	LAWYER	PAINTER
WAITER/WAITRESS	DENTIST	CLEANER	POLICE OFFICER

6B Strip Story

Last year I started university so I could become a vet.

I loved my course, but life on campus was expensive.

I needed money, so I looked for a part-time job.

I wanted one with animals because it would help me with my studies.

I wrote to a vet, but he only offered voluntary work.

Then I rang the director of the zoo and she offered me a job straight away!

My job was to help out with the animal exhibits.

At first I felt very nervous because I didn't know anyone.

After a few weeks, I felt more confident.

Last year I started university so I could become a vet.

I loved my course, but life on campus was expensive.

I needed money, so I looked for a part-time job.

I wanted one with animals because it would help me with my studies.

I wrote to a vet, but he only offered voluntary work.

Then I rang the director of the zoo and she offered me a job straight away!

My job was to help out with the animal exhibits.

At first I felt very nervous because I didn't know anyone.

After a few weeks, I felt more confident.

Last year I started university so I could become a vet.

I loved my course, but life on campus was expensive.

I needed money, so I looked for a part-time job.

I wanted one with animals because it would help me with my studies.

I wrote to a vet, but he only offered voluntary work.

Then I rang the director of the zoo and she offered me a job straight away!

My job was to help out with the animal exhibits.

At first I felt very nervous because I didn't know anyone.

After a few weeks, I felt more confident.

Communication activities

7A WHAT AM I DOING?

Balance on one leg.

Kick a ball.

Climb a mountain.

Play tennis.

Play basketball.

Bounce a ball.

Jump over a wall.

Hit a ball with a racket.

Do karate.

Play golf.

Balance on one leg.

Kick a ball.

Climb a mountain.

Play tennis.

Play basketball.

Bounce a ball.

Jump over a wall.

Hit a ball with a racket.

Do karate.

Play golf.

Balance on one leg.

Kick a ball.

Climb a mountain.

Play tennis.

Play basketball.

Bounce a ball.

Jump over a wall.

Hit a ball with a racket.

Do karate.

Play golf.

Balance on one leg.

Kick a ball.

Climb a mountain.

Play tennis.

Play basketball.

Bounce a ball.

Jump over a wall.

Hit a ball with a racket.

Do karate.

Play golf.

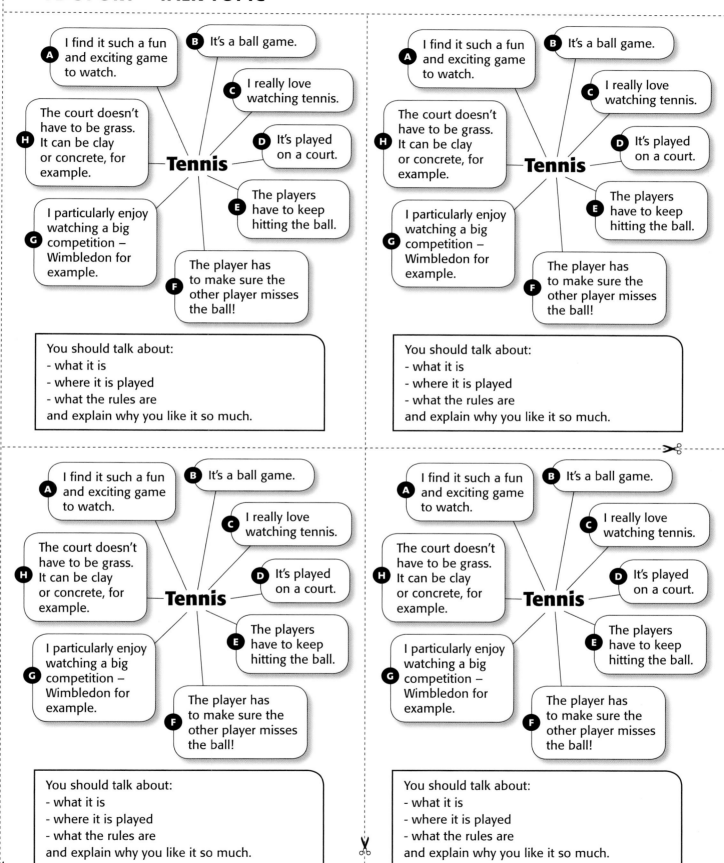

Tennis

A I find it such a fun and exciting game to watch.

B It's a ball game.

C I really love watching tennis.

D It's played on a court.

E The players have to keep hitting the ball.

F The player has to make sure the other player misses the ball!

G I particularly enjoy watching a big competition – Wimbledon for example.

H The court doesn't have to be grass. It can be clay or concrete, for example.

You should talk about:
- what it is
- where it is played
- what the rules are
and explain why you like it so much.

Communication activities

8A PICTIONARY

Student A
cliff   coast   (thick) rainforest   (sandy) beach

Student B
waves   waterfall   (extinct) volcano   (snowy) mountain

Student C
destination   ocean   (spectacular) view   (deep) river

Student A
cliff   coast   (thick) rainforest   (sandy) beach

Student B
waves   waterfall   (extinct) volcano   (snowy) mountain

Student C
destination   ocean   (spectacular) view   (deep) river

Student A
cliff   coast   (thick) rainforest   (sandy) beach

Student B
waves   waterfall   (extinct) volcano   (snowy) mountain

Student C
destination   ocean   (spectacular) view   (deep) river

8B Have you ever ... ?

Student A

1 (*ever climb*) a mountain? _____?
Yes – Question _____?
No – Question _____?

2 (*ever swim*) in the ocean? _____?
Yes – Question _____?
No – Question _____?

3 (*ever see*) a spectacular view? _____?
Yes – Question _____?
No – Question _____?

4 (*ever watch*) _____?
Yes – Question _____?
No – Question _____?

Student A

1 (*ever climb*) a mountain? _____?
Yes – Question _____?
No – Question _____?

2 (*ever swim*) in the ocean? _____?
Yes – Question _____?
No – Question _____?

3 (*ever see*) a spectacular view? _____?
Yes – Question _____?
No – Question _____?

4 (*ever watch*) _____?
Yes – Question _____?
No – Question _____?

Student B

1 (*ever walk*) through a rainforest? _____?
Yes – Question _____?
No – Question _____?

2 (*ever fish*) in a river? _____?
Yes – Question _____?
No – Question _____?

3 (*ever go*) surfing? _____?
Yes – Question _____?
No – Question _____?

4 (*ever see*) _____?
Yes – Question _____?
No – Question _____?

Student B

1 (*ever walk*) through a rainforest? _____?
Yes – Question _____?
No – Question _____?

2 (*ever fish*) in a river? _____?
Yes – Question _____?
No – Question _____?

3 (*ever go*) surfing? _____?
Yes – Question _____?
No – Question _____?

4 (*ever see*) _____?
Yes – Question _____?
No – Question _____?

Communication activities

9A HOT SEAT

Tell us about an aunt or uncle that you are close to.	What is the best age to have children? Why?
Do you enjoy spending time with your family? Why / Why not?	Is it better to live close to your parents when you get married? Why / Why not?
How many cousins do you have? Can you tell us about some of them?	Which birthday has the biggest celebration in your family? Why?
Tell us about a special family occasion that you celebrate. Why?	Should young people look after the older people in their family? Why / Why not?
What is the best age to get married? Why?	Do you come from a traditional or a modern family?

Tell us about an aunt or uncle that you are close to.	What is the best age to have children? Why?
Do you enjoy spending time with your family? Why / Why not?	Is it better to live close to your parents when you get married? Why / Why not?
How many cousins do you have? Can you tell us about some of them?	Which birthday has the biggest celebration in your family? Why?
Tell us about a special family occasion that you celebrate. Why?	Should young people look after the older people in their family? Why / Why not?
What is the best age to get married? Why?	Do you come from a traditional or a modern family?

Tell us about an aunt or uncle that you are close to.	What is the best age to have children? Why?
Do you enjoy spending time with your family? Why / Why not?	Is it better to live close to your parents when you get married? Why / Why not?
How many cousins do you have? Can you tell us about some of them?	Which birthday has the biggest celebration in your family? Why?
Tell us about a special family occasion that you celebrate. Why?	Should young people look after the older people in their family? Why / Why not?
What is the best age to get married? Why?	Do you come from a traditional or a modern family?

Tell us about an aunt or uncle that you are close to.	What is the best age to have children? Why?
Do you enjoy spending time with your family? Why / Why not?	Is it better to live close to your parents when you get married? Why / Why not?
How many cousins do you have? Can you tell us about some of them?	Which birthday has the biggest celebration in your family? Why?
Tell us about a special family occasion that you celebrate. Why?	Should young people look after the older people in their family? Why / Why not?
What is the best age to get married? Why?	Do you come from a traditional or a modern family?

9B Passive voice race

1 They hold a party on the baby's first birthday.

2 Brides wear white dresses in Australia.

3 Many farmers grow rice in China.

4 They pick vegetables from the garden.

5 They give the bride money.

6 We celebrate special events at home.

7 A speech is given by the bride's father.

8 Wedding cake is eaten by all the guests.

9 Fruit is grown by the Hunza people.

10 Fish are caught in that river by fishermen.

11 Their lives are spent moving around.

12 A special kimono is worn by Japanese brides.

---

1 They hold a party on the baby's first birthday.

2 Brides wear white dresses in Australia.

3 Many farmers grow rice in China.

4 They pick vegetables from the garden.

5 They give the bride money.

6 We celebrate special events at home.

7 A speech is given by the bride's father.

8 Wedding cake is eaten by all the guests.

9 Fruit is grown by the Hunza people.

10 Fish are caught in that river by fishermen.

11 Their lives are spent moving around.

12 A special kimono is worn by Japanese brides.

---

1 They hold a party on the baby's first birthday.

2 Brides wear white dresses in Australia.

3 Many farmers grow rice in China.

4 They pick vegetables from the garden.

5 They give the bride money.

6 We celebrate special events at home.

7 A speech is given by the bride's father.

8 Wedding cake is eaten by all the guests.

9 Fruit is grown by the Hunza people.

10 Fish are caught in that river by fishermen.

11 Their lives are spent moving around.

12 A special kimono is worn by Japanese brides.

Communication activities

10A NOUGHTS AND CROSSES

some	how many	there isn't
any	many	there aren't
how much	much	there is

some	how many	there isn't
any	many	there aren't
how much	much	there is

some	how many	there isn't
any	many	there aren't
how much	much	there is

some	how many	there isn't
any	many	there aren't
how much	much	there is

10B Vocabulary race

litter	poster	drill (v)	destroy
waste	jungle	agriculture	conserve
recycle	river	habitat	illegal
leaflet	desert	threat	chemicals
music	landscape	extinct	forest

litter	poster	drill (v)	destroy
waste	jungle	agriculture	conserve
recycle	river	habitat	illegal
leaflet	desert	threat	chemicals
music	landscape	extinct	forest

11A WHICH IS ... ?

✂

Animals: 1 _____ 2 _____ adjective _____
Which is _____?

School subjects: 1 _____ 2 _____ adjective _____
Which is _____?

Languages: 1 _____ 2 _____ adjective _____
Which is _____?

Food: 1 _____ 2 _____ adjective _____
Which is _____?

Jobs: 1 _____ 2 _____ adjective _____
Which is _____?

Public transport: 1 _____ 2 _____ adjective _____
Which is _____?

TV programmes: 1 _____ 2 _____ adjective _____
Which is _____?

Sport: 1 _____ 2 _____ adjective _____
Which is _____?

Music: 1 _____ 2 _____ adjective _____
Which is _____?

Technology: 1 _____ 2 _____ adjective _____
Which is _____?

11B FOUR OF THE BEST

A Talk about the best book you have read.

You should say:
1 what the book is called and who wrote it
2 when you read it
3 what it was about
4 and explain why you enjoyed it so much.

B Talk about the best present you have received.

You should say:
1 what the present was
2 who gave it to you
3 when they gave it to you
4 and explain why it was such a special present.

C Talk about the best film you have watched.

You should say:
1 what the film was called and who starred in it
2 when you saw it
3 what it was about
4 and explain why you enjoyed it so much.

D Talk about the best museum _or_ art gallery _or_ restaurant you have been to.

You should say:
1 what the museum / art gallery / restaurant is called and where it is
2 what kind of museum / art gallery / restaurant it is
3 when you went there
4 and explain why you enjoyed visiting it so much.

A Talk about the best book you have read.

You should say:
1 what the book is called and who wrote it
2 when you read it
3 what it was about
4 and explain why you enjoyed it so much.

B Talk about the best present you have received.

You should say:
1 what the present was
2 who gave it to you
3 when they gave it to you
4 and explain why it was such a special present.

C Talk about the best film you have watched.

You should say:
1 what the film was called and who starred in it
2 when you saw it
3 what it was about
4 and explain why you enjoyed it so much.

D Talk about the best museum _or_ art gallery _or_ restaurant you have been to.

You should say:
1 what the museum / art gallery / restaurant is called and where it is
2 what kind of museum / art gallery / restaurant it is
3 when you went there
4 and explain why you enjoyed visiting it so much.

Communication activities

12A WILL THINGS BE DIFFERENT?

✂----

In the future will cars be different?

In the future will books be different?

In the future will school subjects be different?

In the future will food be different?

In the future will air travel be different?

In the future will computers be different?

In the future will cameras be different?

In the future will clothes be different?

In the future will shops be different?

In the future will music be different?

In the future will going out with friends be different?

In the future will buildings be different?

In the future will birthday celebrations be different?

In the future will learning English be different?

In the future will jobs be different?

✂ In the future will sport be different?

12B Lottery Winners!

1 Where / live? _____
2 What car / drive? _____
3 What holidays / have? _____
4 What / buy? _____
5 / give any money to friends or family? _____
6 / give any money to charity? _____
7 / continue to work or study? _____
8 (your question) _____

1 Where / live? _____
2 What car / drive? _____
3 What holidays / have? _____
4 What / buy? _____
5 / give any money to friends or family? _____
6 / give any money to charity? _____
7 / continue to work or study? _____
8 (your question) _____

1 Where / live? _____
2 What car / drive? _____
3 What holidays / have? _____
4 What / buy? _____
5 / give any money to friends or family? _____
6 / give any money to charity? _____
7 / continue to work or study? _____
8 (your question) _____